Project June

A TRILOGY ABOUT WRITING

Louise Truscott

DEDICATION

For Ava, my niece and a fellow sufferer... ahem, I mean fellow writer

CONTENTS

INTRODUCTION

I was scrolling through Twitter once (as I do several times a day) when I came across a post from either someone I follow or someone who had been liked, retweeted or commented on by someone I follow. (It's hard to tell sometimes.) The poster essentially said that unless you were Stephen King or some other bestselling writer, then he didn't think he should read or follow any advice you might have about writing. Most of the comments agreed with him. Some even thought the only way to improve was to write more (but not to listen to advice on how they might be able to write better).

I have no problem with Stephen King. I have his book *On Writing*. I've read it. I don't consider it a bible on the craft. I've written and published two books on writing myself. As I write this introduction, I'm close to completing a third. (Yes, it's this book you're now reading.) I don't consider any of them definitive guides on writing. (Obviously, if one of them was a bible on writing, I'd be a lot more successful than I am now and I wouldn't have needed to write the other two.) I have many books on writing. None of them render all other books on writing irrelevant.

It's amazing, isn't it, that an off-the-cuff comment by someone on Twitter (who could feasibly be the worst writer in the world) can make me doubt what I've spent almost my entire working life doing (and plenty of years before that). But I suddenly feel the need to justify and qualify the writing advice that I offer.

THE JUSTIFICATIONS

- I've been writing for more than 30 years.
- I've been reading for more than 40 years. (I started reading when I was 18 months old and basically haven't stopped since.)

- I have an Advanced Diploma (a two-year course of study sometimes called an Associate Degree) in Professional Writing and Editing. I majored in novel writing, poetry and editing. I was taught by working writers, renowned poets and one of Australia's most respected editing teachers.
- I have a master's degree in writing, which means I can teach if I want to. (I don't want to.)
- I also have a bachelor's degree in American history and international politics. (Yes, that's three qualifications.)
- I've written, edited and published four of my own books and people have paid money to buy and read them.
- I've ghostwritten, edited and published another.
- I've written two more books that will be published over the next few years.
- My second novel was shortlisted for the 2016 Text Prize for Young Adult and Children's Unpublished Manuscripts.
- I worked as a corporate writer for almost a decade until I couldn't stand it any longer even though I was begged to continue on – to this day, I am contacted by recruiters asking me to return to the field.
- I am the go-to person for everybody I have ever met who has a writing or editing question.
- In addition to my own writing, I freelance as a copyeditor for a magazine as well as writing and editing marketing campaigns for several businesses.

THE QUALIFICATIONS

- My advice is a product of who I am as a writer. Therefore, it may be completely irrelevant to who you are as a writer.
- My advice is also a product of who I am as a reader. Again, this might make it completely irrelevant to who you are as a writer.
- Most of my advice is more like musing. I like to think through things and write down the process of my thinking, as well as any conclusions I come to.
- Two pieces of completely contradictory writing advice might be equally valid, especially when talking about different types of writing. This is sometimes also true when talking about the exact same piece of writing.
- Nobody is under any pressure to accept my advice or implement it or do anything more than give me the courtesy of considering it, even if you choose to disregard it in the end.

- I want to be challenged. It's how I keep learning. It's why I keep reading the advice of other writers even though all those justifications above might suggest I could get away with not doing it.
- I'm not always right.
- You're not always right.
- Nobody is always right, not even Stephen King.
- I'm not telling you what to do. I would hate for anyone to think that any of my advice should be followed word for word. What I'm doing is trying to get you to think about the writing choices you make. Because that's what all writing is. Choices.

I hope you choose to continue reading my advice. And if you don't, thanks for reading up to this point. But I'm not going to stop writing or offering advice. That's my choice.

PART 1

GETTING STARTED… ONE MORE TIME

PROJECT JUNE

"Ideas are like rabbits. You get a couple and learn how to handle them, and pretty soon you have a dozen."
John Steinbeck, interview with Robert van Gelder in April 1947 as quoted in *John Steinbeck: A Biography* by Jay Parini

This is the fifth piece in my Project... series. For anyone who hasn't read my first two books of writing advice or the relevant posts on my blog, here's a refresher for you:

- Project October is all about intensive writing.
- Project November is all about rewriting, polishing and finalising.
- Project December is all about publishing.
- Project January is all about starting over again.

So what is Project June? For the purposes of this series and this book, there had to be another Project... piece. I toyed with the idea of Project February, mostly because February comes after January. But I didn't know what Project February was. I still don't.

Eventually, I realised that the advice I wanted to give and the month that went with it was all about the middle. I'd addressed the start, the sprint to the faux finish and the actual finish; the only thing left was the part in between.

The in-between can sometimes be the most frustrating part. The excitement of the blank page at the very beginning is long gone. The satisfaction of having an entire first draft down on paper feels so far away. And if you're right in the middle and writer's block strikes, then what?

3

The thing I find about writer's block is that it tends to be project specific. It's not that you can't write. It's that you can't write the particular topic or story that you want to write.

So Project June is about how a writer should always have more than one writing project on the go. That way, if you get sick of a project or if you get stuck on a project, you can keep working on another without losing precious writing time.

As I write this chapter, I'm 90% finished a stand-alone novel, I've written 30% of sequels to two completed books and I have 50% of *Project June: A Trilogy About Writing*. I'm also in the development phase of one non-fiction and two fiction books. That's seven projects on the go all at the one time but all at different stages. So if I get stuck on one, I spend some time working on a different one until I get past the writer's block or whatever it is that's preventing progression.

The positives with Project June:

- Having too many ideas is better than having no ideas.
- You'll always have something to work on.
- It relieves the guilt that some writers have when new ideas strike before old ideas are completed.
- Rather than having to abandon a project, you simply put it on hiatus. If it's in the back of your mind that you'll eventually go back to it, it can percolate quietly in the interim. And by the time the percolation becomes an intense boil, that's when you know it's time to pick it up again.
- Sometimes publishers and agents like the way you write but not a specific piece. With Project June, you'll always have something else to give them. It might not be a finished piece but it shows them that you're not just a one-trick wonder.
- It's the mark of a professional to be able to work on multiple projects at the same time.

The problems with Project June:

- You can't just do it, you have to work your way up to it until you have multiple projects on the go and keep starting new ones as you finish old ones or even before you're finished old ones.
- It can pull your attention in multiple directions, which can be annoying, particularly when all you want to do is write one story and your multiple projects are in the various stages of writing, editing, designing, publishing and marketing.

- It doesn't help if you are working on a writing project with a specific deadline.
- You must be able to compartmentalise, that is to completely forget about all other projects for a little while.
- You must be able to remember which storylines go where. If you're constantly having to refresh your memory on where you're picking up the story from, you're going to waste a lot of potential writing time. And you don't want to get them mixed up. A lot of writers have a lot of similarities between subsequent books. You want it to be because they are deliberate themes, not because you couldn't remember you'd already used that plot or that character in another book.
- You might be one of those people who just can't do it (and that's fair enough – it's not for everyone).

Stephen King isn't a fan of working on more than one writing project at a time. I think he must be one of those people who just can't do it, although he says that he thinks it impacts the quality of the work. Maybe when you're pumping out books at the rate he does, that's the case. For the rest of us, it's less of an issue. After all, there are no Project June rules about how quickly you have to turn over your multiple ideas. I suspect a lot of the things I subscribe to when it comes to writing would have to get tossed out if I wasn't able to work at my own pace.

So have as many ideas as you like. As many as you can handle. As many as you need to minimise writing downtime. Whether that's two, a few more than two or dozens is entirely up to you and your imagination. And how to manage them all? Well, that's another subject for another day...

WHAT KIND OF WRITER DO YOU WANT TO BE?

I originally wrote this chapter when I thought maybe I'd do a writing book for children so it has a slightly different tone to the rest of *Project June*. But when I posted it on my blog, plenty of adults told me they had learned something from it, so maybe you will, too.

∞

Saying you want to be a writer is a bit like saying you want to be an athlete. There are lots of different kinds of sports. And there are lots of different kinds of writing. Most kids start out by writing fiction (such as stories about aliens or adventures or animals) and non-fiction (such as essays about what you did over the summer). But by the time you're all grown up, you realise that there are a lot more – sometimes very specific – options for the kind of writer you might want to be.

Here are a few that you will have heard of and maybe a few that you've never even thought about.

ACADEMIC WRITER

To be an academic writer, you need to choose a subject to focus on such as medicine, physics, psychology or geology and become an expert. Then once you know everything about your subject, you do research to try to discover new things that nobody else knows yet. An academic writer usually works for a university and has to write about what new things they have discovered.

AGONY AUNT OR UNCLE

An agony aunt or agony uncle asks people to send in a story of a problem they are having in their life (something they are "agonising" over) and will respond by providing advice on what they should do (like your "aunt" or "uncle" might do).

BIOGRAPHER

A biographer tells the story of someone's life. Usually, the person they are writing about is famous (such as a politician, an athlete or a businessperson) or has done something amazing that readers are interested in reading about (such as being an astronaut, surviving a disaster or climbing a really tall mountain).

BLOGGER

A blogger is someone who writes a blog, which is a personal website. They can write about anything they want to. They can write about themselves, about their favourite hobby, about their favourite TV show, anything! Anyone can set up a blog.

Did you know…?

There are over 500 million blogs on the internet as of 2020 and bloggers post over two million blog posts daily.

COLUMNIST

A columnist usually writes for a newspaper or magazine (named after the "columns" that their writing was formatted to fit into when newspapers and magazines were printed) and they mostly write their opinions about the topics that everyone is talking about.

Did you know…?

Even though a columnist appears in a newspaper or magazine like a journalist, they are very different from journalists. A columnist's job is to tell you what they think. A journalist's job is to tell you what other people think and present the facts of a story.

COMEDY WRITER

A comedy writer tries to make us laugh by writing jokes and funny stories. They might write these jokes or funny stories for a stand-up comedy routine, for a sketch show, for a sitcom on television or for a comedy movie.

Did you know…?

"Sitcom" is short for "situational comedy" and the term is usually used to describe a half-hour television show that follow the lives of a group of people and contains a lot of jokes.

COMIC WRITER

A comedy writer and a comic writer might sound almost like the same thing but they are very different. A comic (which can also be known as a graphic novel) tells a story using words and pictures (like a picture book but for adults). Batman, Superman and most of our favourite superheroes all started out in comics.

COPYWRITER

Copywriters prepare smaller pieces of writing, usually for advertising purposes.

CORPORATE WRITER

Big businesses need writers for a variety of types of writing so a corporate writer could work on proposals (also known as bids or tenders), reports, case studies, articles, prospectuses, speeches, newsletters, websites, brochures and other general marketing materials. A corporate writer's main goal is to make the business they work for look good and deliver the messages the business wants to convey.

CRITIC

A critic is someone who writes reviews – what they liked and what they didn't like – about restaurants, movies, books, television shows, holidays and other things to help readers to decide if they would like to eat at a restaurant, see a movie or television show, read a book or go on a holiday.

CV WRITER

A CV writer writes CVs. What's a CV? CV stands for curriculum vitae, which is Latin for "the course of my life". A CV is also known as a résumé, which is French for "summary". A CV or a résumé is a short description of you, your education, any work you've done and other interesting things about yourself that you give to an employer when you are applying for a job. A lot of people write their own CVs but a CV writer knows how to do it really well to make you look amazing!

DIARIST

A diarist is someone who keeps a diary, usually with the intention of publishing it as a book later on.

ENCYCLOPEDIST

An encyclopedist helps write and put together an encyclopedia.

ESSAYIST

An essayist is someone who writes essays. Essays are a common assessment tool used in high schools and at universities but they are also used in the broader writing world to present thoughts or arguments in a reflective, often literary manner.

FOOD WRITER

A food writer writes about food and recipes. They will often write about going to restaurants and where certain types of food come from. If the food writer is also a good cook, they might even write a cook book.

GHOSTWRITER

A ghostwriter is given a story and asked to write it on behalf of the person who had the idea. When the book is published, they won't be listed as the writer of the book. A lot of people who aren't very good at writing but who have a story that they want to tell will use a ghostwriter to help them do it.

GRANT WRITER

A grant is money available to fund research or support artists or projects. There are more people wanting grants than there are grants available, so applications must be written and submitted so the government departments, charities, foundations and corporations offering the grants can decide who to give the money to. Grant writers work with the people wanting to be awarded the grant money and prepare the grant applications on their behalf.

GREETING CARD WRITER

A greeting card writer comes up with the messages on the front and inside of birthday cards, get well cards, congratulations cards, Mother's Day cards, Father's Day cards, Christmas cards and all those other cards that you see in the store. They work closely with designers so that their messages get matched up with the right pictures.

HISTORY WRITER

History writers write about important events in the past. There is a famous saying that history is written by the victors so sometimes history writers have to do a lot of research to discover true history. History doesn't change but often our understanding or perspective of history can change as society changes and as additional information comes to light.

JOURNALIST

A journalist usually writes for a newspaper or a magazine about what is going on in the world each day. There are many kinds of journalism including politics, crime, health, entertainment, environment, science, sports and many others. Journalists play a very important role in keeping the general public informed, making sure people in positions in power follow the rules and giving a voice to people who aren't in positions of power.

LEXICOGRAPHER

A lexicographer writes dictionaries. "Lexicon" is another word for "dictionary".

Did you know...?

Samuel Johnson was one of the most famous lexicographers. In 1746, he started writing *A Dictionary of the English Language* and in 1755, it was published (yes, it took him nine years and he wrote it all by himself). It was considered the best English dictionary for over 150 years until the *Oxford English Dictionary* was published.

LYRICIST

A lyricist (also known as a songwriter) writes the words for songs. A lyricist will need to work very closely with a musician or composer to make sure the words and the music fit together perfectly.

MEDICAL WRITER

A medical writer writes about medical stories and issues and is usually a doctor, a nurse or a medical researcher. A writer who writes about medical stories but doesn't have medical qualifications is more likely to be referred to as a health writer.

MEMOIRIST

A memoirist is like a biographer but writes about their own life (they are also known as an autobiographer).

NON-FICTION WRITER

Non-fiction is a very broad subject area but is basically everything other than fiction. Journalists, history writers, medical writers, biographers, true crime writers and travel writers all write non-fiction.

NOVELIST

A novelist (also known as an author) writes made-up stories that are usually quite long and there are many novel genres including crime, science fiction, fantasy, horror, historical, western, comedy, romance, thriller and mystery.

OBITUARY WRITER

An obituary writer writes mini biographies about famous people when they die.

Did you know...?

Obituary writers sometimes write obituaries for famous people – such as presidents and pop stars – and for well-known people who are sick or do risky things before they die so they have them ready to publish as soon as the news of their death becomes public.

PICTURE BOOK WRITER

A picture book writer writes picture books for children. A picture book writer will sometimes write the words and draw the pictures but other times they work with an illustrator who draws the pictures to go with the words.

PLAYWRIGHT

A playwright is someone who writes plays, which are then performed on a stage in a theatre with live actors (as opposed to a movie, which is filmed previously with actors and shown on a screen in a cinema).

Did you know...?

The reason it's spelled "playwright" and not "playwrite" is because "wright" is an old English word for a craftsman or a builder. So a playwright is someone who crafts plays.

POET

A poet writes poems. Some of the oldest writing that still exists is in the form of poetry. Poems are hard to describe but they are like songs without music.

PROPOSAL WRITER (AKA BID WRITER OR TENDER WRITER)

Governments and big businesses request proposals from potential suppliers outlining what they can provide, how much it will cost and why they should be chosen to supply it. Proposal writers compile all the required information from the specialists in the business and write any additional information needed, then finalise and submit the proposal.

REPORT WRITER

Big businesses, especially those with multiple shareholders and multi-million-dollar or multi-billion-dollar revenues, have to write reports to keep their investors and business regulators informed on how their business is going. Report writers are specialists in preparing this kind of information, especially for annual reports.

SATIRIST

A satirist uses writing to poke fun, usually at people in positions of power like politicians and especially when they do things that regular people don't think they should be doing. Wikipedia describes satire as a genre "in which vices, follies, abuses and shortcomings are held up to ridicule, ideally with the intent of shaming individuals, corporations, governments or society itself into improvement".

SCREENWRITER

Screenwriters write films and televisions shows. It is a unique form of writing because it is not written to be read, it is written as a set of instructions to be interpreted by actors, set designers, lighting designers, location scouts, producers, directors and all the people involved in making films and television shows.

SHORT STORY WRITER

A short story writer is like a novelist but prefers to write things that are quicker to write and read. They write stories that don't need as many words as a novel needs. Short stories are more likely to be published in magazines and journals or as part of a collection of short stories in a book.

SOCIAL MEDIA WRITER

Do you read messages on Facebook, Twitter and Instagram? Well, somebody has to write them. Yes, a lot of them are from your friends and family but companies and organisations are on social media as well and they need someone to write their messages for them. A social media writer is usually part of a marketing team.

SPEECHWRITER

A speechwriter writes speeches, usually for other people like business leaders, politicians, kings and queens, and activists. These people often have important messages they want to convey to those listening to their speeches and to ensure their speech is impressive and has a lasting impact, they hire someone who is a specialist in writing speeches.

TECHNICAL WRITER

A technical writer writes instructions on how to do something, like learning how to use new software or how to apply for a home loan.

TEXTBOOK WRITER

All classes need textbooks and all textbooks are written by textbook writers. To write a textbook, you need to be an expert in your special subject and you need to be able to explain your special subject in a way that makes it easy to learn.

TRANSLATOR

A translator is someone who speaks and writes and reads another language well enough to be able to translate a piece of writing from one language into another. This book is written in English. For people who don't read English to be able to read it, it would need to be translated into a language they can read and that is what a translator does.

TRAVEL WRITER

A travel writer visits places all over the world and writes about them so we can decide if we would like to go on holidays in that place.

TRUE CRIME WRITER

A true crime writer writes about real-life crime (as opposed to a crime novelist who writes about pretend crime). Reports about real-life crime usually appear at first in newspapers or on television but true crime books delve deeply into all the details to tell the complete story from the history of the person committing the crime, the victims, the crime itself, how it was solved, the resulting court case and the verdict.

VIDEO GAME WRITER

A video game writer works closely with video game designers to write the scripts for video games. This kind of writing is very collaborative because you rely on others to bring your vision to completion.

WEB CONTENT WRITER

Web content writers prepare the text for web pages. They will work closely with website designers to make sure it goes together well with the images and the format.

HOW TO KNOW IF YOU'RE A BAD WRITER

In *Project January: A Sequel About Writing*, I wrote a chapter on what to do when you're a bad writer with a good story. PopCultureGrinch read the piece and asked a follow-up: how do you know when you're a bad writer?

I responded wittily, "There's a reasonably famous quote that says there's no such thing as a bad writer, only bad writing but maybe that's just to make us all feel better about ourselves." It's a little ironic because in that moment, I was a bad writer. There is no such quote, at least not a famous one. I guess it's my quote now. The quote I was actually referring to is by Oscar Wilde, who said, "There is no such thing as a moral or an immoral book. Books are well written, or badly written. That is all."

Which just goes to show that being a bad writer isn't a static state. Someone who has previously been a bad writer can become a good writer. And someone who has previously been a good writer can lapse into moments (hopefully not too many) of being a bad writer. (I hope that it's not something I suffer from all the time and is more closely related to my laziness in confirming that the quote existed anywhere outside of my mind rather than my general ability to write.)

PopCultureGrinch also asked, "Is the quality of the writer based upon their output or their work ethic?" This is easier to answer. It's all about output. Because you can have the worst work ethic in the world and still produce writing of quality. And you can have the greatest work ethic in the world and never produce any writing of quality if you don't have at least a little bit of natural talent.

I think bad writing is a bit like bad art — I know it when I see it. But coming up with some generic rules to identify it is a little more complex.

There's also that pesky problem of beauty being in the eye of the beholder – that is, something that I think is bad writing might be someone else's idea of good writing.

Here's an example of something I think is poorly written:

"The usual 'oohs….aahs' of ours were obvious from the confines of our lonely 4WD parked in the middle of nowhere, with us as co-habitants in way outback. Here we were slap bang in the middle of the lowly occupied Wet Season, miles from anywhere and anyone, in total darkness and dreaming of our near departure from this Heritage Gazetted, Wilderness Park."

Out of respect, I won't name the writer. After all, I'm writing this to help writers identify ways to get better at writing, not to target and ridicule those who haven't achieved that yet.

So why is it bad writing? I think it's because the writer is trying to write something evocative and is getting tangled up in an attempt to integrate a bunch of fancy words instead of keeping it simple. I see this a lot with people who aren't "natural" writers. They want it to sound impressive and instead it ends up sounding nonsensical.

Let's start with the "usual 'oohs….aahs' of ours". "Oohs" and "aahs" aren't generally usual. They're rare. That's what makes "oohs" and "aahs" an expression of something wonderful going on. And when the writer talks about them being "obvious", I think what they actually meant was that the sounds stood out against the quietness of the remote location they were in. But that isn't what was written. The "lonely 4WD parked in the middle of nowhere" is repetition. If the 4WD is lonely, the reader understands the implication that there aren't any other cars or people around. Then "co-habitants"? Co-habiting is something you do in a house, not a car. And "in way outback" is repetition again. Awkwardly constructed repetition.

"Slap bang" is a cliché. It's not the wet season that is "lowly occupied", it's the place in the wet season. After that comes the "miles from anywhere and anyone", which is more repetition. In "total darkness"? If so, how can they see anything? And the reference to "dreaming of our near departure" is confusing. Are they wanting to leave, which is what "dreaming" suggests? Or would they actually rather stay? Each of these individual points contributes to it being considered bad writing. Assessed as a whole, it's extremely and unnecessarily wordy, which just adds more weight to the way the reader already feels.

(The poor punctuation and random capital letters are not evidence of bad writing, just writing that hasn't been edited yet and there are plenty of people considered good writers who need good editors to maintain that reputation.)

It's very difficult to recognise whether you are a bad writer by yourself. That's usually when it's a problem because it's up to somebody else to tell you. Cue hurt feelings if it's not done right. It's strange because I know I'm not a good cook or a good artist but I don't get upset if someone tells me so. Writing, like so many other artistic endeavours, is one of those things that everybody wants to be good at. And because most know their alphabet and the basics of construction, they think that translates into the ability to write. Unfortunately, sometimes, it doesn't. That's why it's important to have honest beta readers, I guess, people who are prepared to tell us the truth about our writing, not just our mums telling us how clever we are.

However, if you're prepared to attempt a self-assessment, here are a few things to look out for:

- Waffle – good writers get to the point.
- Ranting – good writers don't just vent to make themselves feel better.
- Lack of research – good writers support their statements in non-fiction with facts and reasoning and their creations in fiction with authenticity that comes from having at least a vague idea of what they are talking about.
- Poor construction – good writers work hard to make their writing easy to read. (Most people won't go to all the trouble of analysing a piece of writing to understand why it's bad like I did above. They will simply understand it intrinsically because poor construction makes it hard to read.)
- First drafts – good writers don't inflict first drafts on their readers. Multiple rewrites are essential to make sure your writing is as good as it can be.
- Unwillingness to consider viewpoints other than your own – good writers understand that they are not gods, that they can't know it all and that the viewpoints of others may be just as valid. Actually, good people in general understand this. Consider the opinions of others about your writing, even if this means playing devil's advocate against yourself.

The most important thing to remember is that bad writers can get better. Even if a currently bad writer isn't naturally talented, investing the time and effort in learning the basics, practising a lot, asking for feedback and acting on the advice received will really help in becoming a better writer and maybe even eventually a good writer.

WHY I SOMETIMES DON'T WANT TO TELL PEOPLE I'M A WRITER

Imagine this scenario:

"Hi, I'm Rachel."

"Hi, Rachel. I'm John. What do you do?"

"I'm a receptionist."

"So you just sit around talking on the phone all day?"

"It's a bit more involved than that."

"Where do you work?"

"At a small family company."

"Oh. That's a shame. Any chance you might be able to move on to a big corporate?"

"I'm happy where I am."

"Are you a good receptionist?"

"I haven't been asked to do it differently so I guess I am."

"How many calls do you take a day?"

"Um, well, I'm not sure…"

"How much do you earn?"

"That's not really any of your business."

"But how will I know for sure if you're a good receptionist?"

"Call the main switch and I'll make sure I transfer you to the right person."

"But that won't tell me if others think you're a good receptionist."

"I like what I do. I don't really care if others think I'm a good receptionist. And I really don't care what you think."

"That's a pretty poor attitude for a receptionist to have."

"Stop talking to me."

Okay, so it seems like John is a special kind of asshat. But imagine now an almost identical conversation with just a couple of small changes:

"Hi, I'm Rachel."

"Hi, Rachel. I'm John. What do you do?"

"I'm a writer."

"So you just sit around surfing the internet all day?"

"Sometimes. It's called research. But it's a bit more involved than that."

"Where are you published?"

"Through a small independent company."

"Oh. That's a shame. Any chance you might be able to move on to a big publisher?"

"I'm happy where I am."

"Are you a good writer?"

"I haven't been asked to do it differently so I guess I am."

"How many books have you sold?"

"Um, well, I'm not sure…"

"How much in royalties have you earned?"

"That's not really any of your business."

"But how will I know for sure if you're a good writer?"

"Read one of my books or articles and you can make up your own mind."

"But that won't tell me if others think you're a good writer."

"I like what I do. I don't really care if others think I'm a good writer. And I really don't care what you think."

"That's a pretty poor attitude for a writer to have."

"I'm sorry you think so. If you do end up buying one of my books, I'll be happy to sign it for you. Nice to meet you, John."

In the second scenario, John is still an asshat. The difference is that Rachel the receptionist can tell him to take a hike while Rachel the writer has to be nice to her potential reading public no matter how horrible they are. And, of course, Rachel the receptionist would never be questioned about her career choice in this way. Rachel the writer deals with this line of questioning from almost everyone who discovers she's a writer.

I know I have. And that's why I sometimes don't want to tell people I'm a writer. I've had a few other jobs (receptionist, admin assistant, editor, bid manager) but I've never been asked to justify my career choice more since I decided to become a full-time writer.

"It's not stable," people protest. "Neither is acting," I reply.

"It doesn't pay well unless you're at the top," they point out. "Neither does working at McDonald's," I say.

"It's isolating," they continue. "Hardly. I have to interact with more people than ever."

"Eventually, you'll need to get a real job," they snark. "Writing is a real job. Content development is a multi-billion-dollar industry in Australia alone," I respond.

"It's a huge amount of work for little reward," they say. "Being able to do what you love is the reward!" (I've listened to plenty of people talk about how much they hate what they do for a living. Apparently, the fact that I'm passionate about what I do is so much worse.)

I've come to realise it's just easier not to tell everyone what I do. I also justify it by telling myself that the majority of my readers are people I've never met in real life, so it's not like I'm doing myself out of a sale. And anyone who has more than a passing interest can easily Google my name to discover exactly what I'm doing (when you have a blog that gets posted to frequently and multiple books available for sale, it's pretty obvious).

If anyone wants to talk to me about writing without judging me for choosing it as a career, then that would be great. After all, if there's anything I love almost as much as writing, it's helping newcomers to begin their own writing journeys and helping emerging or established writers to get better. (What self-respecting writer who is also a trained editor would feel any other way?)

For everyone else, you can just keep your opinions to yourself. All I know is this: on my death bed, I'm not going to resent a single second of my writing career. Are you going to be able to say the same about the jobs you did just to pay the bills? I highly doubt it.

THE INSULT OF BEING CALLED AN AMATEUR WRITER

It is a well-known fact amongst writers that the majority of us can't earn enough just from our writing to give up all other forms of employment. There are a lucky few but not nearly as many as those of us wanting to join those few would like. It doesn't mean we give up on writing. It just means we supplement our incomes with other work like editing, teaching and, more often than not, jobs that have absolutely no link to what it is we'd much rather be doing.

In 2014, I was lucky enough to be able to begin three years in which I spent the majority of my time writing my own work full-time. During the times I wasn't writing my own work, I was employed as a writer writing for others (six months here, six weeks there but for less than a year of those three years).

Prior to that, I spent six-and-a-half years as a corporate writer and before that, I was a textbook editor for three years. I even have two postgraduate writing degrees.

And in the past decade, I've published four books, written two more, ghostwritten another, written and published over 500 blog posts, and written and published about two dozen articles, one of which had nearly 10,000 views on LinkedIn.

I was even shortlisted for the 2016 Text Prize for my upcoming novel, *Black Spot*, and it was a point of pride for me when one of Text Publishing's employees told me my book wouldn't need a copyeditor because I'd done such a good job.

So imagine my surprise when, as I sat right beside him, my father told a group of his friends and acquaintances that I was an "amateur writer".

We were having dinner, catching up after not having seen each other for a while, when someone I was meeting for the first time asked what I did and when I replied, "I'm a writer," he added, "An amateur writer."

"No," I challenged him, a little bit stunned in light of all of my achievements, "I'm a professional writer."

I know why he said it. Because after those three years of full-time writing, I went back to full-time work that had nothing to do with writing because I couldn't afford not to anymore and because I didn't want to expend my writing energy on projects I didn't care about (i.e. not my own) so I chose not to take on a writing job.

I found it refreshing. It was easy, the people were lovely and the pay was steady. But it meant that I didn't do nearly as much writing as I was able to in previous years. But did it make me any less of a writer? Any less of a professional? I don't think so. But apparently my father did. And I suspect it is entirely to do with the financial aspect.

I have sales here and there and royalties are constantly trickling in but apart from those heady first few weeks after one of my books is released, it's never more than a trickle, certainly not enough for someone paying a mortgage to live off. I always think even that trickle is amazing considering I do little to no marketing (telling those people at that dinner party that I was a writer was the most marketing I'd done in six months).

It's funny that so much of what we think of ourselves is filtered through what our family thinks of us. But in most cases, families have no real understanding of what we do on a day-to-day basis or how we are perceived in our careers, regardless of whatever it is we do. Even when I was working a full-time non-writing job, I was still running my own business after hours. That included my writing (both fiction and non-fiction) and writing, editing, proofreading and project managing primarily marketing materials for others. I don't really talk about my freelance work with my family, mostly because I don't think it's all that interesting as a topic of conversation.

But I get paid for it. Maybe I should talk about it more. Or maybe that's just self-indulgent. Maybe it shouldn't matter how much I earn or what my father thinks. But for some reason, it does. The part about what my father thinks anyway. I want him to be proud of me. And more importantly, I want him to understand that I'm actually doing well at this. Sure, I'm not in the realms of JK Rowling and it's not likely I ever will be, but that's not really the goal I've set for myself, probably because I'm not a big picture or big goal kind of person.

I started out just wanting to write a book. And when I achieved that, I set a goal to publish it. After I published, my new goal was to write another book. And when it was finished, my next goal was to publish it. I think you can see the pattern. Nowhere in my goal setting was getting paid huge sums of money for my writing a factor. That's probably because I'm a realist and because I know it's unlikely. If it ever happens, it will be a bonus.

If it doesn't, that won't make me any less of a writer or any less of a professional. I guess my next goal is to help my father see it, too.

THE QUESTION EVERY WRITER IS ASKED: WHAT'S YOUR REAL JOB?

A couple of Christmases ago, I was talking to my 11-year-old niece about what she wanted to be when she grew up.

"An author," she said. I threw my arms around her, mostly in solidarity but a little in sympathy since I knew what she was in for. A bit of success but more often than not a lot of struggle.

In January, just over a month later, at my sister's birthday party, my niece and I were having the same conversation with my 12-year-old nephew. "You can get paid to play Fortnite, you know," he told me. There was a tournament being held at the Australian Open that weekend with half a million dollars in prizemoney available.

"But what will your other job be?" I asked. He looked at me blankly. "Getting paid to play Fortnite is a pretty sweet gig so there will be lots of people who want that job. But not everyone can get paid to play Fortnite so you'll probably need another job," I explained. He couldn't come up with anything else and that's okay because he's 12.

I was very careful to ask the question that way – "What will your other job be?" – because almost every writer – and even Fortnite players trying to make a career out of it – knows they will need another job and almost every writer, upon responding to the question of "What do you do?" by saying they're a writer, has been asked, "What's your real job?"

It's not just writers without a profile who are subjected to this. When Clementine Ford, a reasonably well-known Australian writer, announced that she would no longer be writing columns for Fairfax newspapers (her decision), conservative media responded by calling her "unemployed". The fact that she'd never been employed by Fairfax in the first place – because she was and still is a freelancer – didn't seem important to them. Neither did the fact that her columns would instead be appearing in other media outlets. Or that she's the author of two bestselling books, *Fight Like a Girl* and *Boys Will Be Boys*. Apparently, if it isn't a permanent role with a salary, superannuation and sick leave, even if it does earn you money, then they think it isn't worthy of being called a job.

For two years between 2017 and 2019, I worked an administration role during the day, did freelance editing work during the evenings and tried to write in the very little spare time I had. When I started that administration role, I made a very clear choice not to add it to my LinkedIn profile or change my description, which reads, "Blogger, Writer and Editor." That's because writing and editing are my career. They have been for a long time – more than 15 years – and that includes permanent roles, temporary roles, freelance roles and my own unpaid writing work (mostly permanent roles actually). Administration is just what I was doing then to pay the bills and save up enough money to write full-time again.

This, I decided, would be my new normal. I don't want a permanent role, writing, editing or otherwise. I want to choose what to write and edit. But I still need to be able to support myself. So I will work a job I don't give two hoots about for as long as I need to reach a certain savings goal (or for as long as I can stand it without wanting to kill all my co-workers). And then I will go back to writing full-time for as long as I can (until the money runs out). And then I will do it all again.

It's not a perfect solution. (In fact, it's one that worries my family – what if I run out of money, can't get another job, have to sell my still-mortgaged house and subsequently move in with one of them? None of us wants that.) But this is the compromise deal I've made with myself. I live an unsatisfactory life for a couple of years so I can live a happy one for a couple of years afterwards.

And in those couple of happy years, when I'm asked what my real job is, I will only be able to say I'm a writer. Just a writer. Nothing more, nothing less, no back-up answer, no socially acceptable alternative. And anyone who doesn't like it can go get a real job.

JUST WRITE, IT'LL BE OKAY! (NO, IT WON'T – WRITERS FOR HIRE NEED A BRIEF)

I think I'm safe enough making a general statement here: most writers would love to be in a position to simply write what they want when they want. Unfortunately, having to earn a living that lifts you above the poverty line often means writers either work a non-writing job or offer their services to write things that under normal circumstances they couldn't care less about. Non-writing jobs result in equal parts financial independence and resentment but being a writer for hire can just as often be a minefield. There are lots of reasons for this but there's one that has stood out for me in several writing requests and that's being asked to write something but not being provided with a brief.

It won't come as a shock to anyone with even a small amount of common sense but professional writers aren't mind readers. We don't have some sort of sixth sense that allows us to automatically know what needs to be written. So when we're asked to write about something that we aren't specialists in or aren't particularly interested in, we need instructions that comprise more than just one sentence.

Anyone with an interest in a positive outcome on both sides of this writing equation will understand. After all, writing is a job like any other. Would we ask a plumber to plumb but not let on which appliance needs attention? Would we ask a doctor to treat us but withhold a description of the symptoms? I suppose we could but it would be just as pointless as asking a writer to write without providing a brief.

On all of the occasions on which I've been asked to write something but haven't been provided with a brief, even after requesting one, the results have been just okay. And it's hardly surprising given how difficult it is to

26

write well when you have no idea if you're heading in the right writing direction.

But there's something else that each of these experiences have had in common and that was the almost sociopathic nature of the person requesting the writing. Since I'm not a sociopath, I don't understand the motivation of deliberately hiring someone in order to see them fail or at least not do the best they can do. But I can see now in retrospect that's exactly the kind of people they were.

If you're a writer for hire or thinking about offering your services as one, you should insist on a brief for any piece of writing you are asked to write and these are the things that should be included:

- The intended audience – a writer needs to know whether what they're writing is for teenagers, CEOs, mothers, current clients, potential clients or even a general audience in order to either tailor a piece of writing or ensure it isn't tailored in a way that will alienate one or several demographics.
- The purpose – a writer needs to know what the piece of writing is intended to achieve; it might be sales, it might be a demonstration of leadership, it might be a demonstration of knowledge but each will result in a different piece of writing.
- The topic – usually this is a given but it needs to be reasonably specific, reasonably detailed; after all, being asked to write about meat is very different to being asked to write about how to make Polish sausages.
- The key points – I'm sure the process for making Polish sausages is relatively simple once you know it but unless the writer for hire is also a sausage expert – and this is going to be reasonably unlikely – then the basics will need to be outlined. (At this point, it might sound like the person hiring the writer could have just written the piece themselves but the whole point is that they can't – or at least that they can't do it well. They might, however, have the knowledge the writer needs and part of the writing process may be conducting an informal interview in order to get it out of them.)
- The preferred writing style – the intended audience may partially dictate the preferred writing style but sometimes a client wants a corporate or conversational or academic tone that isn't necessarily associated with the expected readers or the proposed topic, which is why it needs to be explicit.
- The length – not only does the required length of the piece of writing allow you to estimate your investment of time and quote

your fee, it also prevents you from wasting your time by writing too much or embarrassing yourself by writing too little.

If any person attempting to hire a writer doesn't know or refuses to provide the answers to all these questions, then either they aren't ready to hire a writer or they're one of those aforementioned sociopaths looking to waste your time and make themselves feel better by making you feel bad. Neither is the kind of client a writer for hire wants or needs.

A long time ago when I worked as an admin assistant for an accounting firm, I remember the partners talking about how they had clients who took up an inordinate amount of time but provided few financial rewards and how they had chosen not to provide accounting services to those clients anymore. I can't imagine it's a comfortable conversation for the about-to-be-former clients, being dumped by your accountant, but there's a lesson to be learned from the choices those accountants made. Regardless of the industry you work in, whether it's accounting or writing, everyone has the right to choose the clients they work with. And although the financial imperative sometimes makes writers think we have to take on every client who asks for our services, it's in our best interests to vet them first, especially if it saves us from the heartbreak of working with a sociopath.

MEMOIR VERSUS FACTION VERSUS FICTION

When I enrolled in a master's degree course at university to study writing at the postgraduate level in my late 20s, it came as something of a shock to me that almost all of my fellow students were retired or much older people interested in writing just one thing: their own story. Perhaps it was my relative youth and my correlating lack of life experience that meant I didn't really understand why. After all, nothing much had happened to me at that point. (In fact, it's over a decade later and nothing much has happened to me even now.)

But it wasn't just that I'd stumbled across a rare collection of people focused on telling their own stories. These people, I've since discovered, are everywhere. And since there are just as many – probably a lot more – people wanting to read the real-life stories of others, it makes sense that so many people pursue this avenue of writing.

But it's not just as simple as putting it all out there. Writers who want to tell their own stories have plenty to consider.

MEMOIR

Memoir: a record of one's own life and experiences

In most cases, people wanting to tell their story also want the credit for it, both as the writer and as the person who has lived the events that comprise the story. It's easier to get people to read your memoirs if you already have a profile of some sort – politician, businessperson, sportsperson – or if you've done something outrageous, courageous or almost unbelievable.

Most of those people in my master's course weren't famous. They were just ordinary, everyday people who thought their story was worthy of being told. The advent of self-publishing has certainly contributed to the ease with which people without profiles can write and produce their memoirs, although publicising the existence of the book remains a source of difficulty without a traditional publisher's backing or some specialist marketing knowledge.

Some memoirs are written and published anonymously, usually when the exploits contain sexual elements or explorations. Writing under a pseudonym, Belle de Jour published *The Intimate Adventures of a London Call Girl* and *The Further Adventures of a London Call Girl*, the inspiration for the television series *Secret Diary of a Call Girl*. But it seems as though even if you do publish a memoir anonymously that readers can't stand not knowing who the author is and do just about anything and everything to figure it out. Belle de Jour later outed herself as Brooke Magnanti, a child health scientist who supplemented her income during her doctoral studies by working as an escort, only revealing her real identity when she thought she was going to be exposed anyway.

One thing – one very important thing – to consider when writing your memoir is how much you end up revealing about the people in your life, both those close to you and those on the fringe. These people often haven't chosen for their stories and their secrets to be revealed but in order for you to tell your story, sometimes you have to tell a part of theirs. These people may resent you for exposing them without their consent.

In 2016, I helped John "JJ" Jeffery to write and publish his memoir, *Paula & Me*. In the introduction, he wrote, "Of course, the story of my life is – for the most part – the story of my life with Paula. We were married for 42 years and together for more than 45..." His wife had passed away earlier that year but for those whose stories encompass people still living, their feelings about how they are represented in the story have to be a consideration. JJ partially resolved this issue by naming only family and friends and leaving anyone who may have had a problem with their inclusion unnamed.

FACTION

Faction: blending fact with fiction in creative writing

This is a term I've only recently become familiar with from reading Glenice Whitting's *Something Missing*. Glenice and I studied writing together in the late 1990s and as I was reading her latest book, I realised it was a thinly veiled story of her own life. Later, when I read an interview she'd done, she used the term "faction" to describe what she'd written.

I wondered why she didn't just write a memoir. Perhaps it was because she'd already established herself as a fiction writer with her first book, *Pickle to Pie*. Perhaps she thought her story wasn't quite interesting enough and needed just a dash of fiction to bring it up to publishing standard. Perhaps she wanted to hide behind the altered names. Perhaps, perhaps, perhaps…

There are a number of advantages in this type of writing. You don't need to do a significant amount of research or creation, meaning you can really focus on writing beautiful prose. You can disguise your significant others if the inclusion of their roles in your life might cause them distress. And you don't need to convince a publisher that you're important enough for your story to be published because it's ostensibly fiction, despite the number of included facts that your family and friends will recognise.

But there are also a few potential dangers in choosing to write faction. Readers who don't know that the story is essentially the real story of the author may want to critique the plot and writers might take offence that it has been deemed lacking. After all, the "plot" is their life. Also when editors suggest changes, the author's inclination may be to respond, "But that's not what really happened." It's a valid objection in a memoir but not necessarily in a work of faction.

Faction is very popular these days, particularly using famous historical figures (although writing faction that involves others – instead of yourself – requires huge amounts of research to get the story right and to make sure the fictional components are consistent with the factual ones). But it's always exciting, especially to me, when new types of writing come along. It just goes to show that we haven't quite reached the point of endlessly recycling the same stories in the same ways as is sometimes alleged.

FICTION

Fiction: imaginative narrative, especially in prose form such as novels or short stories

You don't have to be a writer or even a reader to know exactly what fiction is. It might be inspired by real-life events and people but it is writing that is primarily invented, imagined, made up, not true and not intended to be taken as anything other than the work of a creative and fertile mind.

For most writers, our lives aren't anywhere near interesting enough to commit to writing either faction or memoir so we indulge in the wonder of imagining other lives, other people, other worlds, other narratives to come up with a story. And when we do include elements from our own lives, they are usually just starting points that end up completely unrecognisable in the end. I fall into this category. And they have to be unrecognisable. I spend what feels like 90% of my life tapping away on a laptop and nobody in their right mind would want to spend an entire book reading about that.

For those wanting to fictionalise their life story, it usually involves sticking somewhat closely to the events as they happened but adding a lot of imaginary elements to increase the levels of excitement. It also usually means that when an editor suggests a plot change and assuming the author agrees that it makes the story better, there's less resistance to the alteration. Comparatively anyway. When Stephen King advises you as a writer that you need to be prepared to "kill your darlings" in fiction, it's a metaphor, not something that we're also expected to do in faction or memoirs.

∞

I used to be very much against the idea of ordinary people writing memoirs. I thought it was self-indulgent. And I hated being forced to read them in high school (given I'm more of an action adventure, thriller and mystery reader, it makes sense). But I've come to realise it's no more self-indulgent than any other kind of writing. Me wanting to tell my fictional stories is self-indulgent. So good luck to anyone who can find an audience for anything they want to write. That's one of the ultimate determinants of the worthiness of telling your story.

But it's useful to consider the faction and fiction alternatives as a means of presenting your real life in writing in the same way that it's useful to consider a screenplay as an alternative to a novel. Identifying the right format for you and your story is one of the keys to doing it justice.

I AM THE VERY MODEL OF AN UNKNOWN AUTHOR IMMEMORIAL

I'm very bad at marketing and anything promotional
Even though with books I'm always quote devotional
In short, in matters authorial and even editorial
I am the very model of an unknown author immemorial
(And in this case, a bit of a plagiarist and an awful lyricist)

I know I do plenty right when it comes to my writing. If I thought differently, I probably would have given up a long time ago. But I know I do plenty wrong as well. How do I know that? Because I've written three books of writing, editing, publishing and marketing advice and often it's a case of "do as I say, not as I do" because at least 50% of the time, I don't – and sometimes just can't bring myself to – follow my own advice. Which undoubtedly has something (probably a lot) to do with why I remain an unknown author (since time immemorial).

Here's a (hardly comprehensive) list of things I do wrong.

I ONLY WRITE WHEN I FEEL LIKE IT

A lot of writers say you really know you're a writer when you force yourself to sit down and write every day. For several years, I had a nine-to-five job that I sometimes didn't leave until eight o'clock. When I finally got home, I could barely be bothered eating, let alone writing and that was if I didn't have freelance work to get done. So I only wrote when I felt like it. That was usually two to three times a week and mostly on weekends.

The first time I wrote full-time without the distraction (and security) of paid work, I wrote nearly every day (weddings, funerals and family birthdays excepted). And even though I wrote nearly every day, I still only wrote when I felt like it. The difference, of course, was that I felt like writing more often and I had the time to do it. I'm a full-time writer again now but I'm at the stage where I've done so much writing that I actually need to focus on publishing it. So I'm writing a lot less and doing a lot of editing and publishing instead.

Something that I've noticed is that I do my best writing if I only write when I feel like it. I think it's because I spend a lot of time thinking about what I want to say and by the time I get the urge, it all just spills out of me in a form very close to what ends up being the final version.

I'VE NEVER BEEN PART OF A WRITING GROUP

The closest I've ever come to being part of a writing group – sharing my first drafts, reading the first drafts of others, providing and responding to feedback, sharing my second drafts, reading the second drafts of others and so on – was when I was studying for my two writing qualifications. We were all still learning so a lot of what we wrote wasn't great but that was the whole point, I suppose. And while I found it valuable at the time, once I had my qualifications, I just wanted to write on my own.

Part of it is about time. Time spent doing anything else is time not spent writing and I resent that a lot. Part of it is about the diversity of other writers. I'd say at least 75% of all books written don't interest me. I remember that from my time studying; there were so many pieces of writing about things that I wouldn't have chosen to read if we'd been given the choice.

But most of it is about me. I'm a loner, a recluse, a hermit (as much as someone with a very large extended family allows). And I'm also someone who wants to help make every piece of writing she sees the best it can possibly be. I already don't have enough time to do this for my own writing so I have to be kind to myself and keep away from other writers while they're writing.

I DON'T DO ANY NETWORKING

Even when I'm finished writing, I don't seek out other writers or people in the publishing industry very often. I'm as much of a writer as anyone else who claims the title but whenever I'm in the company of other writers and industry people, I feel uncomfortable. I feel out of place. I feel like a fraud.

I'm an introvert and borderline anti-social so it's not surprising I feel that way and a lot of other writers I speak to (when I do speak to them) confess to feeling the same way. The difference, of course, is that they do it anyway because they know how important it is to know and be known by all the right people.

My biggest fear is saying or doing something that means I get remembered for the wrong reasons and so, in the end, I prefer not to be remembered at all. It's counterintuitive and counterproductive for someone who wants to be read. I strongly recommend nobody follows my lead in this respect.

I DON'T HAVE ANYONE ELSE EDIT MY WRITING

Having a professional edit your writing is expensive. I know. As well as being a writer, I'm also a trained editor. I have a side hustle editing books, magazines and marketing materials and my hourly rate is four to six times more expensive than the hourly rate I earned at my previous day job.

All the advice out there says that writers must have their work professionally edited in order to be taken seriously. And it's good advice. Most writers don't have the capacity to edit their own work to the standard required for publishing.

I'm not most writers. I feel very confident that spending money to have someone else edit my writing would simply be an expensive way of having someone read my work. They're not going to find many, if any, errors. Yes, I'm that good. I was told by someone who worked for a publisher and who was part of a panel assessing my book for a competition that my writing didn't need any copyediting. I assumed the fact that it was commented on meant it was rare.

This isn't to say that I don't have anyone giving me feedback on my writing prior to publishing. I have a selection of beta readers who give me feedback on plot and characters and style and all of those kinds of things, amateur manuscript assessors. If they find a mistake, they'll also point it out. But I am, and will continue to be, my own editor for as long as my unknown author status makes it the best financial choice. And maybe even after that.

I PUBLISH WHEN I THINK MY BOOK CAN'T GET ANY BETTER

I know some people can work on a single book for decades, revising and refining and querying agents and publishers until they finally get a bite on the hundreds of lines they've thrown out into the water. I'm not a patient person. I like working on various projects to ward off boredom. And I will eventually get to a point in all my books where I think they're pretty good, good enough that I don't have any more ideas on how to make them better and I'm sick of working on them. That is the point at which I will publish.

I've published four books this way. They could probably all be better. But I'm not going to wait around for my fairy bookmother to come along and tell me how. And since no one else is lining up for the job either, I choose to publish instead.

Maybe they're not perfect but I'm a published author with four- and five-star ratings, which means people have read my books. I think that's better than harbouring the perfect book that no one has ever read.

I DON'T DO ANY PRE-RELEASE MARKETING

Because I self-publish, once a book is ready to go – edited, formatted, book cover designed, ISBN registered – I always publish it immediately. I don't set a schedule a few months in advance and then dangle hints and tweet cover reveals and ask famous writers to review it for some fame by loose association. I just publish. Which means I don't do any pre-release marketing.

I HARDLY DO ANY POST-RELEASE MARKETING EITHER

Once the book is out there, I send an email to all my friends, family and acquaintances, share the news on LinkedIn, tweet an announcement, post another announcement on my blog and add the book to Goodreads. If I'm feeling especially in the marketing mood, I might do some very cheap paid advertising. (I've only done that for two of my four books though.) And then I move onto my next book.

Yes, it would not be uncharitable to label me the world's worst marketer (if the thing I'm marketing is me or my books – I'm a lot better at it when I'm marketing other people and their work). It's partly to do with not enjoying the spotlight but it's mostly to do with not enjoying huge amounts of effort for little reward. That's the chance you take with writing a book, some might say. But, I answer, there's a book at the end of it. That's the reward for writing a book. With marketing, if you put in all that effort and still no one reads your book, there is no reward, just a lot of wasted time.

I DON'T HAVE MY OWN WEBSITE

I have a blog, Single White Female Writer, on WordPress but so do about a billion other people all competing for attention and it's not quite the same thing as having my own website. References to my books are buried further and further back in the timeline each time I post something new and with the over 500 pieces of content on there (mostly writing, editing and publishing advice and book reviews, not specifically about me and my writing), it's not easy to find... well, anything.

I know exactly what my website should have on it. I've helped develop websites for other writers. I guess I just haven't gotten around to it. The thought of having to put even more energy into another online platform is exhausting. Possibly more wasted marketing time. I'll get to it eventually, I'm sure. Just not yet.

I DON'T CAPITALISE ON ANY SUCCESS I DO HAVE

I've written and published four books, I've ghostwritten another, my next two books are nearly ready to go and I've got another few in various stages from development to partly written. I've been paid to write articles. I wrote an article that had nearly 10,000 views on LinkedIn. My upcoming book was shortlisted for the 2016 Text Prize. But every time I have a little bit of writing success, I bask briefly in whatever praise I receive, then retreat hastily back into my precious anonymity. Because while I love the idea of being a full-time writer, to have enough of an income to be able to do that, I really don't like the idea of fame.

And the thing about anonymity and being relatively unknown is that it means you can write whatever you want. My upcoming book clearly has a sequel coming but I haven't written it yet. If it was published through a traditional publisher, there would be significant pressure to write the sequel and get it out there to capitalise on whatever success the first in the series had. It wouldn't matter if the sequel was any good, just that it was ready to go. I know because I've seen it happen. I've had a publisher confirm it to me when I commented on how I hadn't liked a sequel they'd published.

∞

I might be completely delusional but I'm going to continue doing things exactly as I am now because this is what makes me happy and if I'm meant to be anything more than an unknown author immemorial, it will happen regardless of anything I do or don't do. In the end, there's no right way; there's just my way. And your way. And his way. And her way. I hope we all get where we want to go.

SHOULD YOU WRITE A CHRISTMAS-THEMED BOOK?

Clearly, it's much easier to make the decision to write a Christmas-themed chapter (a thousand or so words, a fairly small investment of writing time) but should you write an entire Christmas-themed book? Depending on the type of books you write, it could be another small (or at least smaller) investment of writing time (such as with children's books) or it could be months or years of your life (such as with full-length novels).

As with all writing choices, there are pros and cons. The final decision (and the reasons behind it) for one person will be completely different to the final decision (and the reasons behind it) for another. So this decision needs to be the right decision for you.

REASONS TO DO IT

You have a story that makes no sense without the Christmas theme

The biggest and best reason to write a Christmas-themed story is that you have a Christmas-themed story rumbling around in your head that you just have to get down on paper, one that makes absolutely no sense if you try to take the Christmas theme out of it.

Many of these stories will naturally revolve around families getting together and annoying each other in a way that only families can do. But there will need to be something more than that because everyone, even non-writers, has stories like that rumbling around in their heads from personal experience.

You know exactly when to release and market it

Trying to decide when to release a book can be a marketing nightmare. A lot of people are tempted to simply release it when it's ready but doing that generally means you haven't given enough thought to a marketing plan. But with a Christmas-themed book, the timing of the release and marketing is obvious. A late October to mid-November release gives you enough time to build up to your all-out marketing assault and by the time December comes around, the general Christmas buzz that happens every year will feel a little like it's happening just for you.

It's not an excuse to slack off though. You still have to think about how your Christmas-themed book is going to stand out from all the other Christmas-themed items and events jockeying for attention at this time of the year.

You can do a new marketing campaign each year at the same time

A Christmas-themed book can be the gift that keeps on giving for a writer because each year at the same time, you can do a new marketing campaign to remind people that even though it's not a new book, it's still a perfect read for that time of the year. Many books get forgotten after those heady first months of the initial release but with a Christmas-themed book, you have a legitimate reason to remind people year after year.

Reading a Christmas-themed book every year could become a Christmas tradition

If people enjoy reading the book, it could become one of their Christmas traditions to read it each year at this time of the year. Remaining front and centre in a reader's mind is always a challenge for writers so if your old books can help that process, you'll have an advantage for your future books over other authors who have faded into a little bit of obscurity.

REASONS NOT TO DO IT

You could be trying to force it to be a Christmas story when it isn't really one

There are some stories that can't be told without a Christmas theme but there are just as many, probably more, that don't need a Christmas theme at all. It's important to consider which category your story falls into. Trying to force your story into a Christmas-themed book when it doesn't need to be isn't going to do you or your readers any favours. It's going to be harder to write, harder to market and harder to find an audience for apart from a very specific time of the year.

Christmas stereotypes could make your book just one of millions

There are already an awful lot of Christmas-themed books out there and if yours doesn't have something that sets it apart, it could simply get lost in the crowd. There are just as many Christmas stereotypes – snow, Santa, family dysfunction, turkey, eggnog, gifts – and while these things are worth celebrating, millions of books have done it all before. Christmas is celebrated in many different ways around the world – in Australia, hot weather and seafood are more common than snow and roast turkey; in Japan, KFC (yes, you read that right, Kentucky Fried Chicken) has emerged as a quirky tradition in recent times and there's even a special Christmas menu – so a little research into how others do it could be in order.

People might not want to read a Christmas book at non-Christmas times of the year

Writing a Christmas-themed book may limit its readership at other times of the year. You only have to listen to talk-back radio to hear people annoyed by hot cross buns in bakeries in January or Christmas decorations and paraphernalia when it goes on display too early (in their opinion). So the idea of reading a Christmas-themed book in May might just be too much for their compartmentalised lives and mindsets.

A good book is a good book at any time of the year but convincing readers that a Christmas-themed book can be read at any time other than Christmas is always going to be a challenge.

Releasing a Christmas book at any time other than Christmas doesn't make sense

Part of what makes releasing a Christmas-themed book at Christmas time great is that the marketing is so much easier. Those who celebrate Christmas or who are in countries that celebrate Christmas expect to see Christmas products and you can leverage that. But trying to push a Christmas message at other times of the year can be like pushing a double-door refrigerator up the side of a hill – damn hard if not downright impossible. Christmas in July is a theme in some southern hemisphere countries (just because they want to take advantage of the snow and give people an experience of a northern hemisphere Christmas) but otherwise there aren't any other exceptions.

So you have to be ready to release at a very specific time of the year. And if you miss it, you'll have to wait a full year for that time to come around again.

You could be alienating non-Christian audiences

Less than one-third of the world's population identifies as Christian so writing a Christmas-themed book could alienate non-Christian audiences, who make up a significant portion of the reading world. There are many other religious and cultural celebrations that take place around the same time that Christmas does and there are far fewer books with these themes so it could be worth exploring the alternatives, including Hanukkah (Judaism), Rohatsu also known as Bodhi Day (Buddhism), the Solstice (winter in the northern hemisphere and summer in the southern hemisphere for Wiccans and Pagans) and Kwanzaa (a celebration of African heritage). There are also Muslim holidays, although because they are celebrated according to lunar calendars, they aren't at the same time each year but they still happen on a rough yearly basis.

∞

Let's just add this to the already very long list of things that make writing hard. But the choice is yours. And as long as you've considered all the pros and cons, you'll be in a much better position to make the right one.

SHOULD YOU SET NEW YEAR'S WRITING RESOLUTIONS?

I published this chapter as a blog post initially just before New Year's because I thought to myself, *I should write a New Year's-themed blog post* (just like the Christmas-themed previous chapter that was initially a blog post that was published on the day after Christmas). I've written about New Year's writing resolutions before, setting four goals at the start of 2016 (that I pretended weren't goals to relieve a little bit of the pressure on myself) and writing at the end of 2016 about how successful I'd been (about 50/50 – I achieved some of them, failed entirely at others and achieved things during the year that I'd never even thought about when I was setting those goals).

I wasn't sure I ever wanted to set goals again. Setting goals and then failing is demoralising. And I always fail at goals, especially ones that have definitive and relatively short deadlines. More often than not, I accomplish them but long after any arbitrary time frames I've set. That sums me up really. I'm easygoing. I'm laidback. I'm not ambitious. I'm happy to succeed over years rather than months and pressure to do it sooner doesn't make it happen. In fact, it makes it less likely to happen.

So I asked myself, *Should I be setting New Year's writing resolutions? Should I be setting goals at all?*

Clearly, I have set and met goals in the past. I wanted to write books. I have. I wanted to publish them. I have. I wanted to earn money from my writing. I have (although I'd like to earn more). I know a lot of people would look at my life and say I could have achieved so much more and sooner if I'd set and stuck to goals with deadlines. But I don't know if I would be any happier than I am now.

Almost all of my biggest achievements (the ones that are important in my mind) have come from a reasonably spontaneous place. Yes, writing can take a long time but when I published my first two books, I made the decision to publish and did it all within the space of a week or two. When I was shortlisted for the 2016 Text Prize, it was a competition I entered on the spur of the moment simply because I had an unpublished book ready that met the criteria. I like that kind of spontaneity because it means I don't have a long time to get my hopes up and I don't have huge investments of time and effort to be regretted if everything doesn't go the way I'd hoped.

When I really thought about what I wanted to achieve in the coming year, it all came back to balance. In the past four years, I've been officially diagnosed with an autoimmune condition. (I thought I was putting on weight but actually I was getting swollen from my body attacking itself. Yay!?) My dad's three best friends died. My cat died. My stepmother needed help writing, designing and printing several batches of marketing flyers. I spent a lot of time with my grandfather (like I have since my grandmother died). I babysat. I took on freelance editing work. In short, my life was getting in the way of my writing.

So my goal for the next year, for every year from now on really, is balance. I will continue freelancing but I will also continue writing. I will take care of myself so that I can keep doing both. Life will happen and probably keep getting in the way but it's better than the alternative of life not happening.

And what about you? Should you set New Year's writing (or life) resolutions? Only you can answer that. If you respond well to a little bit or a lot of pressure, then maybe goals with a deadline will help you achieve what you want. If you don't respond well to pressure, then specific goals may be counterintuitive. Whatever you decide, it has to be right for you.

For all writers, the best advice has to be to just keep writing, just keep writing, just keep writing... In the end, you'll get somewhere. It may not be where you planned or when but sometimes that destination is better than the one you thought you wanted.

PART 2

CHARACTERS

CO-OPTING REAL-LIFE PEOPLE TO BE CHARACTERS IN YOUR FICTION

While many authors love the freedom that creating a brand new and completely fictional character offers, others want to tell stories that involve people who exist or have existed in real life. It can be a powerful motivation for readers to want to read it but it can also be a minefield if it's done badly. Here are a few things to think about to help you get it right.

PREPARE TO DO A LOT OF RESEARCH

If you're choosing to use a real-life person as a character, then you'll have to know them inside and out, as much as is possible at least. And that means research. A lot of it. An awful lot of it to get the details right.

Jed Rubinstein's *The Interpretation of Murder* uses several real-life figures in the early 1900s movement of psychoanalysis (which at the time was new, controversial and in competition with neurology) as characters including Sigmund Freud, Carl Jung, Sandor Ferenczi, Ernest Jones and Abraham Brill.

But he didn't just decide to do it on a whim. Rubinstein had been fascinated by Freud for a long time, writing a thesis on the famous psychiatrist during his senior undergraduate year at Princeton. In particular, it seemed he'd been intrigued by Freud's one and only trip to America. Little was known about what had happened while he was there and what, if anything, made him never want to return. It was the perfect gap to fill with a little bit of fiction informed by well-researched assumptions.

The book wove together real and fictional incidents so well that Rubinstein included an essay at the end to separate them out. He didn't want to pretend that he had any idea what had really happened. He just wanted a vehicle for writing a cracking novel and perhaps to find a few new converts to his long-standing fascination with Sigmund Freud.

THE MORE FAMOUS THE BETTER

The more famous the real-life person you choose to include in your story, the more information you'll have access to. After all, if you're going to write about somebody real, part of the reason is that they are already fully developed characters.

And from a marketing perspective, the better known your real-life character is, the wider the automatic audience there will be for your novel. But if part of your motivation is to get a less well-known person some of the recognition you think they deserve, it might be more work but it could be a lot more rewarding, too.

ALTERNATIVE HISTORIES

If you want to write a "what if?" alternative history, then using real-life people as characters is just a given. But remember all that research I was talking about earlier? Triple it.

THE DEADER THE BETTER

Real-life people who are already dead are much less likely to kick up a fuss if they don't like your depiction of them. And the longer they've been dead, the less likely it is their friends, children, grandchildren, associates and acquaintances will still be alive to take issue with your novel either (and try to sue the pants off you).

It also means if you want to use incidents that have no basis in fact that it's easier to get away with. Phillipa Gregory's *The Other Boleyn Girl* was a smash hit and was just one in a series but academics have pointed out its many historical inaccuracies. Of course, none of the books had to be historically accurate because they were fiction, not non-fiction.

These inaccuracies were probably the result of creative choices but many of them were based on the rumours going round at the time and long since afterwards. So it doesn't mean you can get out of doing all that intensive research. It just means you can choose the facts that suit the story you want to tell.

PEOPLE WHO ARE STILL ALIVE

So what if you want to write about someone who's still alive? It's actually quite common to have real-life supporting characters. US presidents and European royalty get a lot of gigs in fiction. The key is usually to put them in stories that have absolutely nothing to do with their real lives. A fantastic example of this is John Birmingham's Axis of Time trilogy. Colonel Harry Windsor (known more commonly as Prince Harry) is part of a military group that gets sucked back in time to the 1940s. It's not really crucial that Prince Harry be in the book but it's certainly a talking point.

NOT A VEHICLE FOR VENGEANCE

If you are going to head down the real-life and still-alive route, it's important to remember that this kind of fiction is not a vehicle for vengeance unless your goal is to hand over to the inspiration for the character all the profits from the book and everything else you own. If vengeance is your goal, then it's important to do everything you can to disguise the real-life person you want to take your revenge on.

Attorney Lloyd J Jassin recommends the four "d"s in order to avoid the fifth "d" (a defamation lawsuit):

- Disclaim – include a legal statement that the characters are not based on or inspired by real people; everyone knows it's very rarely true but it's a common practice.
- Disassociate – that is, change enough about the character to disguise them to everyone who doesn't know them well.
- Depict (but don't disparage) – truth is a defence to accusations of defamation so if you include real events without exaggerating their extent or making judgements, it's hard to claim it's the writer rather than the perpetrator who is responsible for the bad reputation.
- Wait for death – okay, so it might take a while but it's the safest option apart from not writing about the real-life person at all.

WRITERS WHO'VE DONE IT WELL

There are plenty of writers who have paved the way in co-opting real-life people to be characters in their fiction but the king and one of the originals is, of course, William Shakespeare. Julius Caesar, Edwards, Henrys, Richards, King Duncan in *Macbeth*, Antony and Cleopatra. I don't think it's a coincidence, though, that writers who have co-opted real-life characters into their fiction and done it well are good writers generally. After all, why bother with all that effort if you're going to do it badly? So treat your real-life characters with the respect they deserve by putting them into a great story written well. It's the ultimate compliment.

OH, BROTHER! (AND SISTER): NAMING
FICTIONAL SIBLINGS

Naming characters is always a great deal of fun, like naming a baby but without having to go through nine months of pregnancy and a painful labour. Well, naming the first few is fun, at least. But what happens when you have to name hundreds? And what happens when you have to name a very specific group such as brothers and sisters?

Would Edwina ever have a brother named Lebron? It seems unlikely. And why does it matter so much? Let me illustrate with a couple of real-life examples.

I have a brother-in-law named Timothy. Timothy has a younger brother. Perhaps at the time his parents were naming him they didn't realise that calling his younger brother Thomas might draw a few guffaws later in life. But it did. Yes, they are Tim and Tom. And now fairly frequent namesakes in commercials featuring twin brothers advertising indigestion medication.

I also have twin nieces. Fraternal twins but arriving from the same womb on the same day nonetheless. Before they were born, my sister was contemplating names and mentioned she was thinking about calling them Olivia and Vivian. "Liv and Viv?" I piped up. I think it gave her pause and when they eventually came along, they were christened Olivia and Lexi. (Lexi is the name of one of my other sisters' cat but at least that was just something we could joke about within the family, not something that would plague the little girls their entire lives like rhyming monikers.)

The reason it helps to get it right when you're naming siblings in a book, apart from avoiding the sniggers, is that it's a really good way of making sure the reader can differentiate them and remember them. In Anne Tyler's book *Back When We Were Grownups*, there are four sisters nicknamed Biddy,

Patch, NoNo and Min Foo. I couldn't tell you what their real names are even though I've read the book and it is explained. I couldn't even tell you which sister is which, apart from Min Foo, who is the half-sister. But do they sound like related women in their thirties and forties or do they sound like a group of elderly bingo attendees?

Kris Jenner knew what she was doing – from a marketing perspective at least – when she named her five daughters Kimberley, Kourtney, Khloe, Kylie and Kendall. The first three are Kardashians and the last two are Jenners but that doesn't really matter because they sound like sisters. Well-marketed sisters but sisters nonetheless.

One of the keys to remember is that siblings are all named by the same people, their mother and father. So while Edwina and Lebron are implausible, Kimberley, Kourtney, Khloe, Kylie and Kendall make total (although somewhat terrifying) sense.

When I named the sisters in a TV show I developed Minerva, Salome, Dahlia, Jolie, Calista and Valentina, it was completely logical to me (and I hope to others) because their mother was a journalist with a classical education who shunned popular culture. When my mother named me and my sisters Louise, Natalie, Michelle, Stephanie, Elizabeth and Genevieve, it seemed right because they all have that English sound with just a touch of French influence. It's an even better story when you know that I was supposed to be named Elizabeth but that my father vetoed it and made it my second name because he didn't want to upset my paternal grandmother (Alberta known as Betty) since it was the name of my maternal grandmother (Elizabeth known as Betty). And that my mother divorced him (probably not for that reason) and had more children later, finally getting to use the name as she had wanted to all those years earlier. And that she never named Michelle at all because Michelle is actually my stepsister and was named by her biological parents. But we sound like sisters (perhaps because we are).

According to the internet (where else do we do our research these days?), there are several golden rules for naming siblings in the real world and I suppose it should apply in the fictional world as well:

- Each child's name should start with a different initial. "Yes, a certain reality TV family would argue this point, which may just prove it," says Claire Gillespie.
- Each child's name can start with the same initial. "There's a sweetness to siblings' names who share the same first letter," according to J Bartlet.
- None of the children's names should be matchy matchy. Why? "Because name substitutions are increased by factors like name

similarity and physical similarity," according to a study released by the University of Texas at Austin. Even fictional characters should have distinct identities. Sorry, Tim and Tom.

- Similar names are okay. But not rhyming names. Tim and Tom, you're back on. After all, it's not like they're Tim and Kim.
- The names should not have a theme. It's just cruel naming your kids Petal, Daisy and Poppy.
- The names can have a theme. "Nyuh, nyuh, nyuh, nyuh, nyuh," say Jools and Jamie Oliver.
- All the names should have a consistent style. Lebron and Latonya? Yes. Lebron and Edwina? No. Cultural and geographical backgrounds will come into play here.
- Do whatever the hell you want. Look out for little Lebron and Edwina in a future story of mine.

Your real children may hate you for it but at least your family of fictional brothers and sisters will never say a word (unless you write it for them). But do give it a bit of thought. After all, would we have fallen in love quite so deeply with Katniss and Primrose if they were Kathryn and Patricia? Somehow I don't think so.

THERE ONCE WAS A GIRL WHO LOOKED LIKE A HORSE…

During the first year of my first writing course, the Novel teacher set us students an in-class assignment to pick a fellow student, write a description of them the way we would if they were a character in our book and then read it aloud. Then everyone had to try to guess which student was being described.

There were a couple of rules:

- Before we started, we spent an uncomfortable and lengthy minute looking around the room, deciding who to write about and absorbing as much as possible about their appearance as we could but without staring and giving away our hand before we'd even begun writing.
- After that uncomfortable and lengthy minute, we weren't allowed to look at the person we were writing about again during the creative process in case it ruined the guessing game we were shortly about to play.
- We couldn't write a description that was too obvious. If there was only one boy in a blue shirt, then it wasn't going to be much of a challenge guessing who he was.

I'm not now and wasn't then much good at memorising faces. If I am ever asked to describe a criminal after witnessing a crime, I suspect I'm going to be very close to useless. When I do describe characters in my fiction, the details are so minimal that I mostly might as well not bother. So I made a strategic decision for this particular challenge to write about myself. If I wasn't going to be allowed to look at anyone else in the room to refresh my poor visual memory, at least I had a pretty good idea of what I looked like. And I wouldn't be able to break the rules by looking at myself.

I don't remember much about my description of myself apart from a strange focus on my jagged hairline. It was probably my flaw of the month. I do, however, remember that I wasn't the only one who chose to write about me.

Another female student whose name I don't remember and who I couldn't pick out of a line-up if I fell over her now that it's 20 years later (remember, bad with visual details) read her description. She had written about a long, dark ponytail that resembled a tail as it swished around. She had written about my height (taller than most other women in the course) and the proud arrogance of my posture (something I no longer have, if I ever did – I thought I was just sitting there). She had written about my nose, long and prominent. And then she drew it all together by equating my appearance with a horse. A thoroughbred, she explained. But, yes, a horse.

It wasn't my most favourite moment ever. I don't like being the centre of attention on any occasion, let alone one that focuses on how I look. Which is probably why I still remember it two decades after it happened. Thankfully, people don't write about me very often anymore and never in the context of my physical attributes.

Fictional characters, of course, are far less sensitive about the way they're described. That probably has a little to do with the fact that in popular literature most of them are supermodel beautiful and a lot to do with the fact that they aren't real people and don't do anything that their creators don't let them do (fan fiction notwithstanding). Few of them look like horses. Few of them have any physical flaws at all.

Descriptions of real people are usually somewhat less flattering, often because the writer is not just capturing the essence of the person but using their personal attributes as a means of attack. Donald Trump is a prime example. While I think there are many other ways of describing him that adequately portray him without referring to his appearance, the most common are related to the colour orange – "Cheeto-dusted", "carrot cake", "jack-o'-lantern", "pumpkin pie", "Oompa Loompa", "a rapey can of Fanta", "a huge lobster", "a poorly-trained circus orangutan", "watered with irradiated bat urine". It's all very amusing, assuming you don't like Trump's politics, but it's hardly contributing anything important. So he has a bad spray tan. So what? So have a lot of people. Half of women under the age of 25 in the UK have a very similar skin tone. But what is it actually adding to the debate around his performance as president of the United States?

Writers need to ask themselves the same question about any descriptions of people they write, fictional or non-fictional. If you're going to give a fictional character a bad spray tan or point out that a real-life person has one, what is it meant to say? That you want to ridicule them? That they have self-esteem issues? Or that it's evidence of misplaced priorities? In each case, there are probably better ways of doing it.

If your description of a person is borderline character assassination or just plain mean, you're going to have trouble. But if you can justify it on literary merits, then you'll probably end up okay. Because the best defence against an unhappy recipient is a brilliant piece of writing.

HOW MUCH OF OUR CHARACTERS ARE REALLY OURSELVES?

When I was 10 years old, I was in a car accident. My mother, stepfather, siblings and I were on a freeway driving out of the city after visiting my grandparents when a drunk driver sideswiped us.

Considering it happened over three decades ago, I still have a pretty clear memory of it. Our car was a green and creamy white van, possibly ex-army, with lots of khaki double bench seats and an aisle down the right side. Big families need big cars. Because there was so much room, we kids tended to move around a lot, even while we were in transit. Because of that, we weren't always wearing our seatbelts when we should have been.

We lived in a little country town about two hours outside of the city and we were barely on the outskirts. It was just starting to get dark. There was a police car somewhere nearby and my mum turned around in the front passenger seat to look at it. That's the last thing I remember before the accident. When I woke up, I was on the inside lane of the freeway, face down, trapped underneath a car with my foot caught in its engine.

It must have been horribly traumatising for the driver of that car. Not for me. I was unconscious while it was happening. I was told later that a drunk driver sideswiped our van, causing it to roll several times. Because I wasn't wearing a seatbelt, I crashed out of a window and was flung onto the road where the car that hit me couldn't stop in time. The wheels didn't run over me – they did a really good job of steering perfectly so they avoided that – but my foot managed to tangle itself in the engine and they pushed me along the freeway for about 100 metres.

That's when I woke up. I knew something bad had happened. There was pain. And I was stuck. I couldn't free my foot, meaning I couldn't pull myself out from under the car. I passed out again. When I woke up for a second time, I was in the back of an ambulance and they were inflating a temporary cast around my right ankle just in case it was broken.

They needed several ambulances to ferry us all to hospital but, surprisingly, our injuries were relatively minor. My mother had stepped on a piece of glass after the accident and was hopping around the emergency room from child to child, refusing to let the doctors near her (she is very afraid of needles and knew they would try to give her several). My stepbrother Brian had a cut over his eye. A centimetre lower and he would have been blinded. My stepsister Michelle had lacerations around her mouth and couldn't eat, drink or speak without pain. My sister Natalie had bruised ribs. Everyone else was fine. Shocked but fine.

I was the worst hurt. I had a severe abrasion high on my left cheek from being dragged face first down the freeway. And I hadn't broken my ankle but I had chipped off a piece of bone that to this day floats freely in there. I couldn't put any weight through my leg. I certainly couldn't walk without crutches. I stayed in hospital for four days while the swelling went down and the pain abated.

Despite the fact that there was a police officer who had witnessed the entire accident, the drunk driver was never charged with causing it. He had been allowed to speed off, with the police officer electing instead to stop, to help us and to manage the scene. The drunk driver was pulled over several hours later, still way over the legal blood alcohol limit, but nobody could prove definitively that he was the same driver and it was the same car.

I spent several weeks, possibly months (my memory gets a bit fuzzy on the timeline here), on the crutches before graduating to a walking stick. Yes, I was 10 years old and I had a walking stick. I went to sessions with the physiotherapist where they made me balance on a board with a ball stuck through it (and probably other things but that's the piece of equipment I specifically remember). Eventually, I was able to discard the walking stick. My ankle still swells every day, even now, but the pain is long gone.

The psychological side effects were more long lasting. For years afterwards, whenever I sat in the front passenger seat, I was sure the car next to us, the car coming to a stop at the t-intersection as we were driving past, the car approaching us from the opposite direction, was going to sideswipe us. After a few years, I settled down.

At least, I thought I did. What actually happened is that I spent a lot of that time being driven in the back seat or driving myself. What actually happened is that I spent barely any time in the front passenger seat.

In late 2019, my dad invited me to go see his new house in the country. My stepmother wasn't able to come because she was working. So instead of sitting in the back seat like I normally would when I spend time driving with them, I sat in the front passenger seat.

I completely freaked my dad out. I gasped and shrunk back as we drove up and then down the side of a mountain on the way there and on the way back. I closed my eyes and shrieked as he passed slow cars with plenty of clearance, sure we were going to collide. I yelled several times, "Stop, stop, stop!" as I misjudged the speed and how quickly we were coming up behind the cars in front of us.

My dad is a perfectly competent driver, a much better driver than me, but sitting in the front passenger seat and not being in control of the vehicle brought out all those fears I thought I'd gotten over but had just shoved deep down and avoided by hardly ever riding in the front passenger seat.

I hadn't thought about these fears for years. Except subconsciously. How do you think about something subconsciously? Well, when you're a writer, it comes out in your characters. In one of my books, the main character was in a car accident several years ago and reacts very badly whenever she travels in the front passenger seat of a car. Not when she drives. Not when she sits in the back. Just when she's in the front passenger seat. Yet again, I've been writing a main character who is essentially myself.

I actually thought I was past thinly veiled fictional versions of myself. I hope for the most part that I am and that these things just slip through now and then rather than all the time. I'll leave it to people who know me and read my writing to be the judge. Fingers crossed.

NAMING YOUR EVIL FICTIONAL CORPORATION

If there's anything that capitalism has taught us, it's that all companies are evil. They don't start out that way, they don't intend to be evil but somewhere along the corporate path they take, they all seem to end up not very nice. They pollute, they steal (from their workers, from their customers, from their competitors, from taxpayers and many, many others), they manipulate, they plan obsolescence, they cover up management misconduct, they are just generally bad.

Regardless, there comes a time in every writer's career when one of these evil corporations is exactly what a story needs. You can use the *Jennifer Government* (brilliant, brilliant book) method in which Max Barry uses actual big name corporations to skewer the path of consumerism but his publisher felt compelled to include a long-winded disclaimer that the references to real companies were "used simply to illustrate the increasingly important role played by large corporations in the future and not to denigrate them in any way. However, some people (whom we shall call 'lawyers') get very uptight when you describe large corporations masterminding murders. So let's be clear: this is a work of fiction set in the future." So maybe the way forward is to come up with a fictional corporation of your own.

The best place to start is to remember that nobody, not even in the real world, names their company with the intention of scaring the pants off anybody. Intimidate, maybe, but scare, no. And unless it's a fake company being run by a conman, the founders don't intend for their creations to be vessels for evil. So the fear that evil corporations and their names inspire comes from what the readers (and viewers in the case of television and movies) see them doing.

When I began writing *Enemies Closer*, I needed two companies: one that my main character worked for and one that was trying to destroy her. I wanted the company she worked for to be renowned and to resonate with readers familiar with the industry she worked in so I chose a real corporation, Heckler & Koch. A German gun manufacturer with facilities in the US, they were perfect (and as far as I know scandal-free).

But there was never any question in my mind that I would create a fictional evil corporation to represent the company trying to destroy her. I wasn't trying to make a statement about capitalism, I was just trying to write an interesting story. And I certainly didn't want to have to deal with any lawyers. But what to call it? The answer was staring me in the face the entire time.

During the years I was writing *Enemies Closer*, I worked full-time and at my place of employment, there was an official looking folder that sat on one of the shelves of a desk neighbour from an organisation called IBSA. It's more than a decade ago now but I think it stood for Innovation & Business Skills Australia and I think the contents of that folder outlined the requirements of courses to meet the standards for nationally recognised qualifications. IBSA. IBSA. IBSA. And just like that, International Ballistics & Strategic Arms was born, the perfect name for a company in the weapons industry that was being used as part of a plot to bring my main character down.

If you need a little inspiration for your own evil corporation, here are a few beautifully named evil corporations (although it's hard to say now whether they sounded evil before they became well known or if the sense of their evilness developed over time as we got to know them):

- Weyland-Yutani: In the first movie of the *Alien* franchise, the company was originally just known as Weyland but since 57 years passed between the story of *Alien* and the story of its sequel, it's reasonable to assume there was some kind of merger in the intervening years. Indeed, when the story was rebooted in *Prometheus* many years before the events of *Alien* took place, it was back to being just the Weyland Corporation. But I think we can all agree that Weyland-Yutani brings a sense of evilness that the singular name doesn't. Even though we didn't realise it at the time, I think the moment we should have known Weyland-Yutani was an evil corporation was when we heard Burke utter their meant-to-be-inspiring-but-slightly-ominous motto, "Building better worlds." To paraphrase *Serenity*, you'll never get to live there.

- Massive Dynamic: I've been a Joshua Jackson fan since the *Mighty Ducks* days but I've only recently started watching *Fringe* so I'm not 100% sure if Massive Dynamic is an evil corporation or not. They certainly have all the hallmarks: smug employees, missing billionaire founder, access to technologies that no one should have access to, knowledge of just about every bad thing going on in the *Fringe* universe, sometimes before it even happens.

- Cyberdyne Systems: They came along at a time when we were still a little bit suspicious of technology and the evil corporation of the *Terminator* franchise seemed destined to end up that way. After all, technology has no conscience.
- MomCorp: *Futurama*'s MomCorp sounds homey but, of course, if you've watched the show, it's run by a power-hungry woman who dominates her sons and toys with the emotions of Professor Farnsworth. MomCorp produces products such as suicide booths and killbots and has copyrighted "mom" and "love".
- Wolfram & Hart: Lawyers. Need we say more? How about lawyers for demons? They're a thorn in the side of *Angel* for all five seasons of the show.
- Soylent Corporation: Soylent Green is people! It's people!

∞

So why is this chapter in the "Characters" section? Because a corporation is a character. In the same way that a town can be a character. They must be complex and multi-layered and well thought out, not just a place someone works or a place someone lives. Otherwise, they become just another stereotype.

WISH YOU WEREN'T HERE: STEREOTYPES IN FICTION

Have you ever started reading a book and thought, *I know this character from somewhere else?* It might be because stereotypes exist in spades throughout fiction of all genres. The worst of the worst seem to occur in threes. Here are the stereotypical females, males, teenagers and children.

Just a word about where they come from: history. And since historical writing was dominated by men, most stereotypes are how men perceived (and to some degree still do perceive) themselves, the people in their lives and even people they didn't know well or at all. Of course, that means they're not very complex or even accurate but they persist in writing today. They're best to be avoided unless you can make them unbelievably original.

FEMALE

Somewhat unsurprisingly, all of the three main female stereotypes originated in the Bible.

Mother – the ultimate support

It shouldn't come as any great shock that mothers are one of the biggest female stereotypes. After all, until quite recently, there weren't many other options for socially acceptable life goals for women (even in fiction). Still now, there is an expectation that every woman will (and should want to) be a mother (barring infertility).

The mother stereotype goes all the way back to Eve, an instinctive mother who bore and raised many children without having any examples to guide her in her motherhood (what a saint).

Of course, mothers do exist and it's not unrealistic that a female character of a certain age might be a mother. But she won't only be a mother and it's not enough for her motherhood to be her defining characteristic. It's everything else that she is in conjunction with being a mother than helps her escape the clutches of stereotypicality.

Virgin – the ultimate sport

Before a woman can become a mother, she must first be a virgin. Motherhood is a pure calling and therefore virgins are the ones who answer that call. Total bollocks, of course. But what better way to convince women that sex is evil unless it is for the purpose of procreation?

The virgin stereotype, while probably existing long before the New Testament, was really crystallised in Mary, mother of Jesus. Wow, would you look at that, two stereotypes in one! Mother and virgin in one perfect woman.

Nowadays, virginity is code for innocence and wholesomeness and a well-worn trope in romance fiction – women who are saving themselves for "the one". It's horribly unrealistic, especially in light of a figure that says only 3% of women go on to marry the first man they sleep with (there wasn't a citation so I can't verify it but anecdotally it sounds about right). As with mothers, virgins do exist but there are very few of them who are solely defined by it.

Whore – the ultimate slut

If you're not a virgin or a married mother, then that only leaves one other alternative: the whore. Spat on by men, shunned by other women, the whore does not occupy an envied place in history or in literature. Even now, slut-shaming (attempting to humiliate women who do not fall into the first two stereotype categories) is a popular pastime for many.

The Biblical example, at least for the uninformed, is Mary Magdalene. She was one of the unofficial disciples of Jesus and is often erroneously confused with an unnamed "sinful woman" (presumably a prostitute or promiscuous) who anoints the feet of Jesus in the Gospel of Luke. Still, mud sticks, just like in real life.

The whore may also be known as a seductress or a femme fatale and even though she has to be having sex with someone, it's interesting to note that there is no equivalent stereotype – heck, there's no equivalently disdainful term – for a man who enjoys sex with multiple partners.

MALE

It's no coincidence that the three main male stereotypes are all positive, even the marginally negative one.

Brave – big heart

Ah, the traditional hero. He's gorgeous, he's honourable, he's adaptable, he's always got someone to save. James Bond, Jack Reacher, Indiana Jones, Luke Skywalker, Batman. While others cower in the corner in the face of danger, he's busy saving the day. He has no concern for his own safety and he'll sacrifice himself if he has to but he'd rather have the tale of his heroic deeds told and live off the glory for years to come.

The truly stereotypical brave hero will have military, martial arts or law enforcement training because physical strength and skill are generally how they defeat the villains. He might be brave but he's also a bit violent and if we look a bit closer, he likely relishes the biff. Still, it's all a means to an end. And when the violence is over, he'll sweep a girl off her feet and they'll live happily ever after until the next time he feels the need to save someone.

Billionaire – big brain

If a man isn't making oodles of money, then he's just not worth writing about (apparently). After all, you have to be pretty cluey to make a fortune, right? (Or maybe you just need to be part of an already wealthy family that gives you a great starting point.)

Christian Grey of *50 Shades* fame is the most well-known recent fictional billionaire. Yeah, he's a bit of a weirdo (more than a bit) but he's rich so there are certain things Anastasia Steele is willing to put up with, things she never even contemplated. I haven't read the books (apart from laughingly flicking through a few pages of someone else's copy in the work lunchroom one day) and I've only seen the first movie adaptation but I'm still a bit baffled about why he's such a sought after bachelor. Oh, wait, I'm forgetting the money.

The thing about real-life billionaires is that most of them are workaholics who have very little time for anything not business-related, certainly not extended sessions in red rooms or lengthy pursuits of women who don't instantly accept their advances. A realistic account of a billionaire would actually be someone who is rarely seen by friends, family and love interests but the story demands someone who's around a little more often, so the stereotype doesn't let reality get in the way. No bad stereotype does.

Bad boy – big dick

Forgive my crudeness but the recently created phrase "big dick energy" really sums up what it is to be a bad boy. He's sexual, he's only just on the right side of the law, there's likely a leather jacket and a motorcycle thrown into the mix somewhere, and he's not the kind of man you take home to meet your mother. If you do, he's likely to seduce her as well.

The bad boy in fiction is such an appealing character – for a good time, not a long time – because bad boys in real life tend to be awful. The reality of bad boys is usually having to escape from the law, then escape from debt collectors, then escape from him when the domestic violence that was always bubbling just below the surface finally emerges. Thank God for fiction.

If you can get brave, billionaire and bad boy into one character, you've got just about every shorter romance fiction hero ever written and a likely bestseller (but critical failure) on your hands.

TEENAGER

Teenage stereotypes are a much more recent phenomenon (because previously there were children and adults and no real acknowledgement of the precarious years in between) and have mostly developed as a result of people who aren't teenagers anymore trying to remember what it was like. These three main stereotypes are also distinctly American. While other countries may have similar categories, they may be given different labels.

Jock – good at sports

In the stereotype world, almost any problem a teenage boy has can be solved by being good at sports. Because being good at sports leads to scholarships at university, then to professional sports and finally to multi-million-dollar yearly earnings.

The jock is a derivative of the brave man, overcoming insurmountable odds with the support of a good woman (more accurately described as winning the game and getting the girl). It's been done to death. Unlike the mother stereotype, which can be justified by pointing to all the women with children out there, jocks are actually few and far between. Yes, plenty of people play sport but very few are good enough to make it into the upper echelons. Like I said, reality rarely gets in the way of a bad stereotype.

Nerd – good at school

The nerd is the diametric opposite of the jock. He's not good-looking (or if he is, he does everything he can to disguise it). He doesn't have any girls lusting after him. He's hopeless at sports. In fact, most of the jocks and cheerleaders don't even know he exists and if they do, he's their punching bag. But he's got one thing going for him: he's smart as smart can be.

He's top of the class, he's the partner everyone wants for school projects so they can ditch him to do all the work and still get an A, he's the guy in the small town who will leave for an Ivy League university and never come back.

A stereotypical nerd often comes good in the end, losing a pimply complexion and whatever it is that seems to repel girls during the teenage years to become wealthy and attractive thanks to a genius invention or a booming business. Yawn.

Cheerleader – good at sex

The cheerleader is a derivative of the whore with one exception; she is the devoted girlfriend of the jock and spends all of her time motivating, supporting and pleasuring him and him alone. She has no goals of her own that don't revolve around him and all things going well, she will transition smoothly into the mother stereotype.

Snore.

Mother, virgin, whore, cheerleader – the pattern here is pretty clear. All the female stereotypes, even the teenage version, are defined by their relationships with men. Mother, a vessel for the children of a man. Virgin, a vessel for the sexual goal of a man. Whore, a used vessel for the sexual goals of many men. Cheerleader, a vessel for the ego of a soon-to-be man. It truly would be an awful world if this were all women could be.

CHILD

Child stereotypes also suffer from primarily being written by people who aren't children. Even worse, they suffer from being secondary and often incidental characters, people no one would really care about from a fictional perspective if something terrible wasn't happening to them or they weren't doing something terrible to someone else.

Victim – possibly dead

The child victim is simply a chess piece on a very large board, bringing out the maternal and paternal instincts of whoever is trying to either save them or avenge them. They're not old enough to have developed into complex characters themselves yet (or maybe it's just that the writer isn't prepared to devote that much time to developing them into complex characters because it's only the idea of them that appears prominently, not the actuality) so their importance is defined entirely by their relationships with their parents/guardians/saviours.

They're also a shortcut to imbuing adult characters with good traits. Cares about children? He or she must be a good guy or good girl.

Orphan – parents are dead

Aww, so sad, mummy and daddy are gone. What better way to garner sympathy from a reader? Cue tiny violins. There's also their corresponding subconscious fear of abandonment to really ramp up the pity party. And just to make it super confusing, they alternate between being ridiculously clingy and determinedly independent.

The percentage of orphans in fiction is enormous compared to the ratios of them in the real world. And while, yes, just like all the other stereotypes, they do exist, rarely do any of them end up living in the lap of luxury with Daddy Warbucks. Most likely, they will end up living with extended family or going into the foster system and contending with many of the same issues that children with one or both their parents still around do.

Brat – wish you were dead

And finally, there's the child character that everyone wishes would just go away because of how annoying they are. You know the old saying that children should be seen and not heard? These characters are why. Just think Veruca Salt saying, "I want a golden ticket!" and "I want an Oompa Loompa!" and "I want a golden goose!"

The truth is that children generally only behave this way because they have parents who let them get away with it or who have never taught them to have compassion for others. Should we blame the kids or their parents? Or should we blame the writers who create them, usually only for dramatic tension?

∞

Stereotypes will never go away completely. They're too deeply ingrained and also plenty useful as starting points for writers. But if you use them, make sure they don't stay stereotypes for long. Your readers will thank you for it.

HOW MUCH LIVED EXPERIENCE DO YOU NEED
TO CREATE DIVERSE CHARACTERS?

"There's a quote from Julius Caesar at the start of *Area 7*. I made it up. It says fiction on the back. A lot of the books – I stopped it in *Scarecrow* for the sake of pace – have the prologue at the start. Advantage Press doesn't exist. WM Lawry & Co. He was a cricket guy. There are gags in there if you look closely enough. But it says fiction on the back."

Matthew Reilly in *Literati: Australian Contemporary Literary Figures Discuss Fear, Frustrations and Fame* by James Phelan

Truth in fiction seems to be a big debate topic these days, at least some truths. Nobody seems to mind when Matthew Reilly makes things up in his books or when George Lucas writes about an epic resistance and the religion at the heart of it a long time ago in a galaxy far, far away. But when a writer wants to explore a real race or a real culture or a real disability that they have no lived experience of in a piece of fiction, it seems to be more and more of a problem. Verisimilitude, or the ring of truth, apparently isn't good enough anymore. Some writers of those races or cultures or with those disabilities don't want you to read a piece of fiction informed by imagination and (hopefully) a decent chunk of research. They instead want you to read their piece of writing about the same topic (whether fictional or not) so that you can read "the truth" or at least a piece of writing informed by their truth.

I've heard the expression "lived experience" plenty but the first time I saw it in relation to fiction was in a review of the book *Wonder* by RJ Palacio. It's the story of a boy with facial deformities who joins a mainstream school for the first time in the fifth grade after being home-schooled previously and the challenges he faces, particularly bullying. The review didn't dwell on Palacio's lack of lived experience in relation to facial deformities; in fact, it almost seemed more like it was just something being mentioned in passing. But it gave me pause.

Why? Because the writer is also an adult female but there was no mention of her lack of lived experience as a male child. Why then, in a piece of fiction, which is by definition entirely made up, was the writer's lack of shared characteristics with one of her characters worth mentioning?

I've written books with characters who are kidnapped, who get shot, who lose their memories and who are home-schooled, none of which has ever happened to me. They have a variety of jobs that I have never worked in including weapons designer, FBI agent, CIA agent, marine, farmer, doctor. They have a variety of medical conditions including depression, agoraphobia, amnesia and post-traumatic stress disorder, none of which I suffer from. I've done a load of research to try to get as many of the details right as possible. Sometimes I've succeeded. Sometimes I've failed. Some people have liked my books. Some people haven't. But nobody has ever commented on my lack of lived experience with these things.

It seems to be different when we're talking about lived experience of race and culture and disability, the things we are rather than the things we do. I don't know why and possibly that's attributable to the fact that I'm a white, able-bodied, fifth-generation (at least) Australian. My only minority status is as a woman and even I admit that being a woman in Australia is a pretty great thing. So I understand the advantages that I've had.

Still, could you imagine telling a man that he couldn't write a female character? Could you imagine telling an adult they couldn't write a child character? Could you imagine telling a human they couldn't write an alien from outer space? Now envisage telling a disabled writer that you found their imagining of an able-bodied character offensive. It's unthinkable. So why is the vice versa situation any different?

I think what writers with lived experience of particular races, cultures or disabilities really find offensive is bad writing about their races and cultures and disabilities. We can all get on board with this because every writer finds bad writing offensive. But personal attachments to these things being poorly depicted understandably make their offence even more intense.

The problem with any type of lived experience and making any part of fiction writing contingent upon it, of course, is that it really limits the things that a writer, that any writer, can write about. And in the end it amounts to censorship.

So what should writers do? Here's a little checklist:

- Whatever you want – it's your right as a writer.

But if you want your writing to be respected and your mental health to survive, here's a slightly longer additional checklist:

- Make sure the race or culture or disability you're writing about is essential to your characterisation and your story – if it's interchangeable, then you really need to ask yourself why you've chosen that race or that culture or that disability.
- Research, research, research – it's the only way to get the facts right. And while truth will be debated until the end of time, facts are unarguable.
- Prepare for the fact that no matter how much research, how much consideration, how much sensitivity you use in your approach, there will always be some readers that just don't like what they consider "appropriation" – it's their right as a reader.

THE RISE AND RISE OF THE UNRELIABLE NARRATOR

Whenever I meet new people in real life, I always start out with the assumption that they're perfectly pleasant individuals. Even when I might have heard other people's opinions about them, I figure it's only fair to give them the benefit of a clean slate and it's only right that I should form my own judgement based on my experience with them, not simply perpetuate someone else's adoration or resentment, which might be completely prejudiced.

I'm the same when I pick up a book and start reading. I don't read reviews beforehand so that I can avoid being consciously or subconsciously influenced and I begin with the assumption that the person telling the tale is telling it truthfully (not factually, because that's a different thing, but truthfully, which means honestly to the best of their recollection). After all, why wouldn't they? The narrators are fictional characters and will never need to worry about any reader's judgement.

Of course, in both cases, there are plenty of instances of people who don't always disclose the absolute truth or the complete story. Sometimes they're frustrating as hell (in the case of real people, especially when you figure out you've had the wool pulled over your eyes), sometimes they're exactly what's needed (more likely in the case of a fictional character only). In the real world, we would call them liars but in the fictional world, they're known as unreliable narrators.

Wayne C Booth, an American literary critic, coined the term "unreliable narrator" in his 1961 book *The Rhetoric of Fiction*. His obituary in the *New York Times* explained that he felt "literature was not so much words on paper as it was a complex ethical act" and his "lifelong study of the art of rhetoric illuminated the means by which authors seduce, cajole and more than occasionally lie to their readers in the service of narrative". A pretty good description of what it is the unreliable narrator does.

TYPES OF UNRELIABLE NARRATOR

There are actually quite a few types of unreliable narrator:

- The deliberate liar: The deliberate liar is, of course, the most obvious one. The deliberate liar has an agenda and will do and say whatever it takes to achieve it, even if it has no resemblance to the truth and no matter how many other people get hurt along the way.
- The half-truther: The half-truther shares some things in common with the deliberate liar and has an agenda as well but tries to achieve it by simply leaving out the parts of the story that don't suit them.
- The self-deluder: The self-deluder is convinced that things are other than they seem to everyone else. The relationship that's actually more of an acquaintanceship. The significant event that others believe is an innocent coincidence. The connection that exists only in their mind.
- Someone who sees things differently: There are two sides to every story, right? This is the other side, the perspective less commonly considered, the unconventional view as opposed to the mainstream.
- Someone with medically-induced unreliability: Amnesia, multiple personality disorder, psychotic breaks, substance abuse – all can result in a narrator unsure of themselves and the real story.
- The absent narrator: There's nothing more unreliable than someone who is trying to relate a story they don't actually have any first-hand knowledge of, someone who wasn't even there. In non-fiction, it requires huge amounts of research to overcome; in fiction, characters are more likely to jump to conclusions rather than go to all the effort of finding out what happened.

As you can see, not all types of unreliable narrator are trying to deceive. Some of them are actually desperate for the truth.

REVELATION OF UNRELIABLE NARRATOR

An unreliable narrator is not always immediately obvious. In the case of medically-induced unreliability or someone who was completely absent from the event that the novel is based around, it's apparent up front. But with the deliberate liar, the half-truther, the self-deluder and the narrator who simply sees things differently, their unreliable status may not be revealed until very close to the end of the book. Often with novels such as these, the instinct of the reader is to want to read the book again immediately in order to reassess everything they took on face value when they first read it.

EXAMPLES OF UNRELIABLE NARRATOR

- The deliberate liar: Amy in *Gone Girl* by Gillian Flynn can't keep it up for the entire book but she does everything she can in the first half to make the reader feel sorry for her. By the second half, the reader realises she's not the one who should be getting our pity.
- The half-truther: Pi in *Life of Pi* by Yann Martel undergoes a miraculous journey, trapped on a lifeboat and lost at sea for 227 days with a spotted hyena, an injured zebra, an orangutan named Orange Juice and a tiger named Richard Parker. By the end of the book, Pi reveals he hasn't been entirely truthful and gives the characters he's been narrating his story to two options. He will reveal the absolute truth to them and they can decide which version they prefer. Unsurprisingly, once they know them both, they decide they prefer the half-truth version.
- The self-deluder: Changez in *The Reluctant Fundamentalist* by Mohsin Hamid suffers from ideological self-delusion. "I am a lover of America," he states at the start of the book but as he narrates his story, and particularly as he cheers the falling World Trade Centre towers on 9/11, it becomes clear that this is not the case.
- Someone who sees things differently: Christopher in *The Curious Incident of the Dog in the Night-Time* by Mark Haddon has Asperger's (or if you keep up with medical bureaucracy, which says this condition no longer exists, he is on the autism spectrum). In his neighbour's front yard in the middle of the night, he discovers the body of a murdered dog with a large garden fork sticking out of it. He decides he will find out who killed the dog so that the perpetrator can be punished. And so begins a book completely lacking in emotion but entirely logical – in Christopher's mind, anyway – as he begins his detecting. About half the book has absolutely nothing to do with anything as Christopher goes off on scientific and mathematical tangents, which help him stay calm in a chaotic world. About one quarter of the book focuses on his murder investigation and the other quarter of the book follows him as his world unravels around him when he finds out who the murderer is. The main character thinks a lot about stabbing people with the Swiss Army Knife he always has with him and tells the reader that his best dream is the one where everybody on earth who isn't on the autism spectrum has

died and he can go anywhere he wants without running into anyone else.

- Someone with medically-induced unreliability: Rachel in *The Girl on the Train* by Paula Hawkins is an alcoholic who suffers from blackouts – entire chunks of her memory sometimes go missing when she's been drinking heavily. When a woman she knows only by sight goes missing, she involves herself deeper and deeper in the lives of the main players until the police start to think she might have something to do with it. It's even revealed she was in the area the woman was last seen and at the same time but Rachel can't remember what happened. She can barely remember even being there or why she was.

- The absent narrator: Diedrick Knickerbocker in *The Legend of Sleepy Hollow* by Washington Irving tells the story of Ichabod Crane and his encounter with the Headless Horseman. There is a note at the beginning of the story and a postscript describing how it was found in Knickerbocker's papers after his death. It is an interesting device because I kept wondering who he was and why he was so interested in this story. But that is part of the story's brilliance. It feels like so much is left explicitly unexplored so that readers wonder about the importance of what they aren't being told.

CHOOSING TO USE AN UNRELIABLE NARRATOR

Some have posited the theory that all narrators, other than the omniscient kind, are unreliable in one sense or another. But it's important to make the distinction between outright lies, sneaky omissions, forgotten acts and selfish perspectives (which all perspectives are – not in a mean sense but in an awareness sense). And it's not just a matter of intentional misdirection. This is the nature of all stories: everyone remembers them slightly differently. Just ask the police when they're interviewing witnesses.

The important thing for a writer when choosing to use an unreliable narrator is that you must keep track of two stories: the one the narrator reveals and what actually happened. And then you have to decide how many of the narrator's inaccuracies will be exposed at the end of the book. You also have to be careful about how you do it. If the entire book has had only one narrator who has lied all along, then a sudden and complete revelation by that narrator of the truth might seem inconsistent. A sudden and complete revelation by an entirely different narrator might also seem forced since they're only being used for that purpose. It's a very difficult balancing act.

But it's one that more and more writers are attempting and succeeding at. If you're having a go at writing one, good luck to you. And if you come across one in a book you're reading, enjoy the ride. It's not about lies or even damned lies, it's just a rising statistic.

THE CONTINUING CONTROVERSY OF SAME-SEX RELATIONSHIPS IN FICTION

I have a theory that there are two types of writers: those who court controversy and those who avoid it. Controversy can mean many things these days but I was a little surprised to realise that same-sex relationships in fiction are still classified this way. And it has forced me to rethink the number of categories writers can be separated into and add a third: those who are controversial without realising it.

When KK Ness released her debut novel, *Messenger*, Book 1 in The Shifter War series, I was one of the first in line to read it. I'd followed with anticipation her writing journey ever since she did me the favour of reading a draft of one of my unpublished novels and offering some very useful advice. It was even more appreciated since we'd never met before and still haven't to this day. You can read my four-star review of *Messenger* on my blog or on Goodreads. For the purposes of this discussion, this extract was my comment on the way the book had been categorised on Amazon:

"I was a little concerned when I was buying it that its main classifications seemed to be 'gay fiction', 'gay & lesbian fiction' and 'lesbian, gay, bisexual & transgender fiction' when the blurb clearly described a story that easily falls into the fantasy genre. Maybe my concern was because so much fiction classified in that way turns out to be erotic fiction. But it's only because the main character and his love interest are both male. In fact, it was so subtle that I wondered if the 'gay fiction' classification might put off some conservative readers when it really shouldn't. More a marketing consideration than anything to do with the story itself."

Despite my concerns about the way the book was categorised, I have no problem reading fiction with same-sex relationships and I found Ness's depiction of the interactions between the two main characters, Danil and Hafryn, quite understated. So much so that I thought it could have been developed a little further, contained a little more depth. Still, I thought maybe she'd achieved something great: a romance written so well that people who are a bit iffy about same-sex relationships and those who find them completely off-putting might be able to look past it to simply see the beauty of love.

Apparently, that was too much to ask for. A couple of weeks after I finished reading the book and had posted my review on Goodreads and Amazon, I went back to those forums to see how the book was going and I was surprised by two later reviews that specifically referred to the same-sex relationship. The first was this:

"The story line was okay and well written. What has put me off is that the author has no respect towards the readers. And giving us the warning that the story involves a same-sex romance. I have no objection against same-sex couples, but frankly I am not interested to read about them either. So my dear author you have lost me as your potential book buying customer. Two stars"

And the second was this:

"An enjoyable light read from a new author. Well written. Good story line and characters. I am concerned however regarding the inferred potential 'gay' relationship between the two main characters. Should this aspect be allowed to develop or intensify, it would result in my not reading future books in this series which would be a shame as I think this author shows real potential. Perhaps I'm being somewhat conservative but I love reading books which are enjoyable and entertaining to me and that doesn't include gay and lesbian stories. Five stars"

Far from being slightly misleading as I had found it, the first reviewer seemed to feel that the book's categorisation as "gay fiction", "gay & lesbian fiction" and "lesbian, gay, bisexual & transgender fiction" hadn't been warning enough of the same-sex relationship. "Not that there's anything wrong with that," as Jerry Seinfeld would say and which the reviewer seemed to be implying. They had "no objection against same-sex couples" but were "not interested to read about them either". Ness had lost herself a future customer.

But it was the second review that I found more insidious. Despite a five-star rating, instead of bemoaning the lack of an appropriate warning, it seemed to be warning the author against pursuing the same-sex relationship storyline any further. "Should this aspect be allowed to develop or intensify, it would result in my not reading future books in this series…" Ness had already lost one customer and if she pushed her luck, she'd be losing another.

I could understand people having a problem with *Messenger* if it contained explicit descriptions of sex – I'm not particularly interested in reading books full of straight or gay sex scenes either – but there isn't a single instance of that. Danil and Hafryn barely touch each other. It seems as though so many of those people who have "no problem with gay people but don't want to read about them" think that all gay people in fiction do is have sex all day long.

I thought we were long past these ridiculous notions of what it is to be same-sex attracted (FYI, in case you didn't know, apart from the obvious, it's pretty much the same as being opposite-sex attracted). I'm disappointed that we aren't long past these ridiculous notions. Especially because it seems to be impacting a book well worth the read.

All I can hope is that it doesn't impact *Messenger* too much and that readers like this are a dying breed. If a reader doesn't like the story of a book with a same-sex relationship, that's one thing. If a reader doesn't like the story of a book because of a same-sex relationship, that says more about the reader than it does about the book. I know which I'd choose to avoid.

PART 3

WRITING

DO WRITERS NEED TO STUDY PROFESSIONAL WRITING COURSES TO BECOME PROFESSIONALS?

In 2007, I was studying the final subject in my master's degree in writing at Swinburne University. The subject was The Writerly Self (don't ask, I have no idea, not sure if I even understood exactly what the subject was about when I was studying it) and the major assessment piece was a writing journal reflecting on my development as a writer. I really didn't want to do it. It seemed self-indulgent. It seemed like a waste of the 3,000 to 5,000 words required.

I proposed, was given permission for and began writing several alternatives including an article with the title, "Can Writing Be Taught?" It was and still is a question perpetually asked in relation to professional writing courses.

At the simplest level, of course writing can be taught. We teach writing to children all throughout their schooling years. But the focus of my article was going to be undergraduate and postgraduate writing studies. What better way to reflect on my development as a writer than to look into the proliferation of bachelor-, graduate certificate-, graduate diploma-, master's- and PhD-level writing courses, their necessity and their usefulness.

It was during the time when these types of writing courses were popping up in what I described as "the most hallowed of educational institutions" and "multiplying exponentially across the world". And the opening paragraph described "the likelihood of professional success without a university education" as "almost as remote as winning the lottery". "Many companies," I wrote, "refuse to interview (let alone employ) candidates without tertiary-level qualifications. Mathematicians, physicists and even

81

philosophers get nowhere without at least a master's degree and preferably a PhD. So why do the merits of studies in writing – creative or otherwise – continue to be debated with such fervour and ferocity?"

It's funny, isn't it, how much can change in such a short period of time. Almost as soon as I finished my course, I landed a job primarily because of my master's degree. But over a decade later, there are now many companies who will interview and employ people who have never attempted tertiary studies, the reason given being that universities aren't training people in the skills they need so companies prefer to do it themselves without their minds being polluted. And several tertiary education institutions have abandoned their writing courses entirely (including Holmesglen Institute of TAFE where I graduated in 1999 with an Advanced Diploma of Arts (Professional Writing and Editing), my first writing qualification).

But nobody employs writers who can't demonstrate that they already have a high level of writing skill. This is usually demonstrated through a portfolio of writing. But a qualification is also a reasonably good sign of having some ability.

And yet the vast majority of commercially and critically successful writers – the household names of today – never found it necessary to wander down this educational path. Virginia Woolf was entirely home-schooled. Ernest Hemingway refused to attend university after high school. John Grisham studied and practised law for nearly a decade before turning his attention to writing without ever feeling the need the head back to university.

But for those who know they want to write without the proof provided by years spent in a different and often unsatisfying profession, undergraduate and postgraduate studies in writing seem a clear way in. A would-be lawyer studies the law. A would-be doctor studies medicine. Why shouldn't a would-be writer study writing?

"People often seem to think that writers should just be able to do it naturally without being taught," says Tracy Chevalier, author of *Girl with a Pearl Earring*. "Why don't people say this about musicians or painters or sculptors? All of us sang at some point when we were children but no one would suggest that a professional singer doesn't need to train since they already know how to sing! I should think the same would apply to writers, yet people somehow expect writers to write well instinctively."

In October 2005, Oxford University agreed. The renowned and respected educational institution announced the creation of a Master of Studies degree in Creative Writing. "For the first time, talented creative writers will have the opportunity to study for a postgraduate qualification in their craft at Oxford University." The press release boasted the program would be supported by "leading literary figures… prize-winning fiction writers, poets and dramatists". They've maintained their faith (unlike Holmesglen Institute of TAFE) as the course is still running.

Studying at Oxford University is the pinnacle. And with only 30 places on offer for the hundreds of applicants each year, it's not easy to achieve. But some still argue it's entirely unnecessary. Jenny Diski, a prize-winning British writer, cynically describes creative writing courses as a "marvellous money-spinner for cash-strapped universities". She continues, "The dream of the book that could be written seems to be pretty universal... It's always been the case that people will find a way to cash in on daydreams. What's new is that educational institutions are ripping off their students – customers, these days, like any other business."

In Australia, there are mixed feelings regarding the postgraduate writing courses. Literary agent Lyn Tranter once said they were "churning out people who are led to believe they are going to be published". Fellow agent Jenny Darling agreed, complaining those employed to impart wisdom upon impressionable young (and sometimes no-so-young) minds "seem to have no idea of what's publishable".

Jenny Sinclair, an Australian former journalist and primarily non-fiction writer, confessed that she "enrolled in a university writing course to give a socially acceptable face" to her compulsion, even as she railed against the proliferation of "writing courses, writing workshops, writing weekends, writing holidays" and the armies of half-wit graduates.

Even I have previously commented that so many writing courses seem to be filled not with writers but hobbyists (based on my own experiences so it's anecdotal evidence at best). Decades after I first studied, I'm hard pressed to find many of my fellow students have ever been published. No, it's not the be all and end all of being a writer but I wonder if the reason I can't find them is because they're still plugging away quietly somewhere or if those hobbyists gave up when they realised how hard it actually is. Certainly, there's no evidence of them ever becoming professionals.

The truth is that it's not a requirement to have studied a professional writing course to become a professional writer. There are just as many who do compared with those who don't. If you have a genuine talent, then you'll probably make it even if you don't study.

I had a genuine talent (I'm happy enough to admit that without feeling arrogant) but I will also admit that the two writing qualifications I studied made me even better. They forced me to practise. They forced me to network. They forced me into areas of writing I would never have attempted otherwise. They gave me real knowledge about writing and editing and the publishing industry that I might have eventually figured out on my own in later decades by learning it the hard way. But I'm really glad I didn't have to wait that long.

But that's not to say that the same choice will be right for you. Check out the next chapter on the pros and cons of studying writing and make up your own mind.

THE PROS AND CONS OF STUDYING WRITING

I am following the careers of two emerging writers who have both gone back to studying at university in their late 20s/early 30s. I did the same thing, studying a master's degree in writing, starting when I was 27 and finishing when I was 30. But even though they are both very vocal about writing, publishing and wanting to be writers, they aren't studying writing. One is studying archaeology and anthropology 10 years after gaining a bachelor's degree in creative writing and the other is studying astronomy after graduating with a bachelor's degree in criminology.

I find it curious, probably because I'm a literal kind of person. When I decided I wanted to make writing my career, I studied writing. But, of course, there are many paths that can be taken towards becoming a writer. And being a writer while having other specialist knowledge can really expand career opportunities. After all, most writers make most of their money doing things other than writing.

So should you study writing? Should you study something else? Should you study at all? Here are a few things to consider.

PROS

Various study options

If you want to study writing, you don't have to dive in head first right from the start. You can dip a toe in to see if it suits you because there are a variety of levels at which to study writing including:

- Self-education (usually through book learning – buying, reading, learning and implementing the lessons learned)

- One-off lectures (writers' groups run many of these each year and some libraries do, too)
- Short courses (each tends to focus on one small area of writing at a very basic level)
- Lower-level tertiary studies (certificate- and diploma-level courses covering the basics across a variety of writing areas)
- Undergraduate degrees at university (bachelor-level courses expanding on the basics and encompassing classical elements)
- Postgraduate degrees at university (graduate certificate-, graduate diploma-, master- and PhD-level courses that focus on cultural and critical approaches to writing)

Structure

When you study writing, you do a lot of learning by doing. With many courses, it's expected that you are coming in fresh with little to no knowledge. With a writing course, it's expected that you've been writing for many months, more likely years. The first writing course I ever studied was full of students who were already many thousands of words into writing novels. And by the end of that first year, many of those novels were finished. I'm not saying any of them were worthy of being published. But, boy, did we do an awful lot of writing.

In Novel class, we were expected to come in each week with new chapters of our works-in-progress. In Poetry class, we wrote poems every week. It was the same in every class. Before I became a full-time writer, the most prolific I ever was, the most writing I ever did, was when I was studying writing.

The classes and the work requirements provide the structure to do a lot of writing and for some people, that's exactly the kind of help they need.

Peers

Studying writing also exposes you to a lot of other writers. You see what others are doing. You give and get feedback from both teachers and other students. You're amongst people who understand what you are doing and why in a way that you never will be again once you're back in the real world. You will often find a real sense of belonging.

Publication

Both of the educational institutions I studied writing at offered student publications and the first time I was published (both fiction and non-fiction) was in these. There was no money on offer and when I look back at those small press books now, there's a sense of mild embarrassment at how raw I was (how raw we all were) but it was nevertheless a thrill. I still have those books.

Qualifications

At the end of your studies, you'll have a piece of paper that says you're a qualified writer. It will mean more to some people than others but it means as much as any other type of qualification. It proves you have a skill, it may help you get a job, it might help you get a bit of recognition. But what it hopefully means is that you're coming out of your studies a better writer than when you went in.

CONS

Costs

No matter what kind of writing study you do, there will always be a cost. Self-education is, of course, the cheapest (the cost of a few books, which, considering that we are writers and also readers, we were going to spend anyway). A master's degree is the most expensive, tens of thousands of dollars. If you make it to the PhD, you'll get paid (a small amount) but you still have to get there and that's usually through the expense of a master's.

In some countries, education costs are heavily subsidised and/or offered as low interest loans to be paid back later. In others, there are no subsidies and the fees must be paid before starting, putting it out of the reach of many. It's an investment. Each writer needs to decide if it's the right one for them.

Time

All study takes time. One of the drawbacks I remember during my master's was that I eventually ran out of subjects I wanted to study and was forced to do a couple of units I had no interest in to achieve enough credits. And in some subjects that I did want to study, I had to write things I didn't want to write. Both felt like wasted time.

Even when it doesn't feel like wasted time, studies can still be lengthy.

No guarantees

And then there's the big one: no matter how much study anyone does, there are no guarantees that it will lead to anything. The goal of my study was to get better and I've definitely achieved that. It's more than a decade since I finished my master's and I've published four books. But I haven't got a publishing contract and I still have to supplement my income with non-writing jobs.

Still, I don't regret either of the two writing qualifications I have. They are a very big part of the reason I'm where I am today.

HOW TO PSYCH YOURSELF INTO WRITING A BOOK

After I wrote close to 100 blog posts in 2015 about developing ideas, characters and plots, writing, editing, publishing, marketing and reading, I realised I had written enough to fill a book. And when I collated them all together, I realised it flowed nicely enough to seem like I'd done it on purpose. I'd written a book without even trying to write a book. That's how *Project December: A Book About Writing* was born.

After I published *Project December*, I continued writing blog posts in the same vein but, of course, this time I knew I was heading towards writing a sequel. Why wouldn't I? It had been so easy last time. I even wrote a blog post called, "How to Write a Book Without Even Trying."

The problem was that because I knew I was heading towards another book, it wasn't going to be the same process. I wasn't going to be able to write a book without even trying. Because I was trying to write a book.

I set a deadline for myself but as it approached, I knew for various reasons that I was never going to make it. Life, work and other pieces of writing were getting in the way.

Instead of giving up, I told myself that the deadline wasn't important. I was the only person who knew it and I was the only person who would know it was going to pass by unmet. The important thing was that I eventually finished writing the book, regardless of whenever that time came.

So I just kept writing. I wrote when I had something to say. I wrote when I felt like it. I wrote when I had nothing else scheduled. And before I knew it, in less than two months, the first draft was finished. It only took one month more for the text to be finalised. How, I asked, did that happen? How, when I was so sure it would never happen in that time frame?

As I wrote in the introduction to *Project January*, the follow up to *Project December*, I'd psyched myself into writing a book. Normally, we psych ourselves out of doing things but by simply removing the deadline that had been putting so much pressure on me and making me doubt myself, I removed the psychological barrier that was holding me back. And although I wasn't aware of it at the time, there was still a little voice in the back of my mind urging me on. My conscious said it couldn't be done so my subconscious was determined to prove me wrong. (It's complex being me but that's another story.)

I think that you have to be a very specific type of person to be able to psych yourself into writing a book. The kind who won't take no for an answer. The kind who doesn't like to be wrong. The kind who does everything they can to make sure they're more often than not right. The kind who still wants to have a go even when what they're trying seems impossible. The kind who won't listen to reason, even when the person they're reasoning with is themselves.

After all, if you tell yourself it can't be done (whatever "it" is) and a logical assessment of the facts supports that argument so you stop trying to do it, then that's more like psyching yourself out of it. You have to be the kind of person who will respond to a little reverse psychology.

STEP 1

Develop your idea and set a reasonable deadline. Six months is reasonable for a full-time writer and a year is reasonable for someone with other commitments. Then start writing.

STEP 2

Tell yourself you're not good enough. It might – at that moment – be true. The only way to fix it is to practise. So you might as well practise on your book. And the best way to practise is to just keep writing.

STEP 3

Tell yourself you'll never make your deadline. After a few months, you will genuinely feel this way. Keep writing anyway. Missing a deadline is not the end of the world. Giving up because you think you might miss your deadline will, however, probably be the end of your very short writing career.

STEP 4

Tell yourself you don't have enough writing time – it's probably true because it's the one thing that all writers never have enough of. But squeeze in a half hour of writing here and a half hour of writing there anyway. Even if you only write for half an hour every day, even if you only write 250 words a session, that's 1,750 words a week and 91,000 words a year, equivalent to a whole book.

STEP 5

Just keep writing. (You might be noticing a theme...)

$$\infty$$

Yes, it turns out that it's not that complicated. You just have to keep writing. Even when you doubt yourself. Even when you doubt your choices. Even when it feels like life is conspiring to prevent you from ever finishing. The secret formula to psyching yourself into writing a book is really just to write. A little bit of reverse psychology might help you but, in the end, it's all about the hard work of actually sitting down and making the effort.

Unfortunately (or maybe it's fortunate – it all depends on your perspective), writing is one of those things that there aren't any shortcuts to achieving. Supposedly, someone somewhere is working on a software program so that robots can write all our content in the future (I saw this being crowdfunded on Indiegogo, although it didn't seem to be doing too well for some reason) but we're not anywhere close yet. And since none of those monkeys from the infinite monkey theory have yet given us the complete works of Shakespeare, let alone a decent novel, it will remain the domain of humans doing a little hard work. Best of luck.

PRACTICE NOVELS: NOT JUST FOR THE START OF A WRITER'S CAREER

In my late teens and early 20s, I wrote three novels that I like to refer to as my practice novels. At the time that I was writing them, I didn't realise that I was just practising. It was only after they were complete that I knew they weren't good enough, they weren't the genre I wanted to pursue and they were unlikely to ever see the light of day.

I published the sex scene from the last of them, *Liberty's Secret*, in 2015 in conjunction with a blog post on writing sex scenes, mostly to demonstrate that I'm not very good at writing sex scenes. It was full of euphemisms, the highs and lows of waves and crashing, and an overblown sense of emotion. Certainly, it was completely devoid of accurate names for genitalia. (That's one of the big no-no's of the romance genre I was attempting to write in.) And I published the entire book chapter by chapter on my blog in 2017, just because… well, why not? I hate wasting writing.

I thought that was the end of my practice novels. But when I sat down to watch the movie of *50 Shades of Grey*, despite its flaws, I realised these genres and sex scenes more specifically aren't going anywhere. They are popular. And if done well, they can be important components of plot and character development. So I could continue avoiding them in my writing or I could try to get better.

Yes, more than 25 years after beginning my writing career and after publishing three books, I decided to write another practice novel. I had no intention of attempting to publish it for profit, just to improve on this writing area. There were a few conditions I set for myself:

- It had to be about sex. (Duh, obviously if I'm practising getting better at writing sex scenes, that was a given.)

- It had to have a sex scene in every chapter. (Go hard or go home, right? No pun intended. But there's no point writing a practice novel to get better at sex scenes if there are only one or two in the entire book.)
- It had to have a plot. (A good plot. If it doesn't have a good plot, then that's not sex, it's just porn. And I don't want to write porn. I have no interest in being good at writing porn. I'm sure a few people make an okay living writing porn but I don't want to be one of them.)
- It didn't have to be kinky sex. (One step at a time. I just wanted to write about regular people with healthy sex lives. There would be no stepsister-stepbrother relationships, no ménages a trois, no S&M, no dominants, no submissives, no tampon scenes, none of the various scenarios I found – and was slightly traumatised by – when I did a little research about what authors in this genre write.)
- It had to have a hook. (Whilst I didn't want to write about all those sex scenarios that seem so popular these days, it still needed to be more than just a basic sexual relationship.)

So I started writing. It sounds funny to admit it now but the thing I spent the most time on was naming the two main characters. Fletcher Smith and Sadie Van Der Zee. (Yes, a man and a woman. I'm straight and I thought it would be easier on me not to have to try to imagine sex I have no experience with. I encourage everyone to write outside their comfort zones but I still think there is merit in a natural progression from the things you know towards the things you don't. Like I said, one step at a time.)

Fletcher sounded like the name of a middle-class man with muscles who worked in an office during the week and on the construction site of the house he was renovating on the weekends. And I made his last name Smith because of the connotations of couples checking into hotels for some hot sex using the "Mr and Mrs Smith" monikers.

Sadie also sounded middle class but Van Der Zee upped her exotic quotient. It also means "by the sea" and I liked the idea of her using "Lady by the Sea" as her cover name when arranging her anonymous hook-ups. Yes, that was the hook. She liked anonymous sex. And Fletcher just happened to be the lucky soul she mistook for her latest conquest.

I wrote over 11,000 words and despite the fact that I love Fletcher and Sadie as characters, I got sick of writing about sex. I think I improved my abilities to write sex scenes but I also realised that part of the reason I hadn't pursued these kinds of plot points is I don't especially enjoy it. At first, it was fun but by the time I threw in the towel, it was just tedious. I want variety in my writing, for my sake as much as for my readers.

Still, I'm pleased I had a go. Now if I need or want to add a sex scene to what I am writing, I won't be so intimidated by the prospect of it. It won't necessarily be the best sex scene ever written but maybe I'll be able to do enough to avoid a nomination for the Bad Sex in Fiction Award bestowed by the *British Literary Review* each year.

If you feel like you need to practise something or you just want to have a go at something you haven't written much of in the past, here are a few tips:

- You don't have to be a beginning writer to reap the benefits of practising. It should be the goal of every writer to continue getting better, not just stagnating, and this is one way of potentially making it happen.

- You don't have to just practise very specific or obscure things like sex scenes. It's probably a good idea for all writers to practise the big three: plot development, character development and developing writing styles, too. Sure, you can practise on your actual novel or a related side project (think *Four* by Veronica Roth, originally released as prequel short stories to the *Divergent* trilogy) but sometimes it helps to practise on something entirely unrelated.

- You don't have to write an entire novel. Aim for a short story instead to help maintain your sanity, avoid boredom and not get completely distracted from your real writing.

- If your practice writing turns out really well, don't be afraid to pursue it even if it isn't your normal genre or your normal style. It could be the beginning of a brave new writing world for you.

HAVE YOU EVER HEARD OF ZANE GREY?

I was recently reading an article about the biggest fiction sellers going back over the last hundred years and how so few of the biggest sellers at the time are still read all these years later. One name kept jumping out at me: Zane Grey.

I'd never heard of him. But he wrote the bestselling book of 1918. He wrote the third bestselling book of 1919. He wrote the bestselling book of 1920. He wrote the third bestselling book of 1921. He wrote the ninth bestselling book of 1922. He wrote the eighth bestselling book of 1923. He wrote the sixth bestselling book of 1924. From 1917 to 1926, he was in the top 10 of the list of bestselling books nine times. According to Wikipedia, he was one of the first millionaire authors.

His first four novels were rejected by publishers and he self-published the first. In 1910, he wrote his first bestseller, *The Heritage of the Desert*. In 1912, he wrote his all-time bestseller, *Riders of the Purple Saga*. He wrote so much that even though he died in 1939, his publishers continued publishing a new Zane Grey book each year until 1963.

Many of his novels were made into films by early Hollywood. One novel was adapted four different times. He was President Dwight Eisenhower's favourite writer.

So why has he virtually disappeared in the calculation of writing history?

It possibly has something to do with the fact that he wrote mostly westerns and few "classics" seem to fall into this category. But I suspect it more likely has to do with the fact that the critics didn't much like him. Even though he was immensely popular and extremely wealthy as a result of his writing, one critic wrote, "The substance of any two Zane Grey books could be written upon the back of a postage stamp."

Sound like any other writers we know? So, so many. In all likelihood, this means that in another hundred years, writers like EL James, Stephanie Meyer, Ann Rice, John Grisham, Dan Brown and James Patterson will have disappeared onto an obscure list of bestselling authors that nobody remembers or reads much anymore. Not because their books aren't any good – they've all managed to find a niche and exploit it admirably – but because their books don't transcend those niches.

Technically, Bram Stoker's *Dracula* falls into the same niche as Stephanie Meyer's *Twilight* but *Dracula* is the vampire novel while *Twilight* is just a vampire novel, merely one of many trying to emulate what Stoker managed to achieve all those years ago.

The thing about legacy – how long pieces of writing and the authors themselves will be remembered and revered – is that it's impossible to control. A hundred years after the height of a writer's success, the odds of having died are pretty close to 100%. And how they were perceived during their lifetime could be a world away from how they are perceived a hundred years later. While he was alive, Bram Stoker was best known as the personal assistant of an actor and as a theatre manager. And before he was a writer, Zane Grey was a dentist.

Writing with a legacy in mind seems like a perfectly good way to ensure a writer won't have a legacy at all. It's hard enough to predict what will resonate now, let alone long after we're dead. And even though Zane Grey isn't at the top of any list of classic authors now, he's still on the list of the bestselling authors throughout history and has an extensive Wikipedia entry profiling him for when someone like me notices his name appearing over and over on a 100-year-old list. Maybe that's legacy enough.

$$\infty$$

Here's a funny twist. About a week after I wrote this chapter, I popped in the DVD of *The Third Man* and settled in to watch it. I've had it in my collection for a while but never got around to it. About halfway through as the main character, Holly Martins, is giving a talk at a local literature appreciation group, the following exchange takes place:

Man in audience: What author has chiefly influenced you?

Holly Martins: Grey.

Woman in audience: Grey? What grey?

Holly Martins: Zane Grey.

Facilitator: Oh, that's Mr Martin's little joke, of course. We all know perfectly well Zane Grey wrote what we call westerns… cowboys and bandits.

The man in the audience then asks a question about James Joyce, clearly implying he is a much more worthy author for discussion. The movie was made in 1948, about a decade after Zane Grey died and obviously before he finished his progression into relative obscurity.

It just goes to show that no one ever really disappears completely from the public consciousness, no matter how hard the self-proclaimed arbiters of taste might try.

DEVELOPING A GENUINELY TENSE AND SCARY SCENE

I once woke up from a dream – more like a nightmare – frozen in place, unable to move from the fear it had evoked. And in true writer form, the first thing I thought to myself was, *I must remember this feeling so I can put in it into a novel.*

As with all my dreams, it was fairly nonsensical. I arrived at my grandparents' house and noticed a man standing in the street with a gun in his mouth. I went inside where my grandparents, one of my cousins and one of his daughters were unaware of what was going on outside. As I explained to my cousin what I'd seen, he went to look out the window and the man in the street suddenly noticed he had a house full of people at his mercy. He took the gun from his mouth and pointed it at the house.

We all rabbited to a bedroom at the back of the house but the hallway that runs the length of the weatherboard provided a clear view out into the street. Inexplicably, the man was suddenly on the roof of the house across the road and the gun that had been small enough to fit inside his mouth was now a bazooka that had to be carried on his shoulder. Then he was running down the driveway and had found our hiding place. There was nowhere left to run…

Thankfully, that's when I woke up. But it had all the elements of a genuinely tense and scary scene. To frighten the pants off your readers, here are the individual components.

A SCARY VILLAIN

If you haven't read the chapter in *Project December* on developing a genuinely scary and evil villain, go do it before continuing any further here. In a nutshell, it's all about avoiding the clichés. But for the purposes of developing a genuinely tense and scary scene, the villain doesn't have to be a person. It can also be a natural disaster, a man-made disaster, an animal, a robot, an alien... You get the idea.

The scare comes from the unpredictable nature of each of these things. And in the case of disasters, it also comes from the fact that it is physics and not morality (whether bad or good) that decides what happens next. Ultimately, you cannot reason with an evil person, a natural or man-made disaster, an animal, a robot or an alien.

LOVED ONES/VULNERABLE PEOPLE IN PERIL

It's generally not enough for just a macho main character to be in the line of fire. After all, Chuck Norris, Lara Croft, John McClane, Ellen Ripley, the Rock – these people can all take care of themselves. But as soon as you add loved ones – wives, husbands, girlfriends, boyfriends, parents, children, pseudo-children – to the mix, it ups the ante. Because it's one thing to take care of yourself. It's another entirely to have to take care of yourself as well as someone or a group of someones who don't have years of martial arts, military and/or law enforcement training.

The main character can be one of those vulnerable people in peril. Think Sandra Bullock as Angela Bennett in *The Net*. She's virtually a hermit, her mother doesn't remember her, the people who do have all been murdered and the police think she's a prostitute and car thief. Even though she's the vulnerable one, she has to figure out a way to help herself.

SOMEONE CHALLENGING OR EMBRACING THE VILLAIN RECKLESSLY

In *Die Hard*, it's the coke-snorting Ellis. In *Daylight*, it's Roy Nord, the rock-climbing entrepreneur sure he can beat the collapsing Holland Tunnel. There's always someone who thinks they can outsmart or outwit the villain. And they almost inevitably become the cautionary tale for not showing enough respect.

Whether it's stupidity, arrogance or just showing off, it never ends well. And despite the stupidity, arrogance and showing off, it's usually also someone we care enough about to be horrified both by the manner of their death and the reinforcement of the evilness of the villain.

A COMPLETE LACK OF CONTROL

Regardless of the amazing skills of the people in the genuinely tense and scary situation, even they must be convinced of their inability to control or extract themselves from the situation. They must face their mortality, they must expect to die, they must make their peace with it or break down completely. In its simplest form, this is the "peeing their pants" moment.

BEING TRAPPED

The complete lack of control is usually combined with being trapped. In a house, in a forest, in a prison, in a conspiracy, sometimes a character may even be trapped within themselves (catatonia). It's the straw that breaks the trapped camel's back.

It may also involve the villain realising they have some leverage because of the presence of loved ones and a choice between the lesser of two evils.

A CLEVER SOLUTION TO ESCAPE

Unless you're writing the next instalment in the *Saw* movie franchise where nobody ever seems to get away, somebody – usually the main character but sometimes an important supporting character – will come up with a solution to escape. It must seem to be almost plucked from nowhere but it must also make total sense. No deus ex machina, divine intervention endings. You've put your readers and your characters through hell and the payoff must be worthy of both them and you.

SOME SORT OF LOSS NONETHELESS

Regardless, there will be some sort of loss because nobody ever gets away scot-free. The loss of the reckless villain challenger doesn't count. It has to be something or someone that when they meet their demise, the reader never saw it coming and is devastated. The end of *Pitch Black* starring Vin Diesel is a great example. I won't give it away for those who haven't seen it.

∞

If you combine all these elements with just the right amount of each, you'll have a tense and scary scene that will leave your readers simultaneously breathless and begging for more.

HOW TO WRITE A SERIAL KILLER CRIME THRILLER

To me, there is nothing scarier than a fictional serial killer. Yes, real serial killers are terrifying but most people are very unlikely to ever come across one and know this. Fictional serial killers, however, are everywhere: there are more book, film and TV show serial killers than there will ever be real ones (thank God).

I've come to realise that there seems to be a bit of a formula for writing a serial killer story. It's not compulsory, of course, just a set of common steps that run through quite a few of them. The steps don't always occur in exactly the same order. The steps don't always occur in isolation; sometimes multiple steps are happening at the same time. And the steps are abstract enough that despite appearing in almost all serial killer movies, the stories are still distinct because of the details of each different serial killer, their methods, their victims and the people trying to track them down.

I've tested this formula on a few of my favourite serial killer movies (many originating from books) including *The Silence of the Lambs*, *Frequency*, *Jennifer 8*, *Copycat*, *The Bone Collector* and *Kiss the Girls* and it seems to hold true. So if it can help with plot, allowing writers to focus on the specifics instead, maybe we might be lucky enough to come up with a character as iconic as Hannibal Lecter. I've used *The Silence of the Lambs* as an example.

ESTABLISH THE MAIN CHARACTER
It's usual in many stories to show the main character in their normal world before the events of the story force them into an uncomfortable new reality. For Clarice Starling, this means training at the FBI academy. The main character may be an investigator or a witness or someone being

101

framed for the crime. This step usually occurs before the main character is even aware of the serial killer. At the very least, it occurs before their involvement.

ESTABLISH THE UNSOLVED SEQUENCE OF CRIMES

The main character is drawn into the serial killer's crimes, usually as a way of explaining to the reader or watcher the known details. Clarice is summoned to the office of Jack Crawford, head of the Behavioural Science Unit, on a seemingly unrelated matter.

ESTABLISH A SEEMINGLY UNRELATED SUBPLOT

The unrelated subplot is often the key to solving the crime, even though nobody knows it at the time. Jack Crawford asks Clarice to meet with Dr Hannibal Lecter as part of a project to interview all serial killers in custody. But on the walls of his office are newspaper clippings and evidence related to the Buffalo Bill serial killer.

ESTABLISH A BUREAUCRATIC NAYSAYER

The bureaucratic naysayer tends to get in the way of the case being solved, often due to ego, sometimes due to wanting to do everything by the book. It may also be someone who desperately wants to involve themselves in the investigation. In the case of *The Silence of the Lambs*, it's Dr Chiltern.

ESTABLISH AN INAPPROPRIATE RELATIONSHIP

Calling it an inappropriate relationship might not be quite right, but often the relationship will cause the main character to be removed from the official investigation or the person in the relationship with the main character will betray them. It's not necessarily a romantic relationship. Clarice Starling and Hannibal Lecter's relationship is based on professional respect (despite what happens in later books).

ESTABLISH THE TRAUMATIC HISTORY OF THE MAIN CHARACTER

All good main characters are tormented by their past in some way (or at least that's how it seems). In Clarice's case, her socioeconomic background is called out almost immediately by Dr Lecter:

"You know what you look like to me, with your good bag and your cheap shoes? You look like a rube. A well-scrubbed, hustling rube with a little taste. Good nutrition's given you some length of bone, but you're not more than one generation from poor white trash, are you, Agent Starling?

And that accent you've tried so desperately to shed: pure West Virginia. What is your father, dear? Is he a coal miner? Does he stink of the lamp? You know how quickly the boys found you... all those tedious sticky fumblings in the back seats of cars... while you could only dream of getting out... getting anywhere... getting all the way to the FBI."

And then as the film progresses, the story of her father's death and the screaming lambs that give the story its name is detailed by Clarice herself.

DISCOVERY OF SEEMINGLY UNRELATED EVIDENCE

The seemingly unrelated evidence will make sense later on but for now it appears to be frustratingly irrelevant. Lecter telling Clarice to seek out Miss Mofet is a prime example.

OFFER OF ASSISTANCE FROM SOMEONE WITH ULTERIOR MOTIVES

Once Clarice has found Miss Mofet, Dr Lecter offers to provide a psychological profile of the Buffalo Bill killer. He's pretty clear about his ulterior motives – escaping Dr Chiltern's clutches – but there's nothing to say ulterior motives have to be secret motives.

DISAPPEARANCE/DISCOVERY OF THE LATEST VICTIM

In most serial killer cases, real and fictional, the disappearance or discovery of a new victim can be crucial in providing further information towards the discovery of the killer. It's often a 50/50 prospect of whether the victim is named or not. In *The Silence of the Lambs*, there are two latest victims – the woman found in Elk River, West Virginia, who is never named and Catherine Martin, the senator's daughter, who is kidnapped with the intention of being the killer's next dead body.

BEHAVIOUR FROM A SUPERIOR THAT BELITTLES THE MAIN CHARACTER

There is almost always an act of belittlement from a superior or a direction not to pursue a particular lead that only makes the main character more determined. At the funeral home, Crawford asks the local sheriff to discuss the case away from Clarice because of the nature of the crime.

EVIDENCE BEGINS TO EMERGE

Evidence begins drip, drip, dripping in (the moth in the throat, the patches of skin missing from the Elk River victim's body) and suddenly one thing leads to the next, and then the next, and then the next.

EVIDENCE FROM THE FIRST MURDER PROVES CRUCIAL

Because serial killers tend to start close to home, the first victim often proves crucial in getting the investigators very close to identifying the killer. Real-life investigators know this long before it ever seems to become important in fiction but it makes for a dramatic revealing moment:

Clarice: Fredrica Bimmel, from Belvedere, Ohio. First girl taken, third body found. Why?

Ardelia: Because she didn't drift. He weighted her down.

Clarice: What did Lecter say about "first principles"?

Ardelia: Simplicity.

Clarice: What does this guy do? He "covets". How do we first start to covet?

Ardelia: We covet what we see...

Clarice: ...every day.

Ardelia: Hot damn, Clarice.

Clarice: He knew her.

MISDIRECTION

At this point in the story, the killer is close to being caught even if nobody in the story really understands that yet but for some reason, either intentional misdirection from the killer or the wrong evidence being followed leads the police or investigators down the wrong path. In *The Silence of the Lambs*, this is the taskforce flying to Calumet City to raid an old address for the man they've identified as importing the specific types of moths being left in the victim's throats.

MAIN CHARACTER FOLLOWS THE ROAD LESS TRAVELLED

The main character isn't distracted by the misdirection or is asked to follow up on something that isn't thought to be as important in tracking down the killer and unexpectedly comes across the killer earlier than anyone expects. Clarice is in Belvedere, Ohio, reinterviewing witnesses in relation to the kidnapping and murder of Fredrica Bimmel and knocks on the killer's door without initially realising she has found him.

A BATTLE OF WITS AND THEN BODIES

And then comes the brutal and bloody battle of wits and usually bodies as the main character and the killer fight to gain the upper hand. Buffalo Bill escapes down into the basement where he has hidden Catherine Martin and all the evidence of his double life, and Clarice follows him with her gun drawn. When he shuts off the power and all the lights go out, she must beat him against all the odds.

FINAL RESOLUTION

Which, of course, she does. The serial killer is either captured or killed, often after having the chance to avoid both and failing to take it. Buffalo Bill reaches out and nearly touches Clarice multiple times as she fumbles around in the dark, managing to reveal his position and allowing her to shoot him.

RETURN TO NORMAL LIFE

And then everyone returns to their normal life, which isn't really normal because it has now changed forever as a result of the events that have led them here. Clarice graduates from the FBI academy, so her life is back on track, but then Lecter calls her from Bimini after having escaped, where he is "having an old friend for dinner" (Dr Chiltern who is desperately trying to hide, knowing he has tormented Lecter for years and the favour will be returned).

∞

And there you have it. It's not perfect because no literary formula is but it works in so many already successful stories that it is ultimately useful.

WHY DO SOME WRITERS HATE ADVERBS?

"The hatred of adverbs amongst writers, and specifically teachers of creative writing, has become so commonplace, so unquestioned, and so unthinking, that it ranks only with 'show, don't tell' as the most ubiquitous cliché in writing advice."
"Lovingly, Stridently, Unapologetically" by Colin Dickey, slate.com, 2 June 2016

The thing about clichés is that many of them are accurate. It's how they become clichés. "Show, don't tell" is essential writing advice. It is how "He went here, he went there, he did this, he did that" becomes "The crowded train to the edge of the city was oppressive but the only alternative was to take the bus since what he was heading to was the mechanic's workshop holding his car hostage until he paid the enormous repair bill. And the only thing he hated more than mechanics was buses."

But the ongoing campaign against the use of all adverbs isn't helpful at all. So whenever anyone says that writers shouldn't use them, I want to scream, "Stop telling me what to do!" No adverbs in that sentence so they shouldn't be too offended unless the screaming puts them off. But oops! One has snuck in. (Don't see it? It's the "too".) Does that little modifier render everything I've written here unreadable? I don't think so. Apparently, some do. Uh oh, there's another! ("Apparently.")

"The road to hell is paved with adverbs," said Stephen King in his book *On Writing*. "Never use an adverb to modify the verb 'said'. To use an adverb this way (or almost [<adverb] any way) is a mortal sin," advised Elmore Leonard. Mark Twain didn't mince his words. "If you see an adverb, kill it." Ernest Hemingway, well known as a minimalist, and the authors of *The Elements of Style*, well known as the writers' bible, felt the

106

same way. It's a lofty group of writers. But does their loftiness make them unable to be disagreed with?

Of course not. Because all parts of speech (nouns, verbs, adjectives, adverbs, prepositions, clauses, phrases, gerunds, objects, subjects, etc) have their place in language. If they didn't, they would never have been invented in the first place and so widely used ever since. Much like a healthy diet that remains interesting to the eater, the key is to use everything in moderation. The fact that the above hyperbolic advice fails to recognise is that there's a difference between the use of adverbs and the abuse of adverbs.

There is so much iconic writing we'd never have had without adverbs. A great example (and a piece of writing that breaks more than one "rule") is "to boldly go where no man has gone before". (Oh my goodness, it uses an adverb and splits an infinitive!) And Shakespeare was a fan of the adverb; he invented the word "ceremoniously" (and about 2,000 others). I think if we put him on one side of a set of scales and put Stephen King, Elmore Leonard, Mark Twain, Ernest Hemingway and the authors of *The Elements of Style* on the other, it would balance up fairly evenly. So there's no consensus.

However, one area that most agree really benefits from avoiding the adverb is dialogue attribution. Why write "he said loudly" when you could write "he shouted"? Why write "she said quietly" when you could write "she murmured" or "she whispered", depending on how quiet the volume of her speech was? Why write "they said unclearly" when you could write "they mumbled"? Thomas Jefferson said, "The most valuable of all talents is that of never using two words when one will do" and dialogue attribution is the perfect case in point. But using an adverb can also prove this point. "Will you be there?" she asked. Is it better to answer "It is possible" or "Possibly"? Depends how big the stick up one's ass is. Or if it's the queen speaking. Or if your fiction is set in historical times.

There are always reasons to break the rules and since not using adverbs isn't even a rule but a preference for some but certainly not all writers, you shouldn't feel too bad about ignoring this advice. If removing adverbs makes your writing better, then do it. If leaving adverbs in your writing makes it stronger, then do that. The one real benefit of having this discussion is that it raises awareness. It provides writers with another way to assess their writing and possibly improve it even more. It's why writers should never accept or dismiss any advice out of hand but give it due consideration and then make the decision that is best for them.

GETTING AROUND THE CENSORS: MAKING UP YOUR OWN SWEAR WORDS

Let's face it, unless you're a saint, the occasional swear word (also known as curse words in certain parts of the world) will slip out every now and then. Whether you're stuck behind the world's worst driver or you've dropped something on your foot, sometimes it just happens.

But having characters in fiction drop the "s", "f" and "c" words – amongst an array of offensive others – can have some readers, publishers and moral guardians shaking their heads in disapproval. To get around this, certain writers have simply made up their own swear words.

The best of them seem to be in science fiction and fantasy writing, in worlds completely removed from our own, and many of them are clearly a variation of the "f" word we are all familiar with:

- *Battlestar Galactica*: In both versions of the classic sci-fi television show, "frak" is the swear word of choice and what makes it so believable is its similarity to the word it emulates.
- *Farscape*: A combination of the "f" word and "hell", "frell" first appeared in the ninth episode of *Farscape* and is used as both a verb and a noun.
- *Babylon 5*: Another thinly veiled "f" bomb, yet somehow "frag" lacks a little, probably because it lacks the harsh consonant that tends to really sell the profanity of a swear word.
- *Scrubs*: Okay, this one's not science fiction or fantasy and it's also commonly used in the real world by people who need to swear but can't bring themselves to get down and dirty. Still, I defy anyone to come up with a better use of a faux swear word than Dr Elliot Reed,

played by Sarah Chalke, saying "frick" on the many, many, many times her life goes down the crapper.

- *Mrs Brown's Boys*: Another real-world show but not the only one to use the traditional Irish substitution of "feck". There's something almost adorable about hearing an Irish person use this word.
- *Red Dwarf*: "Smeg" is one of several swear words in the *Red Dwarf* universe but it is the best of them, sold beautifully by the character Dave Lister, played by Craig Charles.
- *The Hitchhiker's Guide to the Galaxy*: "Zark" is probably the most swear-word-like swear word in the *Hitchhiker's* books (unlike "Belgium", described as the "rudest word in the universe" and completely banned in all parts of the galaxy except for one where they don't know what it means).
- *The Smurfs*: "Smurf, smurf, smurfety, smurf!" says Patrick Winslow in the 2011 movie and Gutsy responds with, "There is no call for that sort of language, laddie!" "Smurf" replaces a variety of swear words and even not-so-offensive words in *The Smurfs* to save the delicate ears of children and just for general added smurfiness.

Goodness, if I lived in a different universe, I'd need to wash my mouth out with soap after all of that! But we're still not finished:

- *Firefly* (and *Serenity*): While "gorram" (probably a variation on "God damn") and "rutting" seem fairly standard, it's the random Chinese insults where the Browncoat universe really comes into its own. Because this version of the future envisions the English-speaking world and China merging into overarching world dominance, everyone speaks both languages but Mandarin is mostly reserved for the creative expletives the characters pepper their dialogue with. Translations of the insults include "stupid inbred stack of meat", "panda piss", "frog-humping son of a bitch", "filthy fornicators of livestock", "motherless goat of all motherless goats", "holy mother of God and all her wacky nephews", "the explosive diarrhoea of an elephant" and "holy testicle Tuesday".

If you're feeling especially salty but thoroughly uncreative, you can always go with foreign swear words, although it tends to be an issue if and when your writing is being translated into that foreign language. Or if you're feeling salty and don't give a fuck what the readers, publishers, moral guardians and censors think, you can embark on a real-world swear word writing spree and see if you like the results.

George Washington said that "swearing is a vice so mean and so low that every person of sense and character detests and despises it" but sometimes it's exactly what fictional characters need to release the stress of the things writers put them through.

A GUIDE TO DRUNK WRITING

"I was drinking a case of 16-ounce tallboys a night, and there's one novel, *Cujo*, that I barely remember writing at all."
On Writing by Stephen King

One persistent stereotype about writers is their fraught relationship with alcohol. For some, it's absolutely accurate. But for most of us who write, we know it isn't true. While there may be plenty of creatives who struggle with sobriety, it's no greater in percentage terms than members of the general public experience. Still, why let that get in the way of giving it go?

Stephen King is the cautionary tale but what he did was alcoholic writing. Drunk writing is less intense, less destructive to life in general and a much more rare occurrence.

My first (and only) episode of drunk writing (to date) happened coincidentally. I'd just finished a long week at a non-writing job, I was about to start yet another Project October (a month of intensive writing – 31,000 words in 31 days), but before that I wanted to wind down on a Friday night with a couple of cold beverages while watching the football on television.

I'm not much of a drinker. If I want something alcoholic, I have to specifically go out and buy it as I don't keep spares in the house just in case I feel like drinkies. And I usually can't get through more than three drinks before getting tired and falling asleep. I was about halfway through my second drink when I wrote in big wonky capital letters on one of my whiteboards, "DRUNK WRITING."

I was going to leave it at that. Great idea, my tipsy self thought. I'd follow it up in the morning after a good sleep when I was refreshed and ready to write. The problem was that with that full-time non-writing job I mentioned, more often than not when I put off writing until I was refreshed and ready, the writing never got done.

So I kept making notes. I wrote – sometimes clearly, sometimes illegibly – on my whiteboard. Then I would retreat to the couch, take another swig of my preferred Smirnoff Double Black, rest the bottle in my lap, have a cat jump on me and spill the liquid over both of us, clean it up and wait for the next wave of inspiration. This piece of writing is the result.

But it doesn't read like something written by a drunk person, I hope with fingers crossed you are thinking to yourself. Of course not. I don't – and nobody should – publish first drafts even when they're written sober, let alone drunk.

If you'd like to give it a go, here are a few tips.

STEP 1: CHOOSE YOUR MOMENT

I recommend a Friday or Saturday night. Getting drunk during the day, no matter how productive you intend to be, isn't a great look, more pitiable than experimental. Plus the day-time commitments that many of us have (children, jobs, etc) don't mix well with drinking.

STEP 2: GET NICELY DRUNK

Not so drunk that you pass out, not so drunk that you vomit on your keyboard (it's counterintuitive if you have to spend your drunk writing time cleaning stomach bile and undigested food off and out of your computer, even more so if you do so much damage to your hardware that you need to purchase a new machine).

STEP 3: EMBRACE WEIRD IDEAS

Just go with them. After all, if you wanted to be sensible, you wouldn't be trying this drunk writing thing in the first place. The weird ideas might not make sense in the morning but in these inebriated moments, they will be wonderful. And you never know how they might just evolve into terrific plots. A fight-to-the-death reality television show with child contestants probably sounded a little insane to begin with but now it's difficult to imagine a world in which *The Hunger Games* books don't exist.

STEP 4: IGNORE THE RULES

Don't worry about spelling, grammar, punctuation, sentence structure, chapters or generally making sense. Drunk writing is more of a stream of consciousness type of writing. The only thing you should expect of yourself is to get words down on a page (or a whiteboard or a napkin or whatever it is you have to hand). All of the things that need to be fixed to make it understandable for the sober reader can be left for the sober editor. (The sober editor will probably be you as well, just you the next day after the effects of the alcohol have worn off.)

STEP 5: DON'T OVERDO IT

The reason that drunk writing is appealing is because it's something done rarely. If you're drunk writing all the time, then you're not drunk writing anymore, you're just an alcoholic and while it worked okay for Stephen King in the short term, it doesn't do you (or any of your loved ones) any favours over the longer course of your writing (or general) life.

∞

So that's drunk writing. I got this chapter out of it. But I'm not planning to do any more drunk writing for a while. Firstly, it's incompatible with that Project October I mentioned above, which really requires focus and not falling asleep. Secondly, trying to edit 31,000 words of drunk writing doesn't sound all that appealing to my sober editor (me). Thirdly, for every episode of drunk writing that requires three drinks, I could be spending that money on a book (and if you know me at all, you know I'd much rather be spending my money on books). And lastly, if I spent a month drinking, my medical bills would also likely skyrocket. (And since I'm doing this Project October in July – yes, that's Dry July – it wouldn't seem quite right.)

If drunk writing isn't quite up your alley (after all, it is essentially getting drunk alone), then a nice social alternative is the drunk reading group. How does it work? I'll get back to you once I've been to one.

THE MORAL OF THE STORY

In the wake of the mass shooting in Las Vegas in 2017, the deadliest in US history, I was listening to a segment on the radio about research into gun owners in Australia. Rather than reinforcing the idea that weapons were more likely in rural areas where they are necessarily used for farming and predator control purposes, it found that a small number of urban gun enthusiasts and sports shooters were amassing huge arsenals. One owner had 283 guns. All legal, of course, otherwise the researchers would never have known about them.

There are plenty of illegal guns in Australia as well, estimated at about 10,000, but the strict gun control laws in this country mean that gun ownership is seen as unusual, abnormal even. We don't have the gun culture that the US has, I suspect partly because of the different ways in which the countries established their independence from their shared colonial master.

The reason this segment on the radio resonated with me is because the main character in my debut novel, *Enemies Closer*, is a small weapons engineer, a gun designer with a large arsenal of her own, although primarily comprised of historically significant pieces worth a lot of money. In the as-yet incomplete sequel, the novel begins with the opening night of an exhibition of her collection at the Museum of the Confederacy in Richmond, Virginia.

I began writing the character and her story in 2004. There'd been plenty of mass shootings by that time (Port Arthur, Dunblane, Beslan and Columbine just to name a few within my lifetime) and yet I didn't give any thought to making her someone with a passion and a skill for such deadly machinery. I just thought it made her unique, intelligent and determined. She must have been to have made it in such a male-dominated industry. In fact, part of the storyline was that her employer kept rolling her out to be the public face of the business to demonstrate how progressive they were.

So why now, more than a decade after I created her and five years after I published the novel, was I suddenly having a crisis of conscience? The Las Vegas shooting was still very raw, so there was that. My longest non-familial relationship had also just ended in a not unexpected but still devastating death. Grief was at the forefront of everything. And since I'd gone back to a non-writing job four months before that left little spare time and meant I'd written nothing new in just as long, I was doing a lot of reflecting on things I'd already written.

It was Oscar Wilde who said, "There is no such thing as a moral or an immoral book. Books are well written, or badly written. That is all." But despite the many terrible things he experienced as a man who was well ahead of his time, he could never have imagined the world in which we live today, in which something we tweet on Twitter or post on Facebook can go around the globe multiple times in mere seconds. He could also never have imagined the terrible weapons we have at our immediate disposal, particularly in a place like the US where guns in their many and deadly forms are seen as a right and not a privilege.

I'm not arrogant enough to assume that anything I write has influenced or will influence anyone to do anything more than buy my books (or not buy my books, as the case may be) or buy someone else's books (in the case of my book reviews). But I suspect that any writer who doesn't understand the inclination to go on a shooting spree and kill dozens of people will at one point or another in their writing career question their decision to write about the things they write about, especially if the things they write about encompass the horror of murder, rape, pedophilia or war.

But the reality is that fiction is more often influenced by people who choose to do terrible things than people who choose to do terrible things are influenced by fiction. And the fact that we writers wonder about the morality of the things we choose to write tends to suggest we fall into the camp of the traditional "good guys" because the "bad guys" perpetrating terrible crimes spend very little time on morality beforehand or remorse afterwards.

And yet none of this makes us feel much better when terrible things happen. Another sign of being a "good guy". So what can we as writers do?

The answer, to this question and to so many others we ask ourselves in the writing caper, is simply to write. Write what you must. Write what you can. Write whatever it is in your heart to write. If it is faith that inspires you, then write it. If the good deeds of others inspire you, then write it. If an exploration of the darker side of human nature really gets your creative juices flowing, then you must follow where it leads. Pretending it doesn't exist won't get any of us anywhere closer to a better world. But there have been plenty of books that focus on difficult subjects that have changed the world. If you're brave enough, yours could end up being one of them. And if your writing is honest, then morality will take care of itself.

WHEN CREATIVITY ISN'T APPRECIATED: LITERARY HOAXES

One thing I would really love to do is perpetrate a literary hoax. I see it as the ultimate in creativity, pulling the wool over the eyes of the gullible and, for a while, even those with a little more sense. The conundrum of a literary hoax is that you must be discovered in order to become famous for perpetrating it. That seems to be the less fun part though. But for those watching from a little distance, the people involved and the lengths they go to are fascinating.

Here are a few great literary hoaxes.

NORMA KHOURI

Norma Khouri wrote the book *Forbidden Love* (also known as *Honour Lost*) as a piece of non-fiction describing the murder of her Muslim best friend by her friend's father and brother after they discovered she was dating a Christian man. It was a worldwide bestseller. But the book was full of factual errors and was exposed by an Australian journalist approximately a year later.

An absolutely enthralling documentary called *Forbidden Lie$* was made in 2007 with the participation of Khouri herself, who continued to defend the story as truth, admitting only that she had changed names, dates and places to protect people. For the first half, I was absolutely convinced she was telling the truth and throughout the second half, it seemed clear that she was just a very good actor. It's a fascinating tale, particularly because she still hasn't confessed despite mountains of evidence against her.

ERN MALLEY

Ern Malley was the creation of Harold Stewart and James McAuley, two Australian poets who despised the modernist poetry movement and particularly *Angry Penguins*, a poetry journal. In order to expose the editor, Max Harris, Stewart and McAuley created what they considered to be nonsense poems and submitted them for publication. The entire next issue of *Angry Penguins* was dedicated to Ern Malley and his work.

The hoax was revealed shortly after and Harris's career was essentially destroyed but, ironically, so were the careers of Stewart and McAuley, who couldn't shake the notoriety of being Ern Malley's creators. There is a terrific book on the subject called *The Ern Malley Affair* by Michael Heyward.

JACK THE RIPPER

Unbelievably, debate still rages over whether the diary of Jack the Ripper is real or a fabulous hoax 25 years after it was presented to the public. Is James Maybrick really Jack the Ripper or is he the world's unluckiest man, murdered by his wife and unfairly defamed as history's most vicious killer?

It's about as delicious as literary hoaxes come. Read the original book by Shirley Harrison covering the "discovery" of the diary and if you can't get enough, read the latest book by Robert Smith who is absolutely convinced it's true.

THE HITLER DIARIES

Between the late 1970s and the early 1980s, a man named Konrad Kujau forged 60 volumes of journals and sold them for $3.7 million. It would have been a bargain at twice the price considering the supposed author was Adolf Hitler. Of course, with a little forensic analysis, they were quickly confirmed as fakes.

Both Kujau and the intermediary who stole a lot of that $3.7 million were jailed for their fraudulent activities.

JT LEROY

JT LeRoy is not just a pen name but an entire persona presented as the author of three semi-autobiographical books about a teenage boy experiencing sexual abuse, drugs and poverty. The true creator was a woman named Laura Albert who was eventually sued for $350,000 for selling the film rights for the first book as JT LeRoy instead of as herself.

Savannah Knoop, Albert's sister-in-law, later wrote and published a memoir called *Girl Boy Girl: How I Became JT LeRoy*, about how she would appear in public wearing a wig and sunglasses, pretending to be JT LeRoy at Albert's request.

∞

If these snapshots have merely whetted your appetite for literary hoaxes, here are some more that might satisfy you:

- *A Million Little Pieces* by James Frey
- *The Hand That Signed the Paper* by Helen Demidenko
- *A Rock and a Hard Place: One Boy's Triumphant Story* by Anthony Godby Johnson
- *Love and Consequences: A Memoir of Hope and Survival* by Margaret Seltzer
- *Naked Came the Stranger* by Penelope Ashe
- *The Autobiography of Howard Hughes* by Clifford Irving
- *Coffee, Tea or Me* by Donald Bain
- *Go Ask Alice* by Anonymous
- *The Education of Little Tree* by Asa Carter
- The life of Dan Mallory – apparently he wrote a "memoir" but decided not to publish it, yet the fiction author has woven a web of lies about his background that are more fascinating than anything he could write as fiction – enjoy!

TWITTER WRITING WISDOM

Every time I sit down to write a blog post, I aim for approximately 1,000 words. But as I posted my most recent tweet, I realised that writing advice doesn't always have to be quite so lengthy. Here's a selection of my Twitter ramblings (right back to when I started tweeting) to do with writing. Hope you get something out of it. (I got an entire chapter out of it!)

2013

9 January: @znewnham I think the older you get, the quicker you can write quality stuff – something to do with feeling like your time is running out...

25 January: On a self-imposed reading ban because I am distracted when I #amwriting (or supposed to be). Anyone else torn this way over two great loves?

14 February: Every *Enemies Closer* ebook sold makes me think, "Who bought it? I have to know!" I hate not knowing. Thanks for reading, whoever you are...

4 April: I think I realised that I don't want to work as a writer any more than I want to work at anything else – I just want to write. #amwriting

25 June: Secret to book marketing: write article on own divorce/abuse/ general heartbreak, sign off as author of completely unrelated novel. #amwriting

23 July: Just found a terrific word in the #dictionary: afflatus n. creative inspiration, usually thought of as divine. #amwriting

26 July: I know it's an actual word but in my mind "totebags" reminds me so much of "amazeballs" that I can't take it seriously. #weird #words #amreading

10 September: Why I write #fiction – I'm really only important, witty and interesting when I'm pretending to be someone else. #amwriting

18 September: I'm not self-aware enough to have an "everything I learned about #writing, I learned from" person. Everyone taught me. Yes, including you!

24 October: #Writing goals with #deadlines are good – I never meet any of them but they point me in a direction, I follow and I get there eventually.

2014

29 April: I am essentially finished my novel. Hard to tell. When you've read it so many times, you start to lose all sense of good and bad. #amwriting

25 June: Wrote the opening to my new book last night – #amwriting again! After four months of rewriting and editing, it was such a pleasure. :-)

10 July: I don't like titles that refer to someone as their partner's wife or mother or daughter, as if it's their most important trait. #amreading

22 July: May have solved the sequel problem I was having – realised I was trying to write the story from the wrong character's perspective. #amwriting

25 July: Some people (I'm looking at you, @CassandraPage01) have perfect writer names from the start. The rest of us... not so much. #writing

7 August: Classic – I misspelled supercalifragilisticexpialidocious in an article I am writing and Microsoft Word corrected it! #amwriting

2015

14 April: It's weird how relieved I feel when I see apostrophes in the right places in other people's writing. #amreading #grammarnazi

17 April: Figures! I just posted my inaugural guest post and it's instantly the most popular thing ever on my #blog! #writing

18 July: "100 million #readers can't be wrong." Yes, they can. #Bestselling does not always equal good #writing or worthy of my #amreading time.

2016

8 February: @AdviceToWriters You have to go into debt to study anything nowadays. But I wouldn't be where I am without that expensive study.

3 May: I... have... no... words... which could be a problem for a writer. #textprize @readwatchtweet @skbainbridge @pearliestpearl @textpubYA

30 November: Learned a new word today – uxorious – doubt I'll ever be able to use it in a sentence without feeling pretentious though. #amreading

2017

10 February: But finishing a #novel is an amazing feeling! You'll get there if you just keep #writing, just keep #writing... #amwriting

11 August: I want to #read all the #books – all of them! #impossiblegoals #amreading

29 October: People with #jobs like #butterfly #farmer or #violin #doctor make me realise how boring all my work choices have been – still love #writing though

5 November: What the? From a real #book #review: "While I find [the #writer] as a person as bad as nails on a blackboard, her #writing is engaging..."

15 November: Apart from the Yes verdict, the best part of this survey being over is all the misspelled hashtags should be consigned to history, right? #marriageeqality #marriagequality #marriageequaility #marriageequality

21 November: Started filling in an online form and my phone auto completed it for me, including the occupation field as "Writer". Felt like validation. #amwriting #writing #writer

20 December: Bored a colleague stupid at the office Christmas lunch yesterday about how I'm a #writer (thought I did anyway). Today she told me she'd bought a copy of my #novel, started reading it last night and thought it was really good! #amwriting #ammarketing #amselling

21 December: My instinct to correct every misused or missing #apostrophe online is so strong, it's really only my lack of the infinite time required to do it that holds me back. I am on holidays from my day job for the next three weeks though... #amediting #writing #amwriting #grammar #nazi

2018

8 January: Went to buy a t-shirt today and lectured myself before I went that I was not to buy any #books because I already have an enormous #TBR pile. Came home with seven books. #amreading

15 January: I was told face-to-face by the Sales & Marketing Director of a well-known publisher not to even bother trying to get an agent, that's how low her opinion of agents in general was. Every publishing option – including self-publishing – has its pros and cons, its highs and lows.

25 May: Does it say more about me or the state of television that my current favourite show is *The Amazing World of Gumball* (considering a four is the first – and not the only – number in my age)? Maybe it's because it's brilliant #writing!

5 June: Deliberately mean reviews say more about the reviewer than the book.

7 June: My favourite picture book is *The Big Orange Splot* by @DanielPinkwater because I like the message it sends about how it's okay (and sometimes wonderful) to be different from everybody else.

26 June: Saw these while I was #book browsing. Is this a writer's worst nightmare? #amreading #amwriting

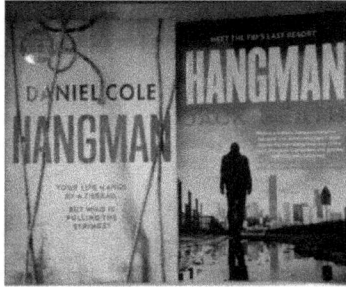

27 June: In honour of #NationalWritingDay, I did some editing. It's the life of a #writer to do things bass-ackwards, right? #amwriting #amediting

27 June: I respect people who just leave out #apostrophes entirely more than people who put them in the wrong place. (My #editing teacher always said, "If in doubt, leave it out.")

30 June: Don't listen to any #writer who professes to know about #writing. They only know about their writing. #amwriting #amreading

3 July: Calling #romance novels a "guilty pleasure" is a passive aggressive way of saying there are better things to read. All #reading should be encouraged, regardless of the content or format that speaks to each individual. It's better than the alternative. #amwriting #amreading

19 November: Sometimes we forget how lucky we are with freedom of speech and expression: "Chinese #writer sentenced to 10 years' jail over book with homoerotic sex scenes" #amwriting #amreading

14 December: Every time I see a book of the year announcement, I think, "There's no way anyone had time to read every book published this year. I'm going to take it with a grain of salt." #amreading

2019

2 August: The nostalgia of the typewriter is so appealing. The reality of the typewriter is bloody hard work. Lovely paperweight? Yes. Functional way to write? Not so much. So say my arthritic fingers.

14 October: Me whenever I see someone announcing they've signed a contract for a #book that will be published next year but hasn't been written yet and thinking about the book I've been trying to finish #writing for seven years:

27 October: Uh oh. Five chapters away from finishing #writing a #book I've been working on for seven years and I've been struck by #inspiration for another book I desperately want to start writing... #amwriting #firstworldwritersproblems

5 December: I have just typed the final words in a book I have been #writing for seven years. Done! Except for... you know... rewriting, editing, beta reads, rewriting again... Maybe give me another seven years just to be safe? #amwriting

2020

29 January: I have never bought a #book based on how beautiful the cover is... until today. *Shell* by Kristina Olsson, cover design by Christabella Designs. #amreading #amwriting

3 March: Me reading a review: "Points deducted for a prologue"!?! I have to respond to this tweet and make fun of that nonsense. *reads responses to tweet first* Wow, every single person beat me to it.

4 March: Just received an email about a store's #book sale and pumped the air in excitement. Then I looked at the roughly four dozen #books in my #TBR pile and decided not to buy any more. Advice on processing the associated grief welcomed. #amreading

7 July: My favourite type of celebrity tweet is the one where they point out the spelling and grammatical mistakes of randoms being mean to them.

18 July: This is why #editors are a non-negotiable:

23 July: This makes me want to cry. What have I been doing with my life? #amwriting "Four-year-old lands book deal for his 'astonishing' poetry"

You can follow me on Twitter at twitter.com/letruscott.

HOW MANY DIFFERENT WAYS ARE THERE TO WRITE ABOUT THE SAME THING?

As the end of another year approached, I sat down to write a Christmas-themed blog post. I started my blog in 2015 and this would be my fifth Christmas-themed blog post in four years (because I did two in 2015 when everything to do with writing the blog was all so new and I had so much to say). I sat down and tried to write... but nothing happened. I decided I just needed to give it a little more thinking time.

I sat down a few weeks later and tried again. Still nothing. Because apart from the fact that I wanted it to be about Christmas and writing, I had no idea what I was going to write.

My four previous Christmas-themed blog posts were about:

- Whether or not a writer should write during the Christmas holidays or take a proper break (December 2015)
- A poem about Santa running into a writer still writing as he was delivering presents – because "the night before Christmas/Was as good night as any/To write a few words/And if possible many" (December 2015)
- What a writer wants for Christmas – time, money, inspiration, motivation and luck (December 2016)
- Writing a Christmas-themed book (December 2017)

This chapter was my third attempt to write another Christmas-themed blog post. But I still had a big fat nothing. After all, how many different ways are there to write about the same thing? Yes, Christmas and writing are pretty broad topics but still, really, how many different opinions can one person have about them? And how many of those opinions will translate into something worth writing (and reading) about?

A handful, a dozen, a hundred, a thousand, tens of thousands, possibly millions? Millions, yes, if we're talking about millions of writers. More likely a handful if we're talking about just one writer. Maybe a dozen if we're talking about a really insightful writer. And obviously that number gets a whole lot higher if we forget about things like being insightful and worth reading.

No, it's not very Christmasey but it was as close as I was going to get.

WRITING THE SAME STORY

Talk to any police officer and they will tell you that a dozen witnesses to the same crime will all have seen slightly different things and therefore will have a dozen slightly different versions of the same story. It's a common writing device to use this approach to tell one story; multiple characters get their turn, each narrating essentially identical stories, the later perspectives revealing a little more, something that the other characters didn't see or didn't understand the importance of.

In a piece of writing like this, it's crucial to develop the distinct voices of each of the characters telling the story. Otherwise, the danger is that readers will start to feel like they're simply reading the same story a dozen times, instead of a dozen slightly different stories.

WRITING THE SAME TOPIC

Clearly, it's problematic for me to write about the same topic too many times (especially when the topics are Christmas and writing) but there are plenty of people out there who have no trouble churning out piece after piece on virtually identical subjects (see the work of every right-wing commentator with a weekly column for evidence of this).

The key is identifying the smaller components that go into the same topic (the A-Z, the top 10, etc) and then fleshing each of them out until they are large enough to make up a complete piece of writing on their own.

WRITING THE SAME THEME

Ainsley Hayes: "He is an Englishman" is from *HMS Pinafore*.

Lionel Tribbey: It's from *Penzance*. Don't tell me about Gilbert and Sullivan. It's from *Penzance* or *Iolanthe*… one of the ones about duty.

Ainsley Hayes: They're all about duty. And it's from *Pinafore*.

"And It's Surely to Their Credit", Episode 5, Season 2, *The West Wing*

Gilbert and Sullivan must have been able to write the same theme over and over if "they're all about duty". They're not the only ones. All writers fall into one of two categories: those who write about the same themes all the time and those who write about a variety of themes. Those who write about the same themes all the time know what they like to write and stick to it. Romance (true love), dystopia (anti-authoritarianism), science fiction (discovery), drama (the meaning of life).

Writing the same theme is a lot easier than writing the same topic because it is so much broader. While romance can seem quite limiting, true love can be about a lot more than just romance. True love can be about parents and children, about friendships, about citizens and countries, about pets and their owners. The same theme is more often than not an undercurrent rather than the easily identifiable plot points.

WRITING THE SAME CHARACTER

Patricia Cornwell and Kay Scarpetta. Lee Child and Jack Reacher. Sue Grafton and Kinsey Millhone. Agatha Christie and Miss Marple. Arthur Conan Doyle and Sherlock Holmes. Jeff Lindsay and Dexter Morgan. Ian Fleming and James Bond. Clive Cussler and Dirk Pitt. Agatha Christie and Hercule Poirot (yes, she was good enough to come up with more than one character to write handfuls of novels about).

Kay Scarpetta, Patricia Cornwell's most famous creation, is referred to in the novels as "doctor, lawyer, chief", a play on the "tinker, tailor" rhyme as well as the fact that she has degrees in both medicine and law as well as being the Chief Medical Examiner for Virginia. Although the focus is on her role as a pathologist, her background gives plenty of scope for a wide range of stories. She also has a past (not a dubious one, just the life that has got her to the jumping off point that is the first novel).

If you have an interesting enough character, you can write about them for the rest of your career. Determining whether you have an interesting enough character, however, can be difficult. It's sometimes just a matter of waiting to see how the readers react to them. And if the readers react favourably, then it's a matter of making sure the character has enough depth to be constantly wheeled out for the next book.

WRITING THE SAME WORLD

I've written before about not letting a world you've already created go to waste. And if you've created a great one and aren't using it more than once, then you're not just doing a disservice to yourself, you're doing a disservice to all the readers who enjoyed immersing themselves in it the first time around.

Writing the same world doesn't mean you have to write the same characters. Harry Bosch, Mickey Haller, Jack McEvoy, Terry McCaleb and Cassie Black have all starred in their own Michael Connelly novels but all exist in the same fictional version of Los Angeles and appear in minor roles or are referenced in other books of which they aren't the main character. JK Rowling has written seven *Harry Potter* books and also released a "textbook" called *Fantastic Beasts and Where to Find Them* that featured in the original novel. A series of five movies based on it, essentially prequels in the Hogwarts universe, are now being made. JRR Tolkien's *The Hobbit*, *The Lord of the Rings* and *The Silmarillion* are all set in the same universe of Eä. What do all these works of fiction have in common? They have been an absolute goldmine – both in terms of earnings for their creators (or their creator's estate) and as a foundation for continuing reinvention. Books have become films, TV shows, plays and merchandise beyond even the most confident writer's imaginings.

Developing a fictional world that can withstand the constant return of a writer to plunder it time and time again is not a simple thing. But done right, it can be a marvellous thing – for both writers and readers.

∞

So how many different ways are there to write about the same thing? Fewer ways if we're talking about really specific topics, many more if we're talking about broad themes. But there are two crucial things when doing it:

- Keeping it all straight in your mind – nobody is better at picking up discrepancies than devoted readers and they will not hesitate to let you know about it.
- Keeping it different enough – even when writing or reading about the same thing multiple times, both writers and readers are looking for something new.

WRITING IS WHAT HAPPENS WHILE YOU'RE BUSY MISSING DEADLINES

In February 2017, I published *Project January*. But I'd actually planned to publish it about four months earlier. Yet as the deadline I'd set for myself arrived, the book still wasn't finished. I had the publishing plans for it and my next four books written on one of my whiteboards:

- *Project January: A Sequel About Writing* – November 2016
- *Black Spot* – November 2017
- *Trine* – November 2018
- *Project February: A Trilogy About Writing* – November 2019
- *Matriarchy* – November 2020

But because it was four months late (or at least four months later than I'd planned to publish), suddenly my subsequent publishing plans were also thrown out. (Obviously, I like the idea of publishing roughly one book a year.)

That wasn't the only thing that changed. I started development of an entirely new book. I changed a title. I moved some things around. So my revised publishing schedule looked like this:

- *Black Spot* – March 2018
- *Motherhood* – May 2019
- *Project June: A Trilogy About Writing* – February 2020
- *Trine* – February 2021
- *Matriarchy* – February 2022

It's been more than three years and until publishing *Project June* (formerly *Project February*) in 2020, I hadn't published any other books. I have the text of two other completed books ready to go: *Black Spot* and *Trine*. *Motherhood* is the entirely new (non-fiction) book, a collection of essays about the many mothers I know with incredible stories (you can read about its development in my 2017 Project October posts on my blog). And *Matriarchy* is something I've been ruminating over for a long time, the story of a small country that expels all men to create a safe place for women. I haven't even written 1,000 words of it but the first third is pretty firmly settled in my mind (if not on paper).

And then, of course, there's my blog. When I first started writing it, I posted three times a week. Then it became two times a week. When I started working a full-time job again, it reduced to once a week. I now write blog posts so infrequently that I can't schedule them in advance and sometimes weeks and months go by without a peep from me. And when I do have something to post, it's usually a book review. Why?

Plans are all well and good but they don't always mean much. Editing, cover design, full-time jobs, freelance jobs, family, health, global pandemics: there are quite a few things that happened between 2017 and now to account for why I haven't published those books.

What's your point? I can hear you asking. The above is my long-winded way of letting you know that it's not the end of the world when the deadlines (otherwise known as goals with time frames) that you set for yourself don't get met. So your book or your blog post gets published later. So what?

The one time it really is a problem is when you're getting paid to write to a deadline. I was a paid corporate writer for over seven years and I never missed one deadline during that time. Probably because I wasn't emotionally attached to what I was writing and everybody else seemed to like the results, so that was good enough for me.

Corporate writing is one thing but a publishing contract is another. I've written previously about how it isn't always what it's cracked up to be. This is from the second of two posts I wrote about why it's unlikely you will and why you shouldn't take it to heart when you don't win writing competitions:

"On offer for the winner of the Text Prize was a publishing contract, which is what we writers think we want. But I spoke to two people at the announcement party who made me wonder if I should be careful what I'm wishing for.

"The first was a writer who has been quite successful and has published a lot. But that writer also seemed very tired, almost on the verge of a burn out, because of contracts with short deadlines that had to be met no matter what. Writers without contracts can sit at home and tinker with our books for years trying to get them right without any such pressure. We bemoan the time as it ticks by without any seeming progress, but now I'm wondering if this is the simpler time we will later fondly look back on and dream of returning to.

"The second person I spoke to worked at a publishing company – there were quite a few different companies represented at the party – and I mentioned that I had enjoyed a book the company had published but hadn't liked the sequel. 'Neither did we,' that person responded. 'Even the author wasn't happy with it.'

"'Then why,' I asked, 'was it published at all? Why wasn't it held back until the author was happy with the final result?' I was told that there were international contracts in place with specific deadlines and that these other publishers didn't care so much about whether it was any good, just that they could capitalise on the success of the first book by rushing out the second."

$$\infty$$

If deadlines work for you, then by all means go ahead and set them. If they don't, you can set them as well and then watch as they go by unmet. As Douglas Adams, author of *The Hitchhiker's Guide to the Galaxy*, said, "I love deadlines. I love the whooshing sound they make as they go by." Maybe you'll learn to love the sound of them, too.

PART 4

EDITING

SPELLING

I originally wrote this chapter when I thought maybe I'd do a writing book for children so it has a slightly different tone to the rest of *Project June*. But when I posted it on my blog, plenty of adults told me they had learned something from it, so maybe you will, too.

WHY IS SPELLING IMPORTANT FOR WRITERS?

Wen a werd iz speld rite, it's eze-er 2 reed. Wen a sintins iz speld rite, the meenin iz eze-er 2 unerstan. wen a howl artycall, storie or bok iz speld rite, ur reedr well no wat u wer tring 2 til thum.

What? Let me make it clear by fixing up the spelling.

When a word is spelled right, it's easier to read. When a sentence is spelled right, the meaning is easier to understand. When a whole article, story or book is spelled right, your reader will know what you were trying to tell them.

WHY IS SPELLING SO HARD SOMETIMES?

Spelling is hard sometimes because the English language breaks its own rules – a lot! Have you ever heard "'i' before 'e' except after 'c'"? It doesn't always work (in fact, it mostly doesn't work). It works in "receive" and "receipt" and "friend" and "believe". But it doesn't work when "foreign feisty neighbours unveil their beige glaciers". Tee hee!

This often means that rather than relying on rules for spelling groups of words, we just have to learn how each word is spelled and try to remember. The second edition of the *Oxford English Dictionary* contains over 300,000 words. That's a lot of words! Plus, new words are being created all the time, sometimes because advances in technology and society make it necessary, other times because young people want a cool secret language their uncool parents and teachers can't understand.

Did you know…?

Some of the world's biggest dictionaries are so big it takes decades to write them. The original *Oxford English Dictionary* was begun in 1888 and was finally finished in 1928. In 2000, the editors of the dictionary began a project to create the third edition of the *Oxford English Dictionary* and they don't expect to finish until 2037.

IS THERE ANY WAY TO MAKE SPELLING EASIER?

With some words, the best way to remember how to spell them is to come up with a rhyme or game or rule that helps you remember. Here are a few examples:

- Separate – the two "a"s separate the two "e"s
- Definite – the two "i"s definitely separate the two "e"s
- Rhythm – rhythm helps your two hips move (see how the first letter of each word spells "rhythm")
- Laugh – laugh and you get happy (a similar method to remembering "rhythm" even though they're not quite all first letters)
- Because – big elephants can always understand small elephants
- Dessert and desert – there are two "s"s in "dessert" just like strawberry shortcake and there is one "s" in "desert" just like a lonely snake in the sand
- Island – an island is land!
- Necessary – there's half a cesspool in "necessary"

Of course, you won't need one of these funny ways to remember for every word. Some words you'll have no trouble with because you already know how to spell them. The best idea is to write a list of the words that you do have trouble spelling and find or come up with a way to remember the spellings of those ones. After all, everybody has words that they struggle with but not everybody struggles with the same words.

Did you know…?

Some people think "antidisestablishmentarianism" is the longest English word, which has 28 letters. But there are a few other words (usually technical or scientific) that are just as long or longer. Perhaps the reason why people like to think this is the longest word is because it's easier to say than some other long words like floccinaucinihilipilification (29 letters), hepaticocholangiogastronomy (28 letters) and spectrophotofluorometrically (28 letters). Hard, right? Well, at least most people know how to say (or sing) supercalifragilisticexpialidocious (34 letters). Thanks, Mary Poppins!

WHAT IF YOU CAN'T REMEMBER HOW TO SPELL ALL THE WORDS?

Don't worry, nobody knows how to spell all the words in the English language and nobody is expected to be able to remember. That's what dictionaries, spell checkers and editors are for.

Dictionaries

As a writer, you should always have a good dictionary with you when you are writing. That way, when you need to look up how a word is spelled, it's right there waiting for you. There are lots of different dictionaries, little ones with just a few words, bigger ones with more words and huge ones with lots of words that are really heavy. The bigger the dictionary, the more words it will have. It's up to you to choose which one you want.

Big dictionaries can be expensive sometimes. If you can't afford a brand new big dictionary, have a look in your local second-hand store for an old one. It might not have all the new words but it will still be pretty good.

There are also dictionaries available online. Make sure when using an internet dictionary that it is for your region (see below).

Did you know...?

If you're Australian, you will need an Australian English dictionary. If you're Canadian, you will need a Canadian English dictionary. If you're American, you will need an American English dictionary. This is because there are little differences in each of these variations of English that have evolved over time.

Spell checkers

If you're writing in Microsoft Word, you can use the Spell Checker to find spelling mistakes in your writing. Make sure you've set the language to the right English for your region and then run the Spell Checker to find any mistakes.

Remember, though, computers are helpful but they're not perfect. If you've used a correctly spelled word that isn't the right word for the sentence (such as "I left the bike hear" when it should be "I left the bike here"), Microsoft Word won't pick it up.

Editors

An editor is someone who has studied the English language (usually at university or at TAFE or at college – at a higher level than high school anyway) and knows a lot about spelling (and grammar and punctuation and all the parts of language). It's their job to find all the mistakes in writing.

Did you know...?

Because being an editor is a job, if you want a piece of your writing edited by an editor, you have to pay them to do it. It can cost a lot of money. At the beginning, the best people to ask for editing help are your parents, aunts, uncles, grandparents and teachers. They will help you for free. But when you want to professionally publish a piece of writing, then it's better to hire an editor. Ask the editor how much it will cost and then decide if you can afford it.

THE INSIDIOUS SIDE OF PERFECTIONISM

My little sister has a lot going for her. She's model beautiful, thin, smart, socially aware, vegan (so much commitment required to do this – I know because I'm vegan as well when I dine with her), loves animals and children, hates injustice and generally wants to make the world a better place and herself a better person. All of this is more amazing when you find out she suffers from chronic fatigue syndrome, rheumatoid arthritis (at the age of 24, mind you), clinical depression, borderline personality disorder, endometriosis and a multitude of allergies. But she still managed to finish Year 12, complete a Certificate IV in Youth Work and begin studying a Bachelor of Social Work.

She's also a perfectionist. I shouldn't be surprised it runs in the family since I'm a perfectionist, too, although our 19-year age gap has given me the time she hasn't had yet to work through my perfectionism and settle on a more reasonable goal of extremely good. I mostly meet that goal but no matter how hard I work, I sometimes don't. Results range from good, okay, not good and complete failure, depending on what I'm doing. (Housework is a complete failure more often than not; I just can't be bothered.)

In the years since she finished secondary school and began her tertiary studies, I've acted as both an unofficial sounding board and official paid tutor (thanks, Mum) to help her out. University hasn't always been the easiest of things for her (she has actually had to change institutions twice, the first time because the campus wasn't disability friendly, meaning she had trouble getting around, and the second time because the compulsory work placements were only offered on a full-time basis, which her disability prevented her from being able to undertake). She's also a self-doubter. If she can't comprehend something, she assumes it must be because she's not smart enough to. It's often because her lecturers and tutors aren't teaching well but the self-doubt always means her default position is to assume there's something wrong with her. A chat with me or Mum or our other sister with a PhD usually gets her to a place of understanding and the ability to move forward.

At a recent meeting, however, when she was struggling with an essay question that I considered poorly written and difficult to interpret (so it was hardly surprising that she was struggling), she said this: "I'd rather not submit anything and just fail than submit something that isn't perfect."

I was disturbed. Firstly, because it was like having a mirror of my own ridiculously perfection-obsessed 20-year-old self pointed straight at me. And secondly, because preferring not trying and failing completely to trying and achieving something – however imperfect – is a dangerous route to take. The sooner everyone can realise that perfection is an impossible goal, the happier their lives will be. Unfortunately, it is a process. You can be told over and over – and I was, frequently – about the impossibility of it but it is something that must be learned, not simply accepted, and it can take years. It took me at least 10, probably closer to 15.

The difference between us, though, was that I was always willing to have a go. I struggled in my first year of university, too. I seriously considered dropping out in the first semester. I was only 17 and although I loved learning and thought I was intellectually capable enough, I didn't have the emotional maturity that would have made that transition from high school to university a bit easier. But I didn't drop out. I stayed. I pushed through. I studied a bunch of subjects that sounded interesting when I signed up but suffered from boring content delivered badly by unengaged lecturers and tutors. My grades often reflected that. But I eventually stumbled into American history, fell in love, finished with a high distinction average in that major and was offered the chance to do honours. I declined and simply graduated with my bachelor's degree without honours because I'd already figured out that the underlying problem was the fact that I wasn't studying writing and had enrolled in a writing and editing course somewhere else.

There are plenty of people more famous than me and my little sister (which is to say actually famous) who failed time and time again before eventually succeeding. Thomas Edison is probably the most famous example of all. Accounts differ about the number of failures he had – 1,000, 2,000, 10,000 – while attempting to perfect the light bulb but his response to these suggested failures is reported pretty consistently: he didn't fail, he just figured out 1,000 [or 2,000 or 10,000] ways not to make a light bulb. Another way it has been put: the process for developing the light bulb had 1,000 [or 2,000 or 10,000] steps.

Imagine if Thomas Edison had decided to give up after the tenth failure. Imagine if he'd decided not to try at all because he couldn't do it perfectly the first time around. We would have been sitting around reading by candlelight for a lot longer than we did. If it were necessary now rather than just nostalgic, we'd have missed out on an awful lot.

That's what I hope my little sister will be able to see, the large number of things that she'd be missing out on if she doesn't give it a go, whatever "it" is. Despite her self-doubt, all of her assignments so far have come back with high distinction grades of 90% or higher. No, it's not perfection but it's pretty damn good. It's certainly a lot better than many other students can claim. And if she considers that as the basis for improvement, then she's going to get very close to excellence.

It's a good lesson for us all. We can allow ourselves to be sidetracked or overwhelmed by the unattainable pursuit of whatever it is we wish we were able to do perfectly or we can give it a red hot go regardless and see where it takes us. It might be even more wonderful than the tediousness of perfection.

DOES YOUR BOOK PASS THE BECHDEL TEST?
DOES IT NEED TO?

The Bechdel test was developed in 1985 in – perhaps unusually – the comic strip of Alison Bechdel, an American cartoonist and 2014 recipient of a MacArthur "Genius Grant". In it, two women discuss going to the movies and one of them outlines her requirements for seeing any of the films being shown. They have to meet three criteria:

- The movie has at least two female characters.
- The two female characters talk to each other.
- The conversation is about anything other than a man.

The Bechdel test didn't gain mainstream recognition until 25 years later (maybe a sign of the times) but Bechdel credits the idea to her friend Liz Wallace, who was in turn inspired by some of Virginia Woolf's writing.

Approximately half of all films meet the requirements of the Bechdel test, including *Alien* and *Aliens*, *All About Eve*, *Die Hard*, *Gone with the Wind*, *The Matrix*, *Raiders of the Lost Ark*, *The Silence of the Lambs*, *Singin' in the Rain*, *Some Like It Hot*, *The Terminator* and *Terminator 2: Judgment Day*, and *The Wizard of Oz*. So we can keep watching many of our favourites without feeling like we're contributing to gender inequality.

However, if about half of all films meet the Bechdel test, this also means that about half of them don't. Some of the films that we might think would – considering their kick-ass female characters – but don't include *The Avengers*, *The Blind Side*, *Breakfast at Tiffany's*, *Lara Croft: Tomb Raider*, *Run Lola Run* and the original *Star Wars* trilogy (*A New Hope*, *The Empire Strikes Back* and *Return of the Jedi*).

And some films that we might think shouldn't pass what is essentially a feminist test (a very basic one) but do include *Anchorman: The Legend of Ron Burgundy*, *50 Shades of Grey*, *Goodfellas*, *How to Lose a Guy in 10 Days*, *Transformers* and *Weird Science*.

The Bechdel test is something I've only become familiar with in the past few years and the vast majority of my fiction writing was done before that so I've had to go back and do some self-assessments to decide if my writing passes it. I'm pleased to say that I think almost everything I've written passes with flying colours.

It's a very low bar so it's not that hard. But having said that, there are some very valid reasons for why some writing might not pass the Bechdel test. *Alien 3*, in which Ripley's shuttle crash lands on a penal colony, doesn't pass the test because she's the only woman in what is essentially a men's prison, the only thing left on a planet that was abandoned by all other inhabitants. In *Gravity*, Sandra Bullock's character, Dr Ryan Stone, is the only woman on a space mission. In a variety of movies based on the battlefields of historical wars, are we really going to be surprised that two women don't pop up and have a conversation? And in the romance genre, which we read specifically to see relationships develop, are we going to criticise two women discussing a man? Usually, these conversations are a means of advancing the plot.

Still, there are lots of measures we use to assess our writing (plot, pacing, character development, etc) and there's no reason why this can't be one of them. Not the only one but part of a holistic process. It will sometimes prove useful. It sometimes won't. But think about it like this. Readers can pick up on the teeniest, tiniest details they don't like and base entire bad reviews around them. If you can remove the possibility of not passing the Bechdel test, then why wouldn't you?

WHO CARES ABOUT THE OXFORD COMMA?

Who cares about the Oxford comma? Plenty of people, it seems. Many writers, editors and language purists have strong feelings about whether or not the Oxford comma should be used. Some have even called it "a hill" they're "prepared to die on", both those who are for and against it.

Mike Pompeo, US Secretary of State, has issued not one but two memos to his staff outlining his preference for the Oxford comma. And under the Trump administration, a preference must be considered an order for anyone wanting to keep their job. However, "[o]n semicolons, Pompeo remains silent; on long dashes — not a tittle." (From "Secretary of State Pompeo Is Mandating His Oxford Comma Preference at State Department, Report Says" by Glenn Fleishman, *Fortune*, 19 September 2018)

So what is the Oxford comma? Called the Oxford comma because it is required usage according to *The Oxford Style Manual*, and also known as a serial comma or a Harvard comma, it's the comma used after the penultimate (second last) item in a list of three or more items.

With the Oxford comma: The shoes were red, shiny, and too small.

Without the Oxford comma: The shoes were red, shiny and too small.

There are two ways in which to use the Oxford comma:

- All the time as a stylistic choice (whether it's your choice or the choice of an organisation you are working for or studying at)
- Only when necessary as a means of preventing ambiguity

Wikipedia has provided the following general formulas:

- The list x, y and z is unambiguous if y and z cannot be read as in apposition to x.
- Equally, x, y, and z is unambiguous if y cannot be read as in apposition to x.
- If neither y nor y and z can be read as in apposition to x, then both forms of the list are unambiguous; but if both y and y and z can be read as in apposition to x, then both forms of the list are ambiguous.
- x and y and z is unambiguous if x and y and y and z cannot both be grouped.

Clear? As mud. The majority of US style guides dictate use of the Oxford comma. The majority of British style guides, despite the preference of *The Oxford Style Manual*, dictate not using it. In Australia, Canada and New Zealand, it is not used as standard. Other languages in which use of the Oxford comma goes against the rules include:

- Bosnian
- Croatian
- Danish
- Dutch
- Finnish
- French
- German
- Greek
- Hebrew
- Hungarian
- Icelandic
- Italian
- Montenegrin
- Norwegian
- Polish
- Portuguese
- Romanian
- Russian
- Serbian
- Spanish
- Swedish
- Turkish

So who is right? Who knows.

The list above demonstrates, though, that bullet points can help to solve the problem of worrying about whether an Oxford comma is required or not because each new line, each bullet point, separates each item. However, bullet points are only appropriate in certain types of writing and not others. They are unusual in fiction, for example.

WHY I MOSTLY DON'T USE THE OXFORD COMMA

- I'm an Australian writing in Australia.
- The Oxford comma is generally redundant in a simple list because the "and" or the "or" serves the same function of separating the last two items.
- If there's doubt because of the inclusion or the lack of an Oxford comma, then I rewrite the sentence so that its meaning is clear.
- The Oxford comma only makes sense if you use it in a list of two as well and nobody uses it like this (nobody who has any idea of what they're doing anyway).

The shoes were red, and shiny. (No)

The shoes were red and shiny. (Yes)

WHY I SOMETIMES USE THE OXFORD COMMA

- Where there are multiple uses of "and" or "or", it needs to be clear which words are being grouped together.

Example: Duties include menu preparation, cooking and serving food, and clean-up.

WHY NOT USING THE OXFORD COMMA CAN SOMETIMES GET YOU INTO TROUBLE

In 2014, the *O'Connor v Oakhurst Dairy* lawsuit was filed in the US state of Maine to interpret a statute under which wages for the "canning, processing, preserving, freezing, drying, marketing, storing, packing for shipment or distribution" of certain goods were exempted from the requirement to pay workers overtime. "For want of a comma, we have this case," commented US appeals judge David J Barron.

The disagreement occurred over whether the phrase "packing for shipment or distribution" meant packing for shipment and packing for distribution (essentially packing only) or if it meant packing for shipment and then, completely separate to that, distributing the goods. Why did it matter? Well, there were 13 million reasons why. If distribution was included, the dairy could keep their money. If distribution wasn't included, then truck drivers were owed $13 million in additional wages.

The lack of the Oxford comma seemed to suggest a certain meaning and the lack of the conjunction "or" before the word "packing" seemed to suggest another. A clear-cut case of ambiguity. A lower court ruled one way, in favour of the dairy, and then on appeal, a circuit court ruled the other, in favour of the drivers.

Eventually, the case was settled when Oakhurst Dairy paid the truck drivers $5 million (better than the original $13 million they could have been out of pocket but no doubt still paid begrudgingly) and the intended meaning of the statute was settled when the Maine legislature amended it to include serial semicolons (which everyone knows are far more definitive than just commas) as well as replacing the word "distribution" with "distributing". It now reads, "canning; processing; preserving; freezing; drying; marketing; storing; packing for shipment; or distributing."

The fact that "distribution" was replaced with "distributing" goes to show that it wasn't just the punctuation that contributed to the lack of clarity. All editors know that lists must be written with identical opening word suffixes (where they exist in the same format) so that it flows; for example, all infinitives or all –ing words or all nouns as below. The fact that the statute originally used "distribution" meant that it no longer flowed with all the other –ing words and could more easily be read as belonging with "shipment" and modifying the "packing" rather than being a separate item in the list.

- Preserve, preserving, preservation
- Store, storing, storage
- Distribute, distributing, distribution

At the time, of the 50 US states, 43 mandated use of the Oxford comma and both the House of Representatives and the Senate, whilst not going that far, did warn against leaving it out, for precisely the reasons described above; in their words, "to prevent any misreading that the last item is part of the preceding one".

WHAT SHOULD YOU DO?

It's probably best to follow the crowd on this one if you want to avoid having punctuation pedants contact you to tell you what you're doing wrong every time you publish a piece of writing. If you're writing in the US, use it. If you're in Australia, Canada, New Zealand or the UK, or writing in any of the languages outlined in the long list above, don't use it unless it is necessary to avoid ambiguity.

And don't worry about getting it right on the first go. After all, the last stage of editing – most writers will be able to tell you this – is all about commas; putting them in, taking them out, putting them in again and then taking them out (and then putting them back in one last time) over several last draft read throughs. The best part about reaching this stage? You know you're nearly ready to finish this piece of writing and begin working on the next.

WHAT TYPE OF EDITING SHOULD YOU ASK FOR? (YES, THERE'S MORE THAN ONE!)

A couple of years ago, I was asked if I might be interested in proofreading a coffee table book for a corporate company. It was the story of their beginnings all the way up to their current-day successes, a glossy thing with lots of pictures, and none of their internal staff had the time to do it. Sure, I replied, providing my hourly rate and the length of time I thought a proofread would take based on the word count I'd been advised of.

But when the first chapter came through, it was clear it was still in its first draft. It hadn't been through any of the other editing stages that should come before a proofread. It wasn't even in the form of a proof (formatted as it will look in the final book with headers, footers, page numbers, columns, photographs, captions, etc). It was just a poorly formatted Word document.

No wonder nobody in the company had the time to do a proofread – they didn't even know what proofreading was. In fact, they thought it was something else entirely. What they should have asked for was a rewrite, a line edit and copyediting, which then could have been sent to a designer or typesetter for preparation of a proof. Because it's only after preparation of a proof that you can undertake a proofread.

I ended up doing a rewrite, a line edit and copyediting for the cost of a proofread because I'd committed to doing the work without asking to see a sample first (that was my mistake – I assumed incorrectly that because they were a professional organisation I could expect a certain level of understanding from them). It was about four times as much work so they got a real bargain. But not all editors are suckers like me. If a writer asks for a proofread and sends through anything except a proof, an editor will more than likely send it back to the writer with either a revised (much more expensive) quote or a request for the proof after the writing has been through the other stages.

So make sure you know what you're asking for when you begin the editing process. It will make your writing life so much easier and so much less embarrassing. Here are the different types and what distinguishes them.

REWRITING

Technically, rewriting is not an editor's job. If you want writing, even if it's rewriting, then ask a writer. But wait, hang on, you're a writer. Shouldn't you be doing it yourself?

Yes, you should. If you want to be credited as the writer of a piece, then you need to be the one doing all the hard writing work. Otherwise, prepare to have another writer's name nestling uncomfortably next to yours on the cover of the final book.

Once you've written a first draft, you might be desperate for feedback from somebody. But all writers have to learn to be their own first port of call for feedback. You're a writer – you should know the basics of writing – but you're also a reader. So read your book. Take copious notes. And then have a go at a second draft based on the things that bothered you when you read it. Essentially, you are doing your own first "edit".

Apart from saving yourself a boatload of money, it's important to get good at this because writers have to do a lot of rewriting. Nobody anywhere has ever written a perfect first draft. And most editors don't do rewrites. They might tell you how to make your writing better but they still won't fix it for you. So being able to get to the second and maybe even third drafts without paying anyone for any kind of edit is in your own best interests.

SUBSTANTIVE EDITING/DEVELOPMENTAL EDITING/STRUCTURAL EDITING/MANUSCRIPT ASSESSMENT

Substantive editing or developmental editing or structural editing or manuscript assessment, whatever you want to call it, is the big picture review. It's the evaluation of the story, the plotting, the pacing, the characters, how they all work together and if they can work together better. At this point, nobody cares all that much if the words are spelled correctly and they certainly aren't going to fix those kinds of mistakes. Suggestions will be made about combining or eliminating minor characters, removing and adding plot points, identifying plot holes, reordering chapters (particularly where flashbacks occur), cutting slow and irrelevant scenes, getting to the exciting scenes more quickly, consistency of each character's dialogue, alternative endings... hopefully, you get the idea.

LINE EDITING

Once your book is in pretty good structural shape, it's time for the line edit. This is about tightening the writing itself – improving the style, removing any instances of poor expression, clichés, redundancies, repetition – and helping it flow. Line editing can be a confronting process because the critique can feel very personal. A plot point that isn't working or a misspelled word, writers can be philosophical about these things (I said can, not will – some writers really resent any suggested changes but that's another subject for another day). But commentary on the style of your writing can be challenging. Try to remember it's all in aid of a better book. And making you a better writer.

COPYEDITING

Copyediting takes care of the basics – correct spelling, appropriate punctuation, good grammar, elimination of typos – and a good copyeditor will prepare a style sheet for consistency – their own and the proofreader's later on.

PROOFREADING

Proofreading is the very last edit to find the final few errors that none of the other edits have picked up. The text should be formatted on pages the size they will be printed (i.e. not A4) with headings in correct font and size, page numbers, headers, etc. This is a review of exactly what the reader will see, not a review of the working documents that all previous edits have worked on. And it is the last edit. It should never be the first.

A NOTE ON PUBLISHING

If you choose to self-publish, it's up to you to know the differences between and the appropriate time to work your way through each of these editing stages. Line editing and copyediting can usually be done at the same time by the same editor for roughly the same cost. Most good editors wouldn't be able to leave something that needs changing alone just because it doesn't fall within the right category of what it is they are being paid to do anyway.

If you've been lucky enough to be signed by a traditional publisher, they will – or at least the trustworthy ones do – guide you on and pay for each of the editing stages. Sometimes though, you may need the assistance of an editor to get your manuscript to a level of quality that elevates you above the writing pack and gets you noticed. A manuscript assessment and rewrites will usually achieve this, if it's going to happen. Everything else will be taken care of by the publisher.

A NOTE ON PERFECTION

About three weeks after I published *Project January*, I was reading a chapter of it out loud to my nephews, the chapter in which I talked about them. There, as plain as the nose on my face (and it's a really plainly, painfully obvious nose), was a straight apostrophe that should have been a curly apostrophe. It was even in my style sheet that there shouldn't be any straight apostrophes. I thought I'd tracked them all down but, no, there was a rogue one staring me in the face.

It didn't make any difference to the quality of the writing and it's likely that most people reading the book wouldn't even realise that it's the "wrong" apostrophe but I was mortified. I really shouldn't have been. Of all the types of mistakes an editor can make, it's the best kind. If that's the only thing wrong with my book, then I'm doing pretty well. (I'm sure there are other mistakes, I just haven't found them yet.)

No matter how many editors you engage, your book will never be perfect. The idea that editors don't make mistakes or don't miss mistakes is ridiculous. The job title is "Editor", not "Perfectionist". And there has never been a "perfect" book in terms of editing. There will always be at least one mistake. That's life.

So then why would you need more than one editor? Because you can get close to perfection. If you methodically work your way through each of the editing stages, you'll get close. You're increasing the probability of finding most of the errors. And by using a couple of different editors, the second will hopefully pick up the things the first didn't and vice versa.

EUPHEMISMS: THE POLITICS OF WORDS

One of the first pieces of advice given to writers is to write from the heart, to write honestly. Most of us take it. Because it's good advice. Honesty helps readers relate to the writer and to what is written.

But, of course, just like anything else, words can be used to manipulate. Through the omission of facts, the selective use of facts, the use of emotive language and, perhaps the most insidious, through euphemisms.

According to the *Macquarie Dictionary*, a euphemism is "the substitution of a mild, indirect or vague expression for a harsh, blunt or offensive one". Sometimes, it's to soften the blow as in the case of saying someone has passed away so that we don't have to say that they died. More often these days though, euphemisms are being used to protect the writer or speaker rather than the recipient of the words.

Perhaps less surprising is the fact that most of these kinds of euphemisms used today occur in the realm of politics. Gone are the days of statesmen and women, replaced by people who are in it for the money and the power. And when they're caught out doing the wrong thing, the euphemisms come out as frequently (and as easily) as breaths.

Have you ever watched a politician being interviewed after it becomes public knowledge that they have done or said something they shouldn't have? You've likely sat through it (if you can stand to) thinking to yourself, *Why don't they just admit they were wrong?* The words "I'm sorry" or "I was wrong" rarely form part of their explanation without being followed by a justification that contradicts the admission of regret or inappropriateness. And if they do, there always seems to be an unspoken component. "I'm sorry (I got caught)."

Here are a few euphemisms currently doing the rounds:

- "You're in my thoughts and prayers" really means "I don't care enough to actually do anything about it so you'll have to content yourself with my thoughts and prayers".

- "You've taken me out of context" really means "That's exactly what I meant but I don't understand why you are getting all up in my grille about it".

- "It's just a witch hunt" really means "All the allegations are true but I don't want to give up my huge salary, cushy perks and/or position of power".

- "Free speech is everyone's right" really means "I'm going to say the meanest, nastiest things you've ever heard and encourage others to do the same and you can't do a damn thing about it".

- "Alternative facts" really means "lies". This is the newest iteration of euphemisms that have been floating around for decades, if not centuries, such as "economical with the truth", "misspeaking", "terminological inexactitude", "post-truth" and "misinformation".

- "The silent majority" really means "most of the people who contact me about this say the opposite to what I'm going to do but I'm going to assume there are a lot of people out there that just haven't contacted me and think like I do because that suits my agenda".

- "Working families" really means "people I've never met and will do everything I can to avoid ever meeting in the future if at all possible".

- "Family values" really means "those things that I talk about in public to shame others while I think about screwing the mistress I have holed up in a million-dollar apartment in the city".

- "Tax relief" really means "a cut so miniscule individually you'll never notice the difference in your weekly wage but so huge collectively that you'll really notice it when you need education or health care".

The great thing about politicians is that they can be (and frequently are) mocked when they use this kind of language and if they don't knock it off, they can be (and frequently are) voted out of office. If we're really lucky, they'll disappear quietly into retirement (less and less frequent these days unfortunately).

The great thing about writers (all good writers anyway) is that if euphemisms have somehow managed to wriggle their way into our work, we can rid our writing of them during the editing process. Once you have an awareness of them, they're quite easy to spot.

I'll give the final word to a man who wrote a rather famous essay on the decline of the English language because of euphemisms and other bad writing habits and wrote the definitive novel, *1984*, on what has come to be known as "doublespeak":

"Political language… is designed to make lies sound truthful and murder respectable, and to give an appearance of solidity to pure wind. One cannot change this all in a moment, but one can at least change one's own habits, and from time to time one can even, if one jeers loudly enough, send some worn out and useless phrase… into the dustbin where it belongs."

"Politics and the English Language" by George Orwell, *Horizon*, April 1946

THE CULTURAL AND HISTORICAL CONTEXT OF WORDS

In August 2018, Senator Fraser Anning of Katter's Australian Party gave his maiden speech in the Australian Senate. In it, he called for a ban on Muslim immigration and a return to the White Australia policy (actually a collection of policies barring people of non-European descent from migrating to the country – the policies were effectively dismantled between 1949 and 1973 and officially legislated against in 1975). That was bad enough in itself. But he then went on to say that the "final solution to the immigration problem" was a plebiscite, a non-binding and hugely expensive opinion poll of the entire Australian voting population.

The speech was widely condemned for its racist overtones and blatant lies but the two words that repulsed people the most were "final solution". I read an article about his speech only hours after he had given it and before the outcry began in earnest. As soon as I saw that he had used those specific words, I was shocked. I am by no means a Holocaust expert but even just from watching a couple of documentaries years ago, I knew that "final solution" was the euphemism used by the Nazis so that they didn't have to call it "our plan to kill six million Jewish people". Thus, those two words, as innocent as they are when used separately, become something to be avoided as a pair regardless of what they are being used to describe.

Senator Anning's response to having this explained to him? "Claims that the words meant anything other than the ultimate solution to any political question is always a popular vote are simply ridiculous. Anyone who actually reads them in context will realise this."

So I must conclude that either Senator Anning did not know that those two words already had a malicious context – in which case he is horribly uneducated (something we all love to see in the people running our countries and making choices that affect millions of lives) – or he knew about the context and chose to use them in spite of (or perhaps because of) the fury he would stir up – in which case he's just horrible.

Words, symbols and even lives in general only have meaning because they are given meaning by the people who use the words and symbols and live those lives. And once a word, a collection of words or a symbol has a well-known context, it's difficult to pry it free from that understanding and imbue it with another. The word "gay" is a good example. It originally meant "carefree" or "cheerful". These days, it is exclusively used to define a type of sexuality. The swastika symbol is another example. The word "swastika" comes from Sanskrit and denotes something that is "conducive to wellbeing or auspicious". And long before the Nazis adopted it, the distinct symbol was widely used in Middle Eastern and Asian religions as well as Byzantine and Christian art. None of that matters because it is now recognised as a representation of hate and bigotry and those who do display it today tend to be embracing Nazi ideals, not ancient religious ones. So the rest of us who don't embrace those ideals understand that using it is considered poor form.

In the previous chapter, I wrote about euphemisms – how they were traditionally used to spare people's feelings such as saying someone had passed away instead of saying someone had died and how they are more and more being used to pull the wool over people's eyes, particularly in politics and the corporate world – but a phrase like "final solution" falls into another category entirely. Because as Todd Haugh explains in *Ethnic Cleansing as Euphemism, Metaphor, Criminology and Law* (2011), the "history of mass atrocity is awash with euphemistic rationalizations". The phrase "final solution" is the most well known of all of them. "Special treatment" is another lesser known euphemism used by the Nazis to describe Jews being gassed to death in extermination camps like Auschwitz and Treblinka.

Perhaps the most concerning part of Senator Anning's use of the term "final solution" is that this does not appear to be a one-off from people of a particular political persuasion. In January 2018, Manfred Weber, the leader of the Centre-Right EPP group in European Parliament used it while talking about immigration as well. And in May 2017, Katie Hopkins, a British tabloid writer, tweeted that a "final solution" was needed in the wake of the Manchester bombing. She quickly deleted it and tweeted the same message again, replacing "final solution" with "true solution" but the damage was already done.

Words are ultimately the most dangerous weapon we – not just writers but all of us – possess and words like "final solution" must be used with caution, with an understanding of how they can wound.

One thing is for sure: there is not a single person unaware of the damage words can do. They are used to hurt others every day. But wouldn't it be great if politicians and journalists and you and me used words to heal instead?

THE THINGS EDITORS LOOK FOR THAT WRITERS HAVE NEVER HEARD OF

I love to edit. I love knowing the parts of speech. Nouns, pronouns, verbs, adjectives, adverbs, clauses, phrases, conjunctions, prepositions, gerunds, subjunctives, infinitives, participles… Have I lost you yet? I wouldn't be surprised. You have to be a particular kind of person to appreciate these things.

Editors are these particular kinds of people. While some of them are instinctive editors and know from experience how words should appear sequentially and the order that gives them their intended meaning, others are trained editors who also know the names of all the mistakes. Here are a few things editors look for that most writers will never have heard of before.

COUNT AND MASS NOUNS

Count nouns are things that can be counted. Flowers, televisions, cats, people. Mass nouns are things that are difficult to quantify and therefore count. Love, chaos, information, freedom.

During a shortage, you would have *fewer* cats. But during peacetime, you would have *less* chaos. During a good harvest, you would have *many* flowers. But during a massacre, you wouldn't have *much* love to go around.

DOUBLE NEGATIVES

Okay, most writers will probably know what a double negative is but do you know how to interpret this sentence from George Orwell in "Politics and the English Language"?

"I am not uncertain whether she will not be unaccompanied by her lawyers."

It took me a while. But the key is to find two negatives that cancel each other out and remove them.

Removal of first double negative: "I am certain she will not be unaccompanied by her lawyers."

Removal of second double negative: "I am certain she will be accompanied by her lawyers."

There is always a place for negative constructions but there are few justifiable uses of double negatives.

SENTENCE FRAGMENTS

Most people probably know about sentence fragments these days thanks to them being Microsoft Word's favourite error. You will also know that sentence fragments aren't always wrong. They're great for emphasis.

Example: They are reminders of the things she has lost. (Full sentence) But not painful reminders. (Sentence fragment)

These two sentences are evoking two different sentiments so separating them gives each sentiment a chance to be experienced properly. However, there are some sentence fragments that just don't make any sense.

Example: Authorities being unable to prevent these cultural changes.

I came up with this example and I'm not even sure what I was trying to say but the correct version of any sentence fragment will have a finite verb or a main clause.

Example: Authorities were unable to prevent these cultural changes.

MODIFIERS

Strong nouns and verbs are always recommended but sometimes we choose to use more basic words and strengthen them with adjectives and adverbs. These kinds of modifying elements in a sentence should be placed next to the word or words they are modifying (or as close as possible at any rate). This is important because one modifier has the potential to modify many, if not all, of the words in one line of text. Consider the following five identical sentences apart from the placement of the modifier:

- Just I saw her at the park yesterday. (I was the only one who saw her.)
- I just saw her at the park yesterday. (But I didn't speak to her.)
- I saw just her at the park yesterday. (But I didn't see anyone else.)

- I saw her just at the park yesterday. (But I didn't see her anywhere else.)
- I saw her at the park just yesterday. (I saw her recently.)

While they are nearly identical, the simple act of moving the modifier into different positions changes the meaning on each occasion.

Misplaced modifiers

A misplaced modifier is an adjective, adverb or adjectival/adverbial phrase or clause in the wrong place in a sentence, causing ambiguity or creating unintended meanings.

Example: At the aquarium, Sarah found a lost child's hat.

Is it the child that is lost? Or the hat? Reorder the modifiers or add additional information for clarity.

Example: At the aquarium, Sarah found a child's lost hat OR At the aquarium, Sarah found a hat belonging to a lost child.

Squinting modifiers

Squinting modifiers could potentially modify multiple pieces of information in a sentence.

Example: She promised not to smoke in September.

Was the promise made in September? Or was the promise not to do it in September? Move the modifier (or even change some words in the sentence) so that the meaning is clear which part of the sentence is being modified.

Example: In September, she promised not to smoke OR She promised not to smoke during September.

Dangling modifiers

A dangling modifier exists in a sentence where the thing that is being modified is in the wrong place or implied but missing altogether.

Example: Summoning the taxi, the car arrived in less than 10 minutes.

Clearly, the taxi must be summoned by a person but there's no person referenced in that sentence. It needs to be rewritten to include the person.

Example: Summoning the taxi, I was relieved when the car arrived in less than 10 minutes.

In the following example, the person is referenced but not in the right place.

Example: Annoyed by Amy's crying, it was easier for Phillip to just leave the room.

"It" is not annoyed by Amy's crying, Phillip is. So the sentence should be rewritten to move "Phillip" closer to the modifier.

Example: Annoyed by Amy's crying, Phillip found it easier to just leave the room.

SPLIT CONSTRUCTION

A split construction is where an auxiliary verb is awkwardly separated from the main verb.

Example: Some people will if provoked by threats retaliate against aggressors.

"Will" is the auxiliary verb and "retaliate" is the main verb and separating them results in a sentence that is more difficult to read. It's better if they stay together.

Example: Some people will retaliate against aggressors if provoked by threats.

However, not all split constructions are awkward. In some cases, the split constructions are easier to read.

Example: Abigail got on the bus to excitedly show her friends her new dress.

If the word "excitedly" is moved before or after the infinitive, the construction becomes awkward (Abigail got on the bus to show excitedly her friends her new dress) or changes the meaning entirely (Abigail got on the bus excitedly to show her friends her new dress).

ELLIPTICAL CONSTRUCTION

An elliptical construction is a sentence where a word or words (usually verbs) are omitted because to include them is repetitious and leaving them out doesn't alter our understanding of what is being said.

Example: The cat was miaowing and the dog barking.

The missing word is "was" between "dog" and "barking" but the sentence still makes sense because the omitted word is the same as a word already in the mix. Problems occur when the word omitted in an attempted elliptical construction is not the same as the word that remains. Those problems become obvious when you try to reinsert the omitted word.

Example: The day was long and the clouds grey.

Example with omitted word reinserted: The day was long and the clouds was grey.

Correct example: The day was long and the clouds were grey OR The days were long and the clouds grey.

FAULTY PARALLELISM

Parallelism is almost like a list. Each of the components should be formed in the same way and when they aren't, the flow of the sentence is disrupted.

Example: My sister is smart, thin and a woman of great beauty.

It gets a bit wordy on the end, right? Condense it down into one word just like the other descriptors.

Example: My sister is smart, thin and beautiful.

The key is to match nouns with nouns, adjectives with adjectives, infinitives with infinitives and clauses with clauses.

∞

If it's all just a little too confusing, that's what editors are for. But I guarantee that knowing what to look for will make finding them a whole lot easier.

HOW TO PROOFREAD LIKE A PROFESSIONAL

You've written and rewritten your manuscript, you've had it assessed, rewritten it again (and possibly again), then had it edited. It's finally time for your book to be published. If you've already paid a manuscript assessor and editor and you can afford a proofreader as well, then go ahead and do it. A professional will always be able to do a better job than you. But if you're looking for a way to save a few bucks and you're confident you have the skills to take on the final stages yourself, then here's how to proofread like a professional. (Note: these steps assume you are using Microsoft Word.)

STEP 1

First, you'll need an electronic proof. A proof is your book laid out in the way it's going to be printed. You can't proofread if you don't have a proof. If you have a publishing contract, your publisher should organise for a proofreader to undertake all the following steps. If you're paying a publisher to print your book, they should provide the proof to you. If you're self-publishing, templates are usually available that you can paste your proof into and apply the appropriate styles (headings, opening paragraphs, following paragraphs, etc).

STEP 2

Turn on Track Changes.

STEP 3

Run the Spelling & Grammar Check (making sure that you've first selected and applied the language you want the Spelling & Grammar Check to look for; if you've chosen US English, then, for example, –ize endings will be considered correct and –ise endings will be considered incorrect and vice versa if you've chosen UK or Australian English). Let's face it, if there are tools available to make the proofreading process easier, then we'd be fools not to use them. And the Spelling & Grammar Check is one of the greatest technologies ever invented to help speed up that process. Remember, though, that Microsoft Word doesn't know English as well as we might like it to. So consider all suggested changes and also remember that it's okay to ignore the ones that don't make sense or that you know are just plain wrong.

STEP 4

Now read the proof for yourself and make corrections on screen as you go.

STEP 5

On the Review tab in Microsoft Word, change the Display for Review setting from "Final: Show Markup" to "Final" so you can't see the changes you've made in Step 4. Now repeat Step 4.

STEP 6

On the Review tab in Microsoft Word, change the Display for Review setting back from "Final" to "Final: Show Markup" so you can see all the changes you've made. Review the changes and if you're happy with them, accept all changes in the document.

STEP 7

Check for widows and orphans. Widows and orphans are where one line at the start of a paragraph is at the bottom of a page or where one line at the end of a paragraph is at the top of page. Publishing etiquette dictates that there must be a minimum of two lines of a paragraph together at the tops and bottoms of pages (not including single line paragraphs). Microsoft Word has a function for automatically ensuring this but sometimes this means the facing pages of a proof are slightly uneven at the bottom. Where this is the case, I like to make slight changes in the text to even it up manually (either by deleting a few words here and there or adding a few in).

STEP 8

If your proof has a table of contents and page numbers, check that the page numbers in the table of contents match up with the page numbers throughout the book. (If you have an automatic table of contents, update it and that should make it accurate. If you have a manual table of contents, first of all, why? Secondly, go through the text and make sure the page numbers in the table of contents match up with the locations in the proof.)

STEP 9

Order a printed proof. This should look exactly like what you will be offering readers for sale.

STEP 10

Read your proof like you would read any other piece of writing for pleasure but have a red pen handy. Circle any final mistakes you find.

STEP 11

In the electronic proof, correct those final mistakes you've found in the printed proof.

STEP 12

Repeat Steps 7 and 8. (You can also repeat Steps 9, 10 and 11 if you want to but if you've done this process thoroughly, you shouldn't need to.)

STEP 13

Approve your finalised proof for printing. Approval is a must. No publisher or printer will print your book without the proof being officially signed off. This way, if there are any mistakes, then you are responsible for them and all the copies of your book that are printed with them in it. If you're printing on demand, then there won't be any upfront costs and you can always make a few more changes and approve a second proof but if you're doing a print run, you will be liable for the cost of any printed books. So try to make sure you're as happy with the book as possible. You don't want to have to pulp hundreds or even thousands of books. Apart from the cost, it's a terrible waste.

∞

And that's it. A final word though: it's impossible for your book to be perfect. Small errors almost always slip through. A good rule of thumb is this: if you eliminate enough errors that only professional editors, proofreaders and pedants are able to find the rest, then you'll have done well. Good luck!

PROJECT JUNE STYLE GUIDE

A

Advanced Diploma of Arts (Professional Writing and Editing)

apostrophes – check to make sure all are curly, no straight apostrophes

article titles – all words initial cap (except prepositions and conjunctions) inside quotation marks followed by "by [author name]" followed by a comma followed by name of publication followed by a comma followed by date published

asshat

Australian English

B

Bachelor of Arts BUT bachelor's degree

backstory

bestselling, bestseller

the Bible (no italics) for the Christian text BUT bible (no initial capital) for references to guidebooks e.g. the writers' bible

black-and-white (adj)

book quotes – quoted text in quotation marks. On the following line, name of the book followed by "by [author name]" e.g. *On Writing* by Stephen King

book titles in italics

bullets – black circles at 0.5cm and following lines indented 0.5cm, 12 points of space after bullets are completed

C

chapters – each chapter starts on a new page

coattails

copyedit, copyediting, copyeditor

counterproductive

E

ebook

encyclopedia, encyclopedist

F

fairy tale

Father's Day

fire-free

first-hand

follow up (verb) BUT follow-up (noun)

font – Garamond 11 point

Fortnite

G

goal setting (noun)

ghostwriter, ghostwritten

Google (verb and noun)

go-to

H

Harlequin

heading level 1 – Garamond 14 point, all caps, centred

heading level 2 – Garamond 11 point, small caps, bold, left aligned

heading level 3 – Garamond 11 point, bold, left aligned

headings – initial capital, lower case following words unless proper nouns

how-to

I

initials of names – no full stops between letters e.g. JK Rowling, EB White

L

long-standing

long-winded

love-hate relationship

M

male-dominated

man-made

Master of Arts (Writing) BUT master's degree in writing

middle-class (adj) BUT the middle class (noun)

Mills & Boon

money – $20,000, $1.00, $0.99

money-making

Mother's Day

movie quotes – name of character speaking followed by a colon followed by the dialogue. On the following line, the name of the movie in italics.

movie titles in italics

multi-authored

multi-billion

multi-layered

multi-million

N

new-age (adj)

nine-to-five job

no one

numbers within text – spell out numbers one to nine and simple numbers over 100 e.g. one million BUT use numerals for complex numbers over nine e.g. 157 OR 942 AND over four digits use commas to separate thousands and millions e.g. 5,047 OR 1,747,222 BUT use numerals when referencing school years e.g. Year 10 and percentages e.g. 100%

numbers referencing decades – use numerals e.g. 1920s, 1950s

numbers referencing age decades – use numerals e.g. 20s, 30s

O

okay (verb and adj)

old-fashioned (adj)

one third (noun) BUT one-third (adj)

one-trick (adj)

P

paragraph formatting – first paragraph after any heading has no indent, subsequent paragraphs 0.5cm indent first line only, 3 points before, 3 points after, justified

parts – each part heading is labelled with its part number (numeral) and given its own page

pedophilia

percentages – numerals and symbol e.g. 100%

poem quotes – text as displayed in the original poem in quotation marks. On the following line, the name of the poem in quotation marks followed by "by [author name]" e.g. "Advice to a Prophet" by Richard Wilbur

postgraduate

practice (noun and adj) BUT practise (verb)

Project December: A Book About Writing in the first instance and then *Project December* in all following instances where talking about the book, Project December where talking about the process of publishing a book

Project January: A Sequel About Writing in the first instance and then *Project January* in all following instances where talking about the book, Project January where talking about the process of starting a sequel or second book

Project June: A Trilogy About Writing in the first instance and then *Project June* in all following instances where talking about the book, Project June where talking about the process of writing multiple pieces at the same time

Project November

Project October

proofread, proofreader, proofreading

Q

quotation marks – doubles NOT singles unless quotation marks required within quotation marks

R

real life (noun) BUT real-life (adjective)

résumé

S

scandal-free

sci-fi

scot-free

second-hand

semicolon

sideswipe

sidetrack

stand-alone

stepmother, stepfather, stepsister, stepbrother

symbol to break up paragraphs – ∞ in Garamond 20 point, centred, 12 points before, 12 points after, no indent in first line of paragraph following symbol

T

television show quotes – name of character speaking followed by a colon followed by the dialogue. On the following line, the episode name followed by a comma followed by the episode number (in numerals) followed by a comma followed by the season number (in numerals) followed by a comma and the name of the television show.

television show episode titles in quotation marks

television show titles in italics

time frame

U

undergraduate

upfront

V

versus – spell out

W

wellbeing

Y

you and your NOT they and their – speak directly to the reader

PART 5

WHAT HAPPENS NEXT?

HOW TO WRITE YOUR AUTHOR BIOGRAPHY

Harry: Why don't you tell me the story of your life?

Sally: The story of my life?

Harry: We've got 18 hours to kill before we hit New York.

Sally: The story of my life isn't even going to get us out of Chicago. I mean, nothing's happened to me yet. That's why I'm going to New York.

Harry: So something can happen to you?

Sally: Yes.

Harry: Like what?

Sally: Like I'm going to journalism school to become a reporter.

Harry: So you can write about things that happen to other people.

Sally: That's one way to look at it.

When Harry Met Sally

It's strange but the one thing writers seem to struggle with the most is the subject they know better than anyone else: themselves. Perhaps that's because writing an author biography is about finding the balance between arrogance and unworthiness (something everybody struggles with, of course, but only writers have to put the results down on paper). Toot your own horn without at least a smidge of self-deprecation and potential readers may write you off as a narcissist. Fail to toot your own horn enough and potential readers may write you off as a nobody who doesn't have the right to ask them for an hours' long commitment.

Perhaps it's also because an author biography tends to be something we dash off at the last minute instead of giving it the thought and attention it really deserves. You've spent months, possibly years, polishing a piece of writing and now that it's being published, you need a few paragraphs that will be appended to the end of it to enlighten readers about the person it came from. But if you feel like "nothing's happened" to you, then it can be tough no matter how long you spend on it.

There is no foolproof template for writing an author biography but here are a few things that might help get your creative juices flowing about your least favourite topic.

FAMILY

If you're married and have children, most people like to mention this in their author biographies. Significant others are good filler. And if you're lucky enough to be related to someone on whose coattails you can ride while you're establishing your own bona fides, then that's good material, too. A grandparent, an uncle, an aunt, a parent or a sibling who is also a writer or some other type of creative goes to show talent runs in the family.

LOCATION

Nobody needs to know your exact address but a city, county, state or country can add some flavour. If you're an American in Paris or a Nova Scotian in Nigeria or a Mongolian in Argentina, you'll certainly seem more exotic than the rest of us. Even if you've lived in the one place all your life, at least the locals will know you're one of them and can get around you.

AGE

Including your age isn't necessary or even important – unless, of course, there's something a little bit different about the stage of your life at which you are accomplishing your writing achievements. If you are younger (before your mid-20s) or older (past your mid-50s), particularly if you are releasing your debut book, then listing your age is really a coded message that it's never too early or too late to start writing and publishing.

QUALIFICATIONS

Qualifications aren't important either, especially for writers because there are plenty of wonderful published authors who have never studied a day in their life since leaving high school. But if you've gone to all the effort of getting them and you're struggling for points of interest in your author biography, then why not include them? Did you study something completely unrelated to writing? So what? The truth is that all study requires the ability to write and edit and receive criticism. What better preparation for being a writer!

I have three qualifications – a Bachelor of Arts (American History and International Politics), which taught me how to research, an Advanced Diploma of Arts (Professional Writing and Editing), which taught me how to edit, and a Master of Arts (Writing), which taught me to introduce more complex components into my writing.

RECOGNISED EXPERT IN A SPECIFIC FIELD

If you have succeeded in a field other than writing and are recognised as an expert, especially if it relates somehow to what you're writing about, then by all means tell the world. A former television star writes a novel about an actress? Sounds like they'll have the inside scoop. A former prisoner writes a crime novel? Should be packed full of details that give it more than just verisimilitude. Just like your qualifications, if you've gone to all the effort of becoming an expert, then figuring out a way to use it to fill out your author biography seems like a no-brainer.

MEDICAL CONDITIONS

If you have been diagnosed with a medical condition and either beaten it or are living with it every day, then that will likely have shaped you and who you are as a writer. It also tends to be a source of pride. A cancer survivor, a disability advocate, a sufferer of a chronic condition. These days, many writers include medical conditions in their author biographies. However, don't feel pressured to do it if it makes you uncomfortable. Your health is very personal and you may not want to be defined by it so specifically.

VICTIM OF A CRIME OR NATURAL DISASTER

Same goes for if you've been a victim of crime or a natural disaster. Surviving difficult challenges is inspirational to those who haven't had it happen to them. Caught up in an act of terrorism or an act of God. Survivor of rape or child abuse. Had all your money stolen by a conman. But if it doesn't sit right with you, then it's perfectly okay not to include it. After all, this is your narrative, not your sob story. The tale you tell is entirely up to you.

OTHER BOOKS PUBLISHED

Apart from anything else, if you've published other books, including that information in your author biography will prompt readers to seek them out if they enjoy the piece of writing your author biography appears in. If you've written only a couple, then list them by name. If you've written dozens, then a statement that you're the author of that number of books will suffice. You can include a list of your other works on a separate page instead of bloating your author profile with them.

WINNER/NOMINEE OF AWARD

This is a gimme! If you or your writing have ever been recognised by being nominated or shortlisted for or winning an award, then you must include it in your author biography. It doesn't matter whether it's the most prestigious award known immediately around the world as soon as it's mentioned or something your local library sponsored, if a panel of judges thought your writing was a class above most others that entered a competition, then that's information worth sharing with your readers.

UNUSUAL FACTS

This is box number three, as Josh Lyman in *The West Wing* would call it. Trivia, ephemera, the stuff that has very little to do with anything but is interesting anyway. My ephemera is crazy cat lady, Collingwood supporter, world's greatest aunt, things I own seem to catch on fire more than I would prefer (my car and my house within a year of each other, although that was a while ago now; I've been fire-free for over a decade). If you've climbed mountains on every continent or had 17 different jobs or invented something or been to space or own an animal refuge or speak a dozen languages, now's your chance to tell your readers.

MY AUTHOR BIOGRAPHIES

From the announcement that my novel *Black Spot* had been shortlisted for the 2016 Text Prize: "Louise Truscott is a blogger and author from Melbourne. Her debut novel, *Enemies Closer*, came out in 2012 and her non-fiction work, *Project December*, in 2015."

From *The Victorian Writer* when they published my article "A Dirty Word": "Louise Truscott is the author of the novel *Enemies Closer* and two non-fiction books, *Project December: A Book About Writing* and *Project January: A Sequel About Writing*. She also writes a blog called Single White Female Writer. *Black Spot*, her upcoming novel, was shortlisted for the 2016 Text Prize."

From the Swinburne University profile of me: "Master of Arts (Writing) graduate Louise Truscott has found the balance between corporate and creative writing. After publishing several books spanning fiction and non-fiction and recognition from the writing world, Louise is more satisfied with her career than ever."

From my blog and used as the author bio in *Project December*, *Project January* and *Project June*: "Louise Truscott was born, brought up and still lives in Melbourne, Australia. She tried not being a writer and editor, then tried being a corporate writer and editor, but she's only truly happy writing and editing when she chooses what to write and what to edit. With a blog called Single White Female Writer, there are lots of hints in the name about who she is. She published *Enemies Closer*, her debut novel, under the name LE Truscott in 2012. *Project December: A Book About Writing*, her second book, was published in 2015 and *Project January: A Sequel About Writing* was published in 2017. *Black Spot*, her upcoming novel, was shortlisted for the 2016 Text Prize."

Each of these biographies says essentially the same thing, although the last is a little more personal (probably because I wrote it) whereas the others were written by someone else using information I had provided and no doubt had word limits that needed to be strictly followed. And the Swinburne University profile is very focused on the master's degree I obtained there and how it contributed to my career because they were trying to sell potential students on doing further studies.

∞

My advice on preparing your author biography is to write a broad draft and then have an independent editor cull it into a short and sweet couple of paragraphs (a relatively inexpensive request since it's a very short piece of writing). As a corporate writer, I prepared a lot of employee biographies for tender submissions and the people who were the subjects of the biographies always seemed to have the same reaction, which was that they never knew they could sound so impressive. The truth is that they didn't sound that impressive when they were writing about themselves but after I took the basic facts they provided and jazzed them up, they were suddenly their own biggest fans. As we all should be.

MISTAKEN IDENTITY: WHEN SOMETHING YOU'VE WRITTEN SHARES ITS TITLE WITH AN INFINITELY MORE FAMOUS WORK

In the early 2000s, I wrote a category romance novel (Harlequin, Mills & Boon, whatever you call them in your region) called *Liberty's Secret*. It was the story of a woman named Liberty Freeman who had successfully reinvigorated a serious magazine from low circulation to being the talk of the industry. Now she was being asked by the publisher to do the same thing for a publishing company he had just bought with the help of a financial whiz named Quinn O'Connell. Cue pounding hearts, stolen kisses and Liberty's insistence that she wasn't interested despite plenty of evidence to the contrary. And her secret was the reason why.

Liberty's Secret was the last romance book I wrote. By the time I finished writing it, I knew I didn't want to continue writing romance or be known as a romance writer. So I shelved it. I put it aside, choosing not to publish it, and I have barely thought about it since.

When I started writing my blog, I was constantly trying to figure out ways to repurpose all of the many, many things I have written. So when I wrote a blog post about writing sex scenes for fiction and admitted that this wasn't a strength of mine, I also posted the sex scene I had written for *Liberty's Secret* to prove it was true.

When I originally posted it, the sex scene from *Liberty's Secret* averaged one view per month. Like I said, it's not great. And because it's just that one scene, completely out of context from the rest of the missing novel, that makes sense to me. Also, because it was an example of something I didn't think I did that well, I didn't mind that much.

So imagine my surprise when WordPress notified me of the following:

180

"Your stats are booming! Single White Female Writer is getting lots of traffic."

And when I checked to find out why, it was all because of the sex scene from *Liberty's Secret*. In one month, my average views from that post had increased significantly. And in just one week, the average views had increased 4,100%! What the heck was going on?

I knew there had to be more to it than the sudden popularity of a sex scene I had posted two years ago and had written over a decade previously. And, of course, there was. In 2016, a film also called *Liberty's Secret* had been released. It's the story of Liberty Smith, an all-American daughter of a family values preacher who is selected as the running mate of a conservative in an attempt to save his floundering presidential campaign. But when she falls in love with a woman, all hell breaks loose on cable news. (I haven't actually seen the film; I got all of that from imdb.com. Apparently, it's a girl-meets-girl musical in the vein of *La La Land* and it was partly funded by an Indiegogo campaign.)

Since I haven't seen it, I can only guess that there's some kind of sex scene in it because there seems to be an awful lot of people Googling "sex scene in *Liberty's Secret*". The only problem is that when you put that in your search engine, the top result is my completely unrelated blog post. And from what I understand about search engine results, the more people who click on my blog post – even though it's not what they were looking for – the longer my blog post will remain the top result when that phrase is searched.

A similar thing happened to my debut novel, *Enemies Closer*. I chose the title in 2005 when I first started writing the book (it was almost the very first thing I came up with) and when I published it in 2012, I didn't find anything else with the same name. But in 2013, the Jean-Claude Van Damme film called *Enemies Closer* was released. And in 2015, Ava Parker released her second book, also called *Enemies Closer*. Of course, the Van Damme film comes up first in search results on Amazon for works called *Enemies Closer*. My book comes up second and Ava's comes up third.

So why am I telling you all this? Mostly as a way to lead in to advice about considering carefully what you decide to call your book or film or any other piece of fiction in case someone else has already used the same title. In my case, I chose the titles *Liberty's Secret* and *Enemies Closer* well before they were used again by the films. When I published the initial post about writing sex scenes, I didn't even bother trying to find out if someone else was using it as well because I was using it for educational purposes, not commercial ones.

Even when I decided to post my old romance novel in full on my blog, I didn't think it was worthwhile spending a lot of time coming up with a different title. After all, I was pretty sure I'd come up with it first and I was really only posting it to fill a gap in my blog schedule.

But if you're planning to publish a novel and you haven't researched the possibility that there are already creative works out there with the same title, then you could really be doing yourself a disservice. While titles can't be copyrighted, if you call your book *Harry Potter and the Philosopher's Stone*, you're probably going to struggle to compete against JK Rowling's well-established novel, you're probably going to confuse a huge number of people and you're probably going to spend an awful lot of money on lawyers (and then lose anyway).

When I was preparing to release *Project December*, I did my due diligence to discover if there was already anything with the same title. There was. One was identical and the other was close enough that I needed to consider it. The identically titled creative work was an album by Endy Chow. I didn't and still don't have a clue who Endy Chow is but I figured the fact that his *Project December* was music and my *Project December* was writing was enough of a difference not to worry too much about it.

The other work was a book called *The December Project: An Extraordinary Rabbi and a Skeptical Seeker Confront Life's Greatest Mystery* by Sara Davidson. While the use of the title in Sara's book had a similar meaning to mine – *The December Project* is about preparing for the end of your life while, of course, *Project December* is about preparing for the end of your book – the subject matter of both is completely different. Again, I felt that there were enough differences to be able to get away with it. But discovering Sara's book did inspire me to add the subtitle, *A Book About Writing*, to clarify exactly what the book was about.

The key with choosing your book's title, as with so many other things in writing and indeed in life, is to make the choice with a full understanding of what it means. If there's something out there with the same or a similar title, if you know it and if you're still determined to continue using it when you release your book, that's entirely up to you. But doing it fully informed with your eyes open will make your writing life a lot easier than discovering it afterwards when it's too late to do anything about it.

IT'S A FINE LINE BETWEEN PLEASURE AND PAIN: DEDICATING YOUR BOOK

All writers devote an enormous amount of time, effort and passion towards writing their books. And while finally holding a completed book in your hands is right up there, one of the other most emotional moments usually comes just before the end of the process: deciding on a dedication.

They aren't compulsory but they appear in almost every book. As a way of showing our loved ones, our peers, our mentors, our inspirations just how much they mean to us. In recognition of a particular period in our lives. As an inside joke.

But deciding on a dedication can also be a little stressful. After all, most of us have support networks of more than just one person and we want to pay tribute to them all. We certainly don't want to put anyone offside. And while a writer can include a lengthy thank you list in the acknowledgements (usually at the back of the book), a dedication that focuses on just one person – or sometimes a couple – (usually at the front of the book) tends to top getting lost amongst the crowd.

Most writers seem to start by dedicating their first books to parents or partners. As I write this, I'm in the middle of reading *The Last Anniversary* by Liane Moriarty and when I opened it up to check, yep, there's evidence to back me up. "For my parents, Diane and Bernie Moriarty, with lots of love." And it makes sense. Parents and partners are usually significant influences on everyone, not just writers.

Some writers know exactly who they want to dedicate their work to, some need a little help. And the more books they write, the closer they might come to running out of easy choices. Here are a few options.

DEDICATION TO YOURSELF

The dedication at the front of *Psychos: A White Girl Problems Book* by Babe Walker reads, "Dedicated to the strongest person I know: me." It's an entirely honest and worthy dedication option. After all, you wrote the book, you did most of it by yourself and you deserve the credit. And it doesn't come across quite as self-absorbed as thanking yourself when winning an award.

DEDICATION TO NOBODY

As Arika Okrent puts it so succinctly, John Neal "had a stubborn temperament that would never let him settle for just a 'screw you' where a 'screw you all' would do". The dedication in his 1822 book *Logan: A Family History* is probably one of the best dedications to nobody ever written.

"I do not dedicate my book to anybody; for I know nobody worth dedicating it to. I have no friends, no children, no wife, no home; – no relations, no well-wishers; – nobody to love, and nobody to care for. To whom shall I; to whom can I dedicate it? To my Maker! It is unworthy of him. To my countrymen? They are unworthy of me. For the men of past ages I have very little veneration; for those of the present, not at all. To whom shall I entrust it? Who will care for me, by tomorrow? Who will do battle for my book, when I am gone? Will posterity? Yea, posterity will do me justice. To posterity then – to the winds! I bequeath it! I devote it – as a Roman would his enemy, to the fierce and unsparing charities of another world – to a generation of spirits – to the shadowy and crowned potentates of hereafter. I – I – I have done – the blood of the red man is growing cold – farewell – farewell forever!"

I have no words (unlike John Neal).

DEDICATION TO YOU

There are plenty of books that are dedicated to you. Sometimes it's the you reading the book, sometimes it's a you the writer doesn't name (but usually accompanied by the immortal words, "You know who you are"). Here's the dedication Neil Gaiman included in *Anansi Boys*:

"You know how it is. You pick up a book, flip to the dedication, and find that, once again, the author has dedicated a book to someone else and not you. Not this time. Because we haven't yet met/have only a glancing acquaintance/are just crazy about each other/haven't seen each other in much too long/are in some way related/will never meet, but will, I trust, despite that, always think fondly of each other! This one's for you. With you know what, and you probably know why."

DEDICATION NOT TO YOU

In EE Cummings's 1935 book *No Thanks*, his dedication was a list of the fourteen publishers who had rejected it in the shape of a funeral urn.

NO

THANKS

TO

Farrar & Rinehart

Simon & Schuster

Coward-McCann

Limited Editions

Harcourt, Brace

Random House

Equinox Press

Smith & Haas

Viking Press

Knopf

Dutton

Harper's

Scribner's

Covici-Friede

Genius!

DEDICATION AS MESSAGE

I couldn't stand waiting for a book to come out if I used the dedication as a message, particularly if it was a question that needed an answer as in *The Invisible Hook: The Hidden Economics of Pirates* by Peter Leeson: "Ania, I love you; will you marry me?" That's dedication in all of its meanings!

NO DEDICATION AT ALL

If it's all just too hard, it's also perfectly fine to have no dedication at all.

MY DEDICATIONS

The dedication in *Enemies Closer*, my first book, was to a fellow writer and his scantily clad women. I'd written the book directly as a response to a book he'd written and entrusted me to read during the draft stages, which seemed to contain an inordinate number of scantily clad women. I wanted to demonstrate that women in action fiction could play a substantial role and not just be the sexual playthings of the hero and the villain. They could be the heroes and the villains! He didn't change his book in any of the ways I'd suggested in this respect but I couldn't be too aggrieved since he was ultimately the reason I wrote my first published novel.

The *Project December* dedication does seem a little flippant in retrospect but since I didn't actually realise I was writing a book at the time – and then compiled, edited and published it within a very short time frame – it felt right to me in the moment. It's dedicated to all the cats I've loved before and names all 16 who have ever lived with me since I became a crazy cat lady. It was right around the time that I was fostering six cats in addition to my own three and I was loving it.

Project January was dedicated to my maternal grandparents. My grandmother died while I was writing the book (and was an avid reader), my grandfather was left bereft without her (and loved reading as long as it was about football) and I knew he would be honoured by the gesture. I lived with my grandparents for 11 years while I studied for two degrees and then ventured out into the workforce at the start of my career; they are like my pseudo-parents.

Black Spot is the only book I wrote the dedication for before I started writing the novel itself. It reads, "For Zac, who didn't make it. For Gen, who did. And for Jess – this book would never have been written without you." I did a lot of planning for this book so I had a very good idea of what it was going to be about, a girl who had struggled with mental health and come out the other side (amongst other things). Earlier in the year I started writing it, my cousin Zac had committed suicide. Prior to that, he had decided he wanted to be a writer and knowing my background, he had sought me out for advice on both his writing and his writing journey. I'd done a manuscript assessment on his novel and recommended he begin a writing course to improve his skills. He was only one term into his studies, which he said he was loving, when he killed himself.

I hadn't known about his mental health issues, I still don't really, I just assume he had them based on what he did. But he didn't make it. My sister Genevieve, however, did. She's struggled with eating disorders, clinical depression, borderline personality disorder and a long history of doctors refusing to believe there was anything physically wrong with her (even though she has now also been diagnosed with chronic fatigue and rheumatoid arthritis – she's still in her very early 20s by the way). She's made it. She makes it every day. And she was a very great inspiration for the main character in the book.

And then there's Jess. Jessica Vigar is not only my book cover designer and marketing go-to person, she is also the reason *Black Spot* exists. We were desk neighbours at a company we both no longer work for and when she found out that I wrote novels, she insisted I should write something to take advantage of the appetite for young adult/mainstream crossover novels (it was around the time that *The Hunger Games*, *Twilight* and *Divergent* were all very big). I had a few ideas but she really helped me by vetoing several and then giving the go ahead to the one that eventually became *Black Spot*. Then she read early drafts and as I write this, she is designing the book cover for it. How could I not acknowledge the essential role she played?

∞

Whatever direction you decide to head in, just remember you don't owe anybody a dedication. It's an honour and a privilege and hopefully a lovely surprise when you give them their copy of the book and they open the front cover to see their name.

A STORY ABOUT DESIGNING A BOOK COVER

If you're anything like me, when it finally comes time to design your book cover, you have a rough idea of what you want but none of the skills necessary to accomplish it. I'm lucky because I once worked with someone with a boatload of design and marketing skills and she has been my book cover designer ever since. She's less lucky because I'm a bit of a control freak (okay, a lot of a control freak).

When I eventually finalised the manuscript for *Project January*, I contacted her to ask if she would do the cover for this one as well and she agreed. She had also done the cover for *Project December*, which looked like this (although it was in colour).

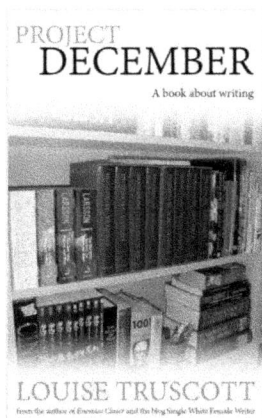

The photograph on the cover is a selection of books from my personal collection that I styled to look interesting. I styled and sent my designer another photograph of a different selection of my books, assuming the cover for *Project January* would be much the same as the cover for *Project*

December. After all, I reasoned, when you publish a sequel, you want the two books to look like they belong next to each other on a shelf.

So I was a little bemused when this book cover draft arrived in my inbox (although it does look better than this black-and-white image suggests).

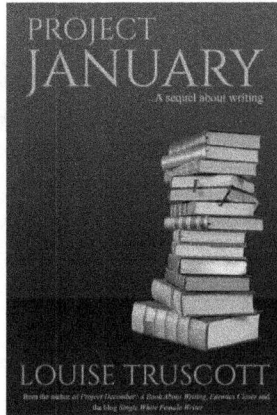

The accompanying message read, "Okay, so bear with me here... I really wanted to have a stab at a different feeling cover. Something a little more modern. I have kept the typography very similar. Feel free to tell me to go shove it and stick to the original design, but just thought I would try."

She also sent me a text message saying, "I've been doing some research into book cover design. I have read that strong, bold colours with contrasting graphics are good for catching the eye. And blues and blacks encourage dependability, trust, authority and intuition."

I actually liked the alternative design and I liked the fact that she'd put so much thought and effort into it. But my designer was at somewhat of a disadvantage in that she hadn't read the book and I hadn't told her anything about it except that it was a sequel to my previous book, which I don't think she read either.

I responded, "It might be a bit too bold and modern. Doesn't really suit the whimsical, conversational nature of what will be between the covers. It looks quite legalistic, especially the anonymous books. If I had to choose between this and the original design, I'd choose the original."

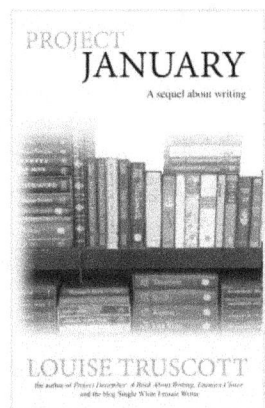

She wasn't bothered and happily went about producing a version that matched the *Project December* cover. This is the ebook cover of *Project January* (again in black and white, not the actual colour version).

189

Normally, that's where the story would end. I ordered five copies of the paperback version (one for me, one for my designer as a thank you, one for my grandfather who the book is dedicated to and two for a couple of giveaways I was planning) and waited the estimated two to three weeks for them to be printed and arrive in the mail.

But when they arrived, the covers were black and white instead of the colourful books and blue font it was supposed to depict. When I contacted the printers, they apologised profusely and assured me this was a rare aberration and five replacement copies would be in my hands within a week via their expensive expedited shipping.

They were as good as their word. I thought they would ask me to return the defective copies but they didn't (perhaps because the printers are all the way across the other side of the world and they didn't want to spend any more money on books that would ultimately end up being pulped). I wondered what to do with them.

In the end, I decided to call them "collector's editions". I wrote pithy messages inside the front covers, autographed them and delivered them to various members of my family. One of my sisters wasn't home when I called past so I left her copy propped up against the front door. A few days later, she called to thank me and I explained why it was a collector's edition.

"Oh, really? I think the black-and-white cover looks fantastic!" Which makes three different preferences of three different covers from three different people.

Well, that's my really long-winded way of getting around to a few pieces of advice when designing a cover for your book:

- When you're ready for a book cover, find a designer whose previous work you like.
- If you know what you want your cover to look like, tell the designer.
- If you don't know what you want your cover to look like, explain what the book is about and ask for a few options.
- Trust your designer – if you've chosen a good one, then they will have good design instincts.
- Ask a few family members or friends what they think about the various options the designer has provided.
- It's your book and ultimately you must be happy with the final design.
- The book cover is your "Director of First Impressions" – make sure it's a good one.

A STORY ABOUT CHOOSING AN AUTHOR PHOTO

Sometimes (okay, more than sometimes), I like to live in a world where the only thing I'm judged on as a writer is my writing. The rest of the time I know I have to play the game. You know the game. The one where what you look like, how cool you are and how good you are on social media seem to be just as important. I resent the hell out it (mostly because I'm not beautiful, I'm a nerd – not one of those cool new-age nerds, just an old-fashioned awkward nerd – and my social media skills could charitably be described as needing work).

So imagine the personal torment I went through as I recently chose a new author photo to go on the back cover of my upcoming book, *Black Spot*. If you know my history with author photos, it's not that hard.

That history is this. In 2012, as I was preparing to release my first book, I asked a friend of mine if she wanted to be the public face of my writing. She was blonde, bubbly and beautiful, people responded well to her without exception and, most importantly, if she was willing to do it, that would mean I wouldn't have to. She graciously declined and instead offered to lend her professional photography and marketing skills to take (and lightly Photoshop) this image of me.

Ever since, I've been using it for my book covers, my social media, pretty much everything related to my writing and professional lives. When *Black Spot* was shortlisted for the 2016 Text Prize and I had to provide a photograph to Text Publishing for promotional purposes, I supplied them the same picture, only in colour.

In February 2017, I used it again when I released *Project January*. Then I enlisted the 10-second delay function on my camera to take a photograph of me holding the book for the announcement.

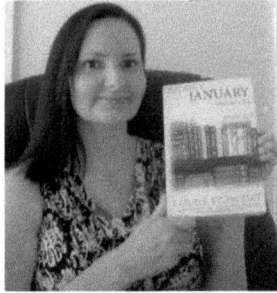

In the uncropped version, you can see my laundry on the left (and a fraction of the garage) and the downstairs toilet on the right. "The toilet roll in the background is distracting," my sister Stephanie commented when I circulated the raw image asking for feedback from family and friends on potentially using it again for the publication of *Black Spot*. "It's going to be cropped!" I replied.

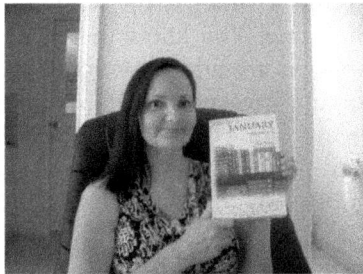

In April 2017, when I was profiled on the website of Swinburne University, I used the 10-second delay function again and took this image. "It looks like you've been crying," said my sister Genevieve when I asked for her help choosing the best image. "I swear I haven't," I told her. "I don't hate having my picture taken that much. Unfortunately, that's about as good as it gets."

And as I prepare to release *Black Spot*, I went back through all these images and realised none of them quite suited the young adult genre of the book. That meant it was time for another horrible attempt to take a picture in which I don't have crazy eyes, chicken neck, caveman forehead, slumped shoulders or that weird smile that strangely emulates my now long-deceased dog after he was hit by a car. Yes, Chandler Bing and I have a lot in common when it comes to sitting for a portrait.

So even though I usually only wear makeup for weddings, I spent half an hour applying it badly (the only way I know how), half an hour taking pictures of myself, five minutes scrubbing my face (only realising at that point and after I'd taken about 75 pictures that I'd forgotten the mascara, more important than you might think for someone once described by a makeup artist as having "the shortest eyelashes" she'd ever seen) and the next day regretting it as I had a massive allergic reaction (the reason I don't wear makeup). These are the best of a pretty bad bunch.

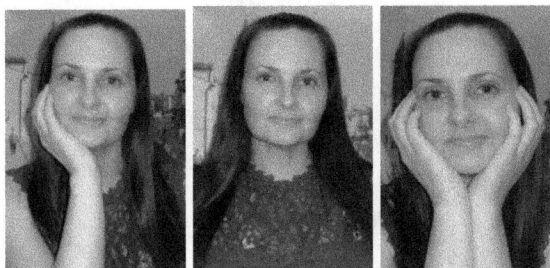

Worse still, even though the whole point was to take a picture that suited the young adult genre of the book I was publishing, none of them were even remotely appropriate for that purpose. What a waste of an evening one day and a box of tissues the next.

Those I enlisted to help me choose a photo agreed by not agreeing. There was no consensus about which image I should use but the two most popular were the ones I'd taken a year earlier for the announcement of *Project January*'s release and the Swinburne University profile. But neither of those screamed "Young Adult Author" either.

My sister Elizabeth, although she was the only one who picked it, said that this was the image that most closely suited the type of book I'd written.

I don't think it's the best picture ever taken of me but it's casual and relaxed, there's no forced cheesy smile, I look confident that I've produced a good book (or possibly like I don't care whether anyone else thinks I've produced a good book) and like someone a teenager might be able to relate to, more than in any of the other pictures anyway. For a few hours, this was the image I chose.

And then I decided that even though the concept of the image was right, the image itself wasn't. It was a little fuzzy and while that usually wouldn't bother me, it's the sort of thing that my cover designer likes to put her foot down over. After all, it's her reputation, too.

So I cleaned a window in my house that I like looking out of, did my makeup again, dressed similarly, posed similarly and sat for another timer-delay photography session. And I finally managed to come up with this.

Nobody is ever going to ask me to be on the cover of *Vogue* and that's okay because it isn't a goal of mine but at least I look better than a dog that's been hit by a car (yes, I set the bar pretty low but when you're not photogenic, you have to be realistic).

I don't know, however, that I'll be following the advice I've seen to splash this image everywhere on my blog, social media, Amazon and Smashwords profiles, Goodreads, etc for the sake of consistency. Because I'm not a young adult author. I'm just someone who happens to have written a young adult book. I might write another in the future. But apart from *Black Spot*, my next few will be non-fiction about motherhood and a literary crime novel. I'm not sure which author photo will best suit the covers of these books but there's a good likelihood that it might not be the one I chose for *Black Spot*.

Yes, I make my marketing life hard by not sticking to one genre but I make my writing life so much more interesting by writing and publishing whatever the hell I want and figuring out which picture goes with it later on. I wouldn't have it any other way.

WHY IS "SELF-PUBLISHING" STILL A DIRTY (HYPHENATED) WORD?

A few years ago, one of my sisters dragged me along to a game show audition. After filling out a four-page questionnaire that asked such insightful questions as "What's the most embarrassing thing that's ever happened to you?", "Have you ever been caught out in a lie?" and "Do you have an unusual bucket list item?" (presumably so that they could be discussed and laughed at on national television) as well as what we did for a living, we were then grilled by a producer.

"You're a writer?" he asked me.

"Yes," I answered.

"What do you write?"

"Books – novels and how-to guides on writing novels." I could have given him my entire writing résumé – articles, websites, marketing collateral, corporate tenders, ghostwriting, short stories, song lyrics, poems – but I was trying to keep it brief.

"And you've published three books?"

"So far."

"Who with?"

"I'm self-published," I said.

"Oh," he replied with a disapproving tone in his voice. "So you just sell to friends and family?"

"No, I sell all over the world." In fact, I'd been looking at a royalty statement just a couple of days prior that listed a sale in Italy, which surprised me a little because the majority of my sales come from English-speaking countries. But the obviousness of his disapproval made me feel like I needed to defend being a self-published writer. "And my upcoming novel was shortlisted for the 2016 Text Prize. Do you know Text Publishing?"

"Sure," he said but I'd already lost him and he moved onto the auditioner standing next to me. In just a few moments, an insignificant television producer had managed to reduce my greatest achievements to some sort of inconsequential side note in my career. Worse than that, I stood there and basically took it.

So why is "self-publishing" still a dirty (hyphenated) word?

Amongst writers of all levels and many in the publishing industry, I'd argue it isn't. After all, it's how a lot of famous authors got their start. Matthew Reilly (*The Contest*). Hugh Howey (*Wool, Shift and Dust*). Lisa Genova (*Still Alice*). EL James (*50 Shades of Grey*). Andy Weir (*The Martian*). They've all gone on to be published by traditional publishers eager to get on the money train. But to people outside of the industry, who don't know (or really care) how these and many other writers got their start, it's still something that people who aren't good enough for traditional publishing do.

I forget sometimes that ordinary readers almost never know the background, the private jokes, the inside stories that those of us in the industry take for granted. (I was talking to another of my sisters and she didn't know that *50 Shades of Grey* was *Twilight* fan fiction, which I thought everybody knew by now. "Really?" she said. "Of course," I replied. "And it's obvious. Take out the vampires and add in all the kinky sex and they're virtually identical." I went on to list several examples. "Oh my God, you're right!" she exclaimed.)

When I finished writing each of my last two books, I didn't ever consider traditional publishing. I didn't submit to a single publisher. I didn't see the need to. Instead, I edited and proofed the manuscripts myself (being a trained editor really helps with this), registered my own ISBNs, engaged a book cover designer, finalised the paperback and ebook templates, sent the first to the printer and the others to online ebook platforms and when they were all ready, I did my own marketing. (Yeah, I mostly suck at marketing but a lot of the time, so do traditional publishers.) And my books are indistinguishable from all those lining the book shelves in stores because I'm nothing if not a perfectionist.

I know not all self-published writers have the same sensibilities as I do. Some publish first draft ebooks full of errors, trite characters and derivative plots, usually for free or for $0.99, which I think is the required minimum price on some platforms. And you don't need to buy and read them to know they aren't quite up to scratch. Because the blurbs are badly written with just as many errors as the books themselves. They're usually reasonably easy to avoid. But to lump us all in together just because we self-publish is like saying Justin Bieber, 5 Seconds of Summer and The Weeknd aren't musicians because they were discovered on YouTube and Ed Sheeran shouldn't be taken seriously because he recorded and released his songs independently for the first six years of his career.

I've also read plenty of traditionally published books that have boring characters, no plot, terrible writing and so many typos, misspellings, poor punctuation and bad grammar that a high school English teacher would fail the author.

To avoid the unsavoury reputation of self-publishing and its vanity publishing connotations, some writers prefer to call it indie publishing (you know, like indie films, which are cool; Robert Redford founded both the Sundance Institute and the Sundance Film Festival to support indie films and filmmakers and he's cool, too). But would it have made any difference to that television producer if I'd said, "I'm independently published" instead of "I'm self-published"? I think he'd already made up his mind about self-published authors long before I ever came along and no fancy euphemisms were going to change it.

The way we self-published writers change it (his and everybody else's minds) is to make sure that when we do self-publish, we don't do it indiscriminately. We follow the same processes that traditional publishers do, which means not publishing first drafts but fourth or fifth drafts that have been through multiple rewrites and assessments and that have then been edited and proofed to be as perfect as it is possible for them to be and have professionally designed covers.

The way we change minds is simply to prove them wrong.

It's not going to happen quickly, especially because traditional publishers want us to think they are essential and have convinced most readers (AKA the people who buy books) of this. But we will gradually get there. Look how far self-publishing has already come in the past decade. Imagine how much further we will have gone in the next decade. And how much further again we'll be in the next 20 years.

In the meantime, if you're a self-published author and someone gives you attitude about it, give it right back. My favoured approach (now that I've gotten over the shock of that moment and had some time to think about it) will be to ask how many books they've published. None? "Oh," I will say in a disapproving tone, then walk away with my head held high.

THE PROS AND CONS OF A PEN NAME (WITH A LITTLE HELP FROM KK NESS)

In 2012, when I released my debut novel, *Enemies Closer*, I decided to use the pseudonym "LE Truscott". The book was action adventure and I was concerned (perhaps unnecessarily) that male readers wouldn't be interested in reading a woman writing in the genre. I didn't think too long or too hard about what the drawbacks might be. But just as there were benefits, there were also disadvantages.

In 2017, KK Ness released her first book, *Messenger*, in The Shifter War fantasy series and her pseudonym is a complete departure from her actual name (as opposed to the partial disguise I chose). I asked her a few questions about her choice to help illustrate the pros and cons of using a pen name.

PROS

Anonymity/freedom

"I feel an immense freedom writing under a pen name," KK Ness told me when I asked why she'd decided to do it. "I've wanted to be an author for years but I've placed so much pressure on myself that I often become frozen at the thought of releasing anything that isn't perfect (an impossible goal, right?). Using a pen name has somehow released me from that unrealistic pressure. KK Ness had no emotional history and could do whatever she wanted and write what she wanted."

It makes sense, doesn't it? Writing isn't just writing – it's complete exposure. Writers expose the inner workings of their minds, the secret and sometimes guilty pleasures they indulge in, even their talent (or their lack of it – at least that's what they worry people will think). So using a pen name gives them the freedom to explore without letting those worries impact directly on their everyday life.

EL James is a great example. The subject matter of her books isn't to everybody's taste – not something they would admit to publicly anyway – so her initial anonymity allowed her to bring her work and a genre that had pottered on the fringes of fiction for a while into the mainstream without worrying about embarrassing herself, her family, her co-workers and her friends. By the time her real identity came out, it was such an enormous hit that the only embarrassment was how much money she was making. Besides, if everyone was reading it, they could all be embarrassed together.

Anne Perry is another example, although for very different reasons. In 1954 in Christchurch, New Zealand, Anne Perry – then known as Juliet Hulme – and her best friend murdered her best friend's mother. She was just 15 years old at the time. It's a reasonably well-known story within the publishing industry and became even more so after Peter Jackson's *Heavenly Creatures* movie about the crime. Anne Perry's name change wasn't just anonymity; it was freedom from her infamy.

Differentiating yourself for diverse audiences in multiple genres

JK Rowling was so famous for her *Harry Potter* series that when she wrote *The Cuckoo's Calling*, she decided to publish it under the pen name Robert Galbraith. She didn't want to confuse the children who had grown up on her magical adventures with the adult crime fiction she was now writing. And she's not the only one (although there are many reasons thrown about). Stephen King wrote four books as Richard Bachman. Ruth Rendell wrote multiple novels under the name Barbara Vine to separate them from her immensely popular Inspector Wexford series. Nora Roberts has written dozens and dozens of romance books but she publishes her crime under the name JD Robb.

Is KK Ness planning to do the same? "Hmmm, I've got a heap of sci-fi and urban fantasy stories rattling around in my brain that I want to write. As for whether I'd write them under the same pen name... I don't know. Many authors recommend using different pen names for different genres so that your readers of war stories don't end up purchasing your steampunk comedies by mistake. Multiple pen names are also important for developing multiple streams of income. Other authors, however, seem to do perfectly well having all of their genre-diverse publications under one name. I'll need to research more on it before deciding."

Disguising gender

This was certainly my motivation and JK Rowling's publishers were the ones who asked her to publish under initials, thinking that the target audience of young boys might not want to read a book written by a woman (just goes to show you how much publishers know). She didn't actually have a second name and had to pick an initial (she chose "K" for her grandmother, Kathleen).

It's conventional wisdom that readers of one gender won't read books written by writers of the other in particular genres – men writing romance, for example. But this seems to be less and less an issue (Nicholas Sparks certainly doesn't seem to have any problems) as quality is prioritised over stereotypes.

I asked KK Ness if this was one of her considerations. "I haven't disguised my gender (anyone who reads my 'About the Author' page will know I'm female). I thought it was important to indicate my gender because anyone can write about any topic or relationship. The aim is to do it thoughtfully and well."

Disguising multiple authors

Frank and Wendy Brennan, a husband and wife romance writing team, published as Emma Darcy (the inimitable Emma Darcy – sigh!) until Frank's death in 1995, after which Wendy continued using the name for her solo writing. Nicci Gerrard and Sean French are another husband and wife team who write as Nicci French.

But this seems to be another one that is falling by the wayside. The recently feted *Illuminae* and its sequels *Gemina* and *Obsidio* were co-written and co-published by Amie Kaufman and Jay Kristof (although both were already established authors in their own rights so it makes sense to leverage their existing popularity). David Levithan is also establishing a routine of publishing multi-authored books (*Will Grayson, Will Grayson* with John Green, *Dash & Lily's Book of Dares* and *Nick & Norah's Infinite Playlist* with Rachel Cohn).

Differentiating yourself from other authors or famous people in general with the same or similar names

I'm not sure I know of anyone specifically in writing who has done this but it's very common for actors. Michael Keaton's real name is Michael Douglas but, of course, Michael Douglas, the son of Kirk Douglas, was already using it and according to Screen Actors Guild rules, only one person can register under any one name. He chose Keaton as a tribute to Buster Keaton.

KK Ness has an academic namesake and given the protocol for listing academic authors by initials and last name, that's how she appears in her many contributions to articles. I asked if she was aware of this when choosing the name. "I knew of Kristen K Ness and figured our target audiences were unlikely to cross paths. I Googled my real name and ironically discovered that there is also a woman of the same name working for Amazon, which is where my ebook is exclusively available at the moment. It seems most names are entangled with other names in some way. It's a small world."

Cons

Inability to trade on the reputation you have established under your real name

Regardless of what industry you have worked in or community you are known in, the networks and connections you have built are often crucial to starting the ball rolling when you publish and begin marketing your book. However, if you've chosen a pen name and you don't want to reveal your true identity, you're automatically at a disadvantage. It's hard enough to get people who know you to buy and read your book, let alone people who don't have or don't know they have an association with the author.

KK Ness agrees. "Marketing a book under a pen name with no existing online presence is hard. It's difficult to build an audience, but I think that's true for most new authors. Personally, I would have struggled even under my real name, since I don't spend any time on social media, and have been neglectful of my blog as well. That being said, savvy advertising and producing more books will impact sales far more than any number of Twitter and Facebook followers."

Potentially having to market multiple names

It's hard enough marketing one name, let alone multiple identities. If you choose to publish under a pen name or multiple pen names and your real name as well, you might have to repeat the same marketing step for each name and I don't know about anyone else but I barely have time to market just one. Multiple names can mean multiple websites, multiple author profiles on Amazon, Goodreads and Smashwords, multiple social media profiles. I'm getting tired just thinking about it.

Difficulty consolidating works published under different names

It can be difficult to consolidate works published under different names if you decide you don't want them separate anymore. After initially publishing as LE Truscott and realising it made almost no difference, I published my next two books under my full name. Goodreads nearly had a conniption fit and in the end told me that I could either establish another Goodreads profile under my "new" name or stick with "LE Truscott" until they can figure out how to achieve changing the name (something their system doesn't currently allow).

Amazon has a similar problem. Even though I published all three of my Amazon ebooks under the same KDP account, the online giant didn't understand that "LE Truscott" and "Louise Truscott" were the same author. I had to apply to "claim" my own books and even though my profile links to my two most recent books, they don't link back to my Amazon Author Central profile. It's enough to make me want to tear my hair out.

Initials can be difficult for search engines

Many authors writing and publishing under pen names choose to use initials, like JD Robb, like KK Ness, like LE Truscott and many more. But how exactly should these names be searched? Is it "LE" or "L.E." or "L E"?

When I found out that KK Ness had published her first book, I went to Goodreads to add it to my list of "Want to Read" books. But when I searched "*Messenger* by KK Ness", Goodreads told me it had no results. Was I jumping the gun? I wondered. Perhaps she hadn't put it on the site yet? But, no, it was just that I wasn't searching the right name. If I added a space between the "K"s or even a full stop (just one, the second doesn't seem to be necessary), the entry came up.

Google was friendlier in this respect, bringing up her website, her Facebook profile, her Twitter profile, the Goodreads entry and the UK Amazon site for *Messenger*. Perhaps Goodreads just needs to pick Google's brains.

CAN'T GET ANYONE TO INTERVIEW YOU
ABOUT YOUR BOOK? INTERVIEW YOURSELF!

As part of the announcement of the release of *Project January*, I sent an email to the alumni group of Swinburne University where I studied and graduated with a Master of Arts (Writing). I'd done the same thing when I published *Project December* and they'd been kind enough to include a mention of it in their newsletter and a link to where it could be purchased. I hoped they'd do the same this time.

Instead, I got an email asking if I'd be interested in being interviewed and profiled as part of a series on their past students. I thought, *Why not?*

But once I'd agreed to do it, I did what I always do, which is panic. I sometimes feel like I have proverbial foot-in-mouth disease (not literal foot-in-mouth disease – gross!) and am prone to say things I shouldn't. I aim for witty and end up coming off like a weirdo. It's why I'm a writer, after all. I like having the chance to revise. And revise. And revise again. Speaking off the cuff doesn't give you that chance.

To keep myself calm and to try to prepare for an interview where I didn't know exactly what the questions were going to be, I decided to attempt to pre-empt what might be asked and come up with answers. That way, if they did come up, I'd have something that didn't make me sound like a gibbering idiot.

Yes, essentially, I interviewed myself.

It was actually a lot harder than I thought it would be. Not answering the questions but coming up with questions that people might be interested in hearing the answers to. But I have to admit that when the phone rang and the interviewer and I had our chat, I felt relaxed, reasonably comfortable and also like I had an answer for everything he asked. Some of them I hadn't anticipated but most I had and when I needed to prompt myself, I quickly looked over the responses I had typed out and it helped me continue on.

So what sort of questions should a writer ask when interviewing themselves? Here are a few that I came up with:

- How long have you been writing?
- Who are your favourite writers?
- Are you self-published or traditionally published? Why?
- Did you always know you wanted to be a writer?
- Why do you love writing so much?
- How did your book come about?
- Why did you decide to write this genre?
- Will you stick with this genre or are you planning to explore others?
- What is your next book about and when will it be available?
- What advice do you have for others wanting to write?

You can throw a few into the mix that are specific to the writing you do and the answers you give – after all, like any piece of writing, it should flow and feel like it transitions naturally from here to there. And since an interview is essentially a conversation, a good interviewer should pick up on parts of the answers you give that require a follow-up or elaboration. Even when the interviewer is you!

You can read the profile Swinburne University wrote about me online and you can read the interview I did with myself on the following pages for a comparison. There are differences because when I interviewed myself, I was only thinking about me but the Swinburne interviewer was very interested in how my master's degree had helped me get where I was going in my writing career.

The most important thing to take out of all this is that when you release your book, tell everyone! Don't be humble or embarrassed or concerned about bothering people. If they're not interested, fine. They can go talk to someone else at that party or they can delete your email. But if they are interested, great! You just never know where the next step, the next connection, the next marketing opportunity might come from.

HOW LONG HAVE YOU BEEN WRITING?

I don't know where the time has gone but it's been over 25 years now. I started, like all children, writing adorable yet cringeworthy stories for my primary school English class, progressed to angsty poetry in high school and by Year 12, I was writing a novella. When I started university, I moved into writing romance. I was so sure that I was going to be the next queen of Australian romance fiction. But I found the confines of the genre very limiting. I didn't want to write one thing, I wanted to write everything.

WHO ARE YOUR FAVOURITE WRITERS?

Joss Whedon and Aaron Sorkin. *Buffy*, *Angel*, *Firefly*, *The West Wing*, *Studio 60*, *The Newsroom*. The writing and premises in these television shows are consistently close to perfection. There are plenty of novelists I enjoy reading but if we're talking about writer envy, Joss Whedon and Aaron Sorkin are the two I wish I could write like. They do witty dialogue and suckerpunch storylines better than anyone.

YOU'VE SELF-PUBLISHED ALL THREE OF YOUR BOOKS SO FAR. WHY?

I tried half-heartedly to get my first book into the hands of the "right" people but it all seemed too hard. And when I started looking into it, self-publishing seemed so easy. Especially for someone like me who is also a trained editor. Right up until the point that I need a book cover, I can do it all myself. And I know a great designer, so even that seemed pretty simple. I'm not great at marketing myself but I know so many writers who say that traditional publishers don't help you out much in that respect anyway. And a senior person at a publishing company told me I'd be better off not having an agent. So who am I to argue?

DID YOU ALWAYS KNOW YOU WANTED TO BE A WRITER?

I think I did but I tried to suppress it because writing wasn't and still isn't considered a stable career option. But even when I was studying non-writing subjects and working non-writing jobs, I would go home and spend my evenings writing. Because I didn't know how not to write. And then I got a job editing accounting textbooks and a job after that writing corporate tender responses. As much as I like to believe in free will, there has to be a little bit of fate in that.

WHY DO YOU LOVE WRITING SO MUCH?

It's more of a love-hate relationship! But I don't really know. It must be linked to how much I love reading but there are plenty of people who love reading and have no desire to write. I love creating something from nothing but, most of all, I love that I don't need anyone's permission to write. I can do as much of it as I like and nobody can tell me not to write. Well, I suppose they can tell me but I'm unlikely to listen to that sort of advice.

YOU'VE PUBLISHED TWO BOOKS ABOUT HOW TO WRITE NOVELS. HOW DID THEY COME ABOUT?

I never had any intention of writing books about how to write novels. Back in 2015, I started a blog as a means of increasing my profile and as a place where I could house samples of my writing. It became evident pretty quickly that I would need to generate a lot of new material to stay fresh. So I started writing blog posts about writing, editing, publishing, marketing and reading. There was no rhyme or reason, it was just my random thoughts and advice. I got so into it and wrote so much ahead of schedule that I realised I had enough to fill a book. And that's how *Project December* came to be. There was literally one week between me realising I had enough to fill a book and me releasing the book. All I had to do was arrange the articles into chapters so that they flowed, do some short rewrites, copyedit it, get my designer to do the cover and it was done. I even wrote a chapter for *Project January* inspired by the process: how to write a book without even trying.

WHAT ABOUT *PROJECT JANUARY*?

It was a similar process but because I'd done *Project December* a year earlier, I knew another book was a possibility so it wasn't writing a book without even trying. It was a bit more stressful especially because I set a date for when I wanted to release it and that date went whooshing by without me meeting it. I've since become a fan of simply letting the writing dictate the release date. I release when I'm ready. That's another advantage of self-publishing. No publishers putting pressure on me for my next book.

WHEN WILL YOUR NEXT BOOK BE OUT AND WHAT IS IT ABOUT?

I'm trying to work according to a schedule of one book a year but if it's longer, so be it. My next book is called *Black Spot* and it was shortlisted for the Text Prize for Unpublished Children's and Young Adult Writing in 2016. It's a young adult mystery about a teenager named Livia Black. She lost her memory in a car accident six years earlier that killed her mother. Ever since, she and her father have been living an isolated life on the family farm and that suits her because the accident left her with terrible scars. For some reason, some of her memories start coming back – not many, just a few – but they don't match up with what her father has told her. She has to decide whether her former identity is important enough to her to pursue it, especially since the things she is recalling don't paint a rosy picture of her life before the accident.

WHY DID YOU DECIDE TO WRITE A YOUNG ADULT BOOK?

A friend suggested it. She saw the explosion in popularity that young adult books were having, even crossing over into the mainstream like *Twilight*, *The Hunger Games* and *Divergent*, and said I should give it a go. I think she thought it was a potential money-making endeavour but I looked at it more like an artistic challenge. I was in the middle of writing another book and it was proving hard work so I put it aside to see what came of going down the different route. I wrote the first draft of the book within six months. The pace with which I was able to write it excited me and the story I came up with excited me, too. So it ended up being a good suggestion.

WILL YOU CONTINUE WRITING YOUNG ADULT BOOKS?

I said earlier that when I first started writing, I didn't just want to write one thing. My first novel was an action adventure, my next novel will be a young adult mystery, the one after that will be literary crime and the one after that will be speculative dystopian fiction. I wish I was better at sticking to a genre because it would be kinder to my reading base and my ability to develop a reading base but I tend to go where the writing takes me. When I try to force myself into a mould or to write things that I'm not feeling, it just doesn't work. I've tried writing the sequels to my first novel and to the young adult novel – I've written about a third of both actually – but I was only doing it because I felt compelled to and I ended up getting to a point where I was stuck. I just didn't know what the story was, only that I had these characters who my readers felt should continue on in other books. I hope I'll figure out their stories eventually but in the meantime, I'll continue writing other books.

WHAT ADVICE DO YOU HAVE FOR OTHERS WANTING TO WRITE?

Buy *Project December* and *Project January* and read them! It's two whole books full of my writing advice and they contain a lot more than I could ever squeeze into an answer to an interview question. But my general advice on writing is to just do it. Very Nike, I know, but they were onto something. The people who bug me the most are those who talk about wanting to write but never actually do it. Why? There's nothing stopping them. Just sit down and write. Then write some more. And continue writing. There's no big secret to being a writer other than actually writing. Whether you're any good or not, that's a separate issue entirely. If you take pleasure in writing, then you take pleasure in writing regardless of whether or not you end up published and feted.

PREPARING FOR PEOPLE WHO WON'T LIKE YOUR WRITING (AND HOW NOT TO TAKE IT PERSONALLY)

I've written before about how writers seek criticism when what they really want is praise. Who doesn't? Everybody wants their endeavours – regardless of what those endeavours are – to be validated. But no matter how hard a writer works on a piece of writing, there will be people who won't like it. Not necessarily because it's bad but just because. That's life.

A writer can solve this problem by choosing not to release their writing. But it smacks of cowardice and self-perpetuating redundancy. Most people who write want to be read. So we find the courage from somewhere while reminding ourselves that universal popularity just isn't possible. Because for every person or book or movie or decision that seems to have plenty of admirers, there will always be a group of people who vehemently dislike or disagree with them or it. Their dislike or disagreement may be valid. It may have carefully considered logic behind it. But it may also simply be a reflection of personal prejudices or specific preferences.

I know I'm in a very small minority of people who find Brad Pitt and Jude Law not attractive but smarmy and a little bit creepy. Possibly there's some long repressed episode in my past that explains why. But let's not get sidetracked. Here's a more literary example. I'm not really a fan of the *Harry Potter* franchise. I've read the first book and wasn't inclined to read any more in the series. I've seen the first movie and fallen asleep multiple times trying to watch the second so I haven't bothered with any of the others. It's not that I hate Harry Potter. I don't have a problem with the fact that so many other people love him. He's just not my cup of tea. I don't think JK Rowling would have any problems with me expressing that sentiment (and if she did, I expect her hundreds of millions of dollars in income from all the people who love Harry Potter would really help soothe any pain).

Readers aren't under any obligation to like what a writer has written. And still it will be hard for a writer to be confronted by the evidence of this. So here are a few things to remember when it does eventually happen that might soften the blow.

TARGET AUDIENCES

Certain storylines, characters, genres and styles of writing will have a clearly defined target audience. Romance is more predominantly read by women. Christian fiction is more predominantly read by Christians. Young boys are more likely to be the primary audience of books with "underpants" and "bum" in the title. So when a man reads a romance or an atheist reads Christian fiction or a 30-something woman reads *The Day My Bum Went Psycho*, the likelihood is that they aren't going to respond to it as favourably as those target audiences will.

As a writer, you will rarely know who your readers are unless they reach out to you. You'll get a royalty statement listing the platforms you've been sold on and the quantities and that's about it. It can be frustrating as hell. Even when your books are reviewed, a Goodreads or Amazon account name or a Twitter handle aren't going to tell you much. And knowing something about the people who haven't responded to your writing the way you had hoped they would won't achieve anything anyway. You just have to remember that you can't please all of the people all of the time.

GENRE SNOBS

Whenever I review a book in a genre I don't particularly enjoy, especially where I haven't enjoyed that book specifically, I always start my review by stating that. I think it's only fair to the author and other potential readers to let them know that my personal preferences may have contributed to why I feel that way. I don't think I'm a genre snob – I read pretty much everything apart from erotica – but fantasy isn't my favourite, I find romance a bit repetitive and steampunk a little strange. However, I still read them occasionally.

Some people, though, really don't like reading outside of their preferred genres. And when they do, instead of being able to objectively assess what they've read, they can only look at it subjectively. They didn't like it and that's that.

Just like being read by those outside of your target audience, you're not likely to know anything about those reading outside of their preferred genres. Perhaps your marketing was good enough to tempt them to cross the boundary, so that's something to console yourself with. But it's far more important to please those who like reading the genre you're writing in.

TROLLS

Once upon a time, trolls had to invest the time to write a physical letter and the money for a stamp in order to be mean. And a quick-thinking manager could weed them out before they got to the author. Now, it's as simple as opening a browser and finding a target and their abuse immediately hits home. There's not much I can say about trolls except that they are sociopaths who don't deserve to be acknowledged.

The best course of action is to report them to the administrators of whatever online platform they are harassing you on, block them if possible, report them to local law enforcement if it becomes threatening and move on knowing you are in some very good company. It's often the best and the brightest who are trolled.

READING YOUR OWN REVIEWS

A lot of famous people advocate not reading reviews for the sake of maintaining mental health. So should you? On the one hand, it's a way of potentially improving. On the other, it could be a long dark slide into depression. It can depend on whether you take criticism well or not. It can also depend on whether you can differentiate between what should be taken on board and what should be ignored entirely. (Most platforms like Goodreads and Amazon have rules about what is appropriate and mechanisms for flagging inappropriate reviews for removal. Of course, a bad review isn't necessarily inappropriate.)

The problem with ignoring reviews is that you end up ignoring the people who liked your writing as well as those who didn't. Maybe you can get your partner or your mum or your friend to preview them for you and help make the decision. Maybe you're brave enough to do it on your own. Maybe you can make a "mean tweets" segment out of it.

Even if you're determined to avoid your own reviews, it's likely you're going to come across them at some point so it's best to be prepared. Take the fawning adoration as well as the bitter hatred with a grain of salt and focus on the thoughtful reviews that fall somewhere in the middle. But don't take any of them – good or bad – to heart.

∞

The most important thing to remember is that you are not your writing. Yes, your writing is intrinsically linked with who you are, it's great when it is liked and it sucks when it isn't. But there is no correlation between talent (or a lack thereof) and your worth as a person. Reviews and reactions from the general public should recognise this, too. If they don't, this says more about them than it does about you. And if you can manage not to take it personally, you'll go a lot further with your writing than somebody who lives and dies with every reaction from the reading public.

PREPARING FOR THE FIRST TIME YOU'RE ASKED FOR YOUR AUTOGRAPH

Anna Scott: Oh, signed by the author, I see.

William Thatcher: Um, yeah. Couldn't stop him. If you can find an unsigned copy, it's worth an absolute fortune.

Notting Hill

Rufus: Can I have your autograph?

Anna Scott: Sure. What's your name?

Rufus: Rufus. [She writes something and hands it to him.] What's it say?

Anna Scott: That's my signature and above it, it says, "Dear Rufus, you belong in jail."

Rufus: Right. Good one.

Notting Hill

There is nothing quite so humbling for an author as the first time you are asked for your autograph. I distinctly remember my first time. It was just a few weeks after I'd released my debut novel and it was a guy who worked with my mum. But since I'd released *Enemies Closer* as an ebook only, I couldn't sign a copy of my book for him. Instead, I printed a copy of my one and only professional headshot, wrote a message about how this was the best I could do until I did publish the book physically, autographed it and emailed it to my mum so she could forward it on to him.

For some, though, being asked for an autograph can also be a little bit frightening. After all, if you haven't prepared for that moment, it can be flustering. Why? Here are a few reasons.

YOUR AUTOGRAPH IS NOT YOUR SIGNATURE

Unless you want every unscrupulous fan out there to attempt to steal your identity, your autograph must not be the same as your signature. You know that scribble that got you your credit card, your home loan and went on the contract for your house when you finally bought it? Yeah, that one. It's the power to be you officially (and usually has money and assets attached to it). The fewer people who know what your signature looks like, the better.

SO YOU NEED TO PREPARE A DIFFERENT SCRIBBLE TO BE YOUR AUTOGRAPH

In 2017, I took my nephew to a football clinic run by his chosen AFL club and after about 200 kids were put through their paces by the players, they all lined up to get hats, jumpers and autograph books signed by their favourites. Predictably, the well-known players were swamped and the more junior or slightly less feted players stood around awkwardly waiting. My nephew wanted every player's autograph (he even got autographs from the few women players who were there – in the first year of the AFLW, so even though he doesn't know it, he's got a significant piece of history there) so when we got to those junior and slightly less feted players, there was a little bit more time to chat.

"Do they send you to some sort of class to work on developing your autograph?" I asked one of them, tongue firmly in cheek.

"No, it just sort of happens." And to demonstrate the unthinking ease with which the autographs flowed from their hands, he pointed to the teammate standing next to him, a recent transfer from another club, and continued, "For a while, Caleb kept signing his old number." (Many AFL players include their number so that the kids can remember whose autograph was whose.)

Mine has evolved over time from my entire name (a sort of lightning strike for a joined together "L" and "T" and then "ouise" on top and "ruscott" on the bottom) to now just my first name in a very cursive, loopy, easy-to-sign-over-and-over-again script. I'm a doodler from way back and I was always scribbling loops so it makes some sense that the "L" in my autograph is very loopy. And apart from the dot on the "i", my autograph is also one quick and continuous line. I could sign it a hundred times and barely break a sweat or need to shake a cramp out of my hand.

It's an important consideration, especially if you're planning to hold book signings where people don't want to be kept waiting forever for their mini moment with you.

YOU MIGHT ALSO WANT TO THINK ABOUT YOUR HANDWRITING

Some people don't just want an autograph, they also want a personalised message. I can't say I do a lot of handwriting anymore (unless you count scribbled reminders and shopping lists that end up going into the recycling). But when I published *Project January* and gave a few copies to family and the designer who did the cover, I wanted to personalise each one and to say, "Thanks."

You would not believe the stress I went through trying to decide which version of my handwriting I should use. I practised and practised and practised and decided on one. But after using it on the inside of the first book, I changed my mind because even after that practising, I didn't like how it looked. All the inscriptions in the books after that were in a different handwriting.

You might think I'm just a bit of weirdo but I know I'm not alone in spending all this time worrying about my handwriting. When my sister proudly handed out copies of her thesis to family members, she didn't autograph them. And when I asked why, she said she wanted to keep them pristine, not desecrate them with her terrible scrawl.

AND DON'T FORGET YOU NEED COPIES OF YOUR BOOK TO SIGN

Unless you've broken into the stratosphere of uber-famous authors (and by that stage, you've probably already worked your way through all your autograph uncertainties), most people are going to ask for you to sign a copy of your book, not an autograph book or a random piece of paper. You are going to need copies of your book for this. Lots and lots and lots of copies of your book. You can direct people to online places to purchase but by the time they've ordered and received their copy, either you're long gone or their interest in having you sign their copy is. And you can't sign an ebook, can you? Or can you?

There is software available that allows authors to electronically sign an ebook but it's not quite the same thing. And since I'm writing this in the same week that Albert Einstein's scribbled note to a Tokyo bellboy (in lieu of a tip for which he had no cash at the time and which read, "A calm and humble life will bring more happiness than the pursuit of success and the constant restlessness that comes with it") sold for $1.7 million, I'm thinking about both the immediate joy that the recipient of a physical autograph has as well as the potential financial benefits in the future of some lucky inheritor of it. (We can dream, can't we?)

∞

If you prepare a little (and if you're not a weirdo worryhead like me), being asked for your autograph can be a lovely experience. I wish you all many autograph seekers now and in the future.

CONTROVERSY IN WRITING

Without having any real evidence to back up the theory, I have always thought that writers could be divided up into two categories: those who court controversy and those who avoid it. (I later realised there was a third category – writers who are controversial without realising it – you will already have read about that in the chapter on same-sex relationships.)

I also figured out a long time ago that getting involved in any type of controversy tends to leave me upset in greater proportion to any change I may be able to effect in advocating for one side or another. So I generally try to stay quiet unless I feel very strongly. And even then, I moderate myself and think long and hard about how to phrase what I want to say in order to avoid reactions from trolls and people who never change their minds about anything even in the face of overwhelmingly logical arguments. After all, the vitriol of stupid people can be vicious and my greatest ambition is an easy life.

Besides, how much controversy is there in writing really?

Okay, sure, there's plenty of controversy in writing when opinion pieces are considered. It's the nature of opinion by definition. *Macquarie Dictionary* defines it as "judgement or belief resting on grounds insufficient to produce certainty". And since there's no certainty, it's almost guaranteed people will come down on both sides of the argument.

But controversy in fiction? In novels? Surely not? Surely not much, in any case?

It was partly why I chose writing (or why it chose me, the definitive answer may never be known on that score). I could sit at home tapping out words that turned into sentences that turned into paragraphs that turned into chapters that turned into entire books. If people liked what I wrote, great. If they didn't, not so great but I could cope. (My foremost reaction to my first – and only to this stage – one-star rating was not anger or offence or sadness but curiosity. Why? Since it wasn't accompanied by an explanation, I'll never know what it was about my book that had so greatly disappointed that reader.) But I would mostly be shielded from the (nowadays) online yelling matches that erupt from time to time, particularly in relation to politics and social justice and education and the law and morals and… well, just about everything else. The world of fiction writing would be a place where I could retreat from all that.

It's taken me a while but I've realised, as I should have from the start, that there's as much controversy in fiction writing as in anything else. I have social media to thank for that. I follow a lot of other writers and they aren't nearly as squeamish as I am in getting involved in controversy. Here are just a few recent examples.

COCKYGATE

This is a strange one. One of the very first things writers learn about the legalities of writing is that titles can't be copyrighted. And yet in the first half of 2018, a self-published writer by the name of Faleena Hopkins trademarked the use of the word "cocky" as an adjective in the title of romance books and wrote to several authors asking them to remove their books with "cocky" in the title from sale, rename them or face legal action. Some of them did because they didn't have the resources to fight against it.

The trademark was then challenged through legal avenues by retired lawyer and writer Kevin Kneupper because:

- The word "cocky" was used in romance novel titles long before Faleena Hopkins ever used it.
- Generic terms generally aren't able to be trademarked.
- It's "a dick move" (according to Joanne Harris, the author of *Chocolat* – "…if it were really possible to legally forbid authors from using a certain common word in their book titles, then the whole publishing industry would be down the drain in a matter of days").

Romance Writers of America also worked with an IP attorney to resolve this issue and the trademark was eventually cancelled.

EBOOK STUFFING

Ebook stuffing is when writers publish supposedly new content that is primarily composed of previously published material. For example, the first 250 pages might be never before seen but the remaining 3,000 pages are not. Because of the way Amazon was paying authors that are part of the KDP Select program (based on a percentage of page views to disperse a limited fund of money), it meant serial book stuffers were often earning up to $100,000 a month and reducing the funds going to other writers who weren't doing the same thing.

It violated KDP's terms of service but not much was ever done about it, some say because it wasn't really hurting Amazon. They paid out the same amount of money, regardless of where it was going. In early June 2018, they implemented some new guidelines in an attempt to prevent ebook stuffing from continuing but as David Gaughran reported, some offenders claimed almost immediately they had found a loophole, simply by adding the word "compilation" to the title.

There will always be people who operate according to the letter of the law but flaunt the spirit of it and this is a perfect case in point.

JENNIFER WEINER AND JONATHAN FRANZEN

I will freely admit I have never read books by either Jennifer Weiner or Jonathan Franzen. In fact, I only know who both of them are because of this controversy. In 2010, when Franzen was releasing his novel *Freedom*, Weiner complained about the wall-to-wall coverage it was receiving (dubbed "Franzenfrenzy"), including not one but two reviews in the *New York Times*, saying it was evidence of the over-representation of white, middle-aged, male writers in a fawning literary scene. Jodi Picoult backed her up, saying the *New York Times* "favours white male authors". Although he was probably just unlucky to be at the apex of a conglomeration of feeling about the attention these white male authors receive, Franzen became a lightning rod for it and the term "Franzenfreude" was coined by Weiner, becoming a rallying cry for female writers and authors of colour. As Jennifer Haigh pointed out when nominating Jonathan Franzen as *Paste Magazine*'s 2010 Person of the Year in Fiction, "Though he may well benefit from it, sexism within literary culture is no way Franzen's fault."

However, instead of calmly making that point himself, Franzen has ever since engaged in personal attacks on Weiner, saying, "There's something about [her] that rubs me the wrong way, something I don't trust..." Therefore, it's hard to begrudge Weiner when she says, "Okay, I don't hate Jonathan Franzen. What I hate is the way the *New York Times* transforms itself into his personal PR machine when he has a book out, to the exclusion of the books people are actually reading, so he's sort of a symbol for a whole binary hierarchical... oh, fuck it, I hate that smug motherfucker, and I vote we TP his house."

∞

The one thing that all these – and most other – controversies have in common is that they divide the writing community that so often benefits from remaining a strong and united front, particularly given that the majority of us will never make it into the JK Rowling-level stratosphere and rely on the kindness of a few random readers (often other authors). It's a shame. Especially because if we're devoting our energies to picking sides, then it doesn't leave a lot of time for the things that will deliver the most benefits to our careers, our royalties and our mental health: writing.

A LITTLE TOO CLOSE TO HOME: WHEN
FANTASY BECOMES REALITY

"Spare us all word of the weapons, their force and range,
The long numbers that rocket the mind."
"Advice to a Prophet" by Richard Wilbur

I mostly follow other writers on Twitter, people I've never met or generally even heard of but who are the most supportive community you could ever hope to be a part of. There are also a few people I follow that I do actually know.

One of them, a friend and former non-writing colleague who is obsessed with things like renewable energy, electric cars and advances in technology, tweeted a link to a Gizmodo article with the headline "China Claims to Have a Real-Deal Laser Gun That Inflicts 'Instant Carbonisation' of Human Skin". His accompanying comment was, "Sounds too good to be true. The ability to put such an effective laser in such a small form and to be able to fire it, at least multiple times, has to be questioned until we see it." A picture of the laser assault rifle, which looks a lot like those brick mobile phones from the 1980s except with a scope attached, was also included.

I'd seen a less descriptive headline and the same image on another website and scrolled past it earlier that same week. But the additional information in my friend's tweet piqued my interest. I responded to him, "This sounds a lot like the storyline of a certain debut novel of mine..." He replied, "Ha ha yes."

So I opened the article and started reading. "As the US prepares for war in space, China's bringing the space war home. Its ZKZM-500 laser assault rifle is reportedly capable of hitting a target from a kilometre away, igniting flammable objects, and burning through human skin. And it's ready for production, the researchers behind the project claim.

"A weapon that fires a destructive laser beam has been a dream of military researchers for decades. The US military has recently had some luck with huge laser-firing cannons that are intended to be mounted on ships or trucks and can take down a drone by burning through its body. But effective laser rifles for use by individual soldiers have been stuck in the land of fantasy.

"The *South China Morning Post*, however, spoke with researchers at the Xian Institute of Optics and Precision Mechanics (at the Chinese Academy of Sciences)…" This was the point at which I had my "Holy fuck!" moment. I actually said, "Holy fuck!" out loud. Then I went into my files, opened the final version of my debut novel, *Enemies Closer*, and confirmed what I had suspected. The story that I'd started writing in 2004, finished in 2007 and published in 2012 with the outlandish plot that (spoiler alert) a prototype for a laser assault rifle had been developed by none other than the Chinese Academy of Sciences. (You can read the prologue on my blog and see it for yourself – the organisation, at least; the plot reveal obviously comes much later in the book.)

I'm not vain enough to think that anyone at the Chinese Academy of Sciences had actually read my book and been inspired by it. Considering the complex nature of the technology of lasers, the research necessary to get them to this stage of weapons development has no doubt been going on since long before I ever had this idea for the story. Still, it is freaky weird coincidental how many similarities there are between the article and my novel.

But I am vain enough to be proud of how much I got right. I did an awful lot of research into lasers (as much as a lay person could understand, at any rate) so I knew back in 2004 that extremely large lasers designed for mounting on ships were a reality. I knew that China was heavily involved in research and development of technology. Alluding to this fact, at the start of *Enemies Closer*, I included a quote from George J Tenet, the former Director of the Central Intelligence Agency, from a publication entitled *The Intelligence Community's Damage Assessment on the Implications of China's Acquisition of US Nuclear Weapons Information on the Development of Future Chinese Weapons*:

"China's technical advances have been made on the basis of classified and unclassified information derived from espionage, contact with US and other countries' scientists, conferences and publications, unauthorized media disclosures, declassified US weapons information, and **Chinese indigenous development. The relative contribution of each cannot be determined**." [Emphasis mine.] And obviously I did enough research to know that it would be the Chinese Academy of Sciences who would be overseeing this development. Yay me!

However, my celebrations were tempered by the fact that the weapon I imagined, the weapon now being described as a reality ready to go into production, is utterly altogether too horrible to envision being unleashed on the world. According to the article, "the technology is expected to be restricted for military and police use only. Even that level of use could face pushback from other countries. As the *Morning Post* points out, the United Nations' Protocol on Blinding Laser Weapons came into force in 1998 and has been signed by 108 nations around the world." Hmmm, I'm sure China will take that fact into consideration in making its final decision on what to do (or maybe not).

In my book, the Chinese researcher who successfully develops the laser technology deliberately but covertly blows up three laboratories she works in and then tells the authorities that it's highly unstable and unable to be harnessed in order to prevent it going into mass production. As she puts it later on when the technology is discovered to be working perfectly, she didn't want "to be known as a destroyer of worlds". I suspect no such real-life equivalent currently exists.

It's all just a little too close to home for comfort. One of the reasons we write stories like this (or at least why I did) with heinous villains and terrifying weapons is that it's a way to control them. They exist only on the pages of the book and when we scare ourselves to the point of overload, we can simply close the cover and return to the real world. But at the moment, the real world and the fictional world I created are dissolving into one and the same thing.

When the Las Vegas shooting occurred, I had a moral crisis about having written a book focused so much on weapons without ever considering whether I was glamorising them. Now I'm having another. In 2012, I was so proud of this book. I published it. I became – and nobody could ever take this away from me – a published author. I'm now also someone who imagined awful things and lived to see them become reality. It's taken just a little of the shine off.

WHEN WRITERS BECOME THE NEWS

What's so hard about writing? All you need is a working knowledge of the language you want to write in, a computer (or a typewriter if you're nostalgic or a pen and paper if you're old-fashioned) and a little bit of time. Or maybe a lot of time. However long it takes, the words will eventually come. And you'll be left with a piece of writing. You'll be proud (and you should be).

Okay, yes, it can get harder after that. Editing, publishing, marketing, readers – there will always be someone who doesn't react quite the way you had hoped they would to what you've written. Of course, that's nothing compared to those who think the appropriate reaction to words on a page that they don't agree with or don't like is to pick up a gun and track down their author.

You might think it's a rarity for writers to be targeted and killed for what they've written but it's actually quite common. More common in countries that don't embrace freedom and democracy, less common in those that do but by no means non-existent. In June 2018, a man walked into the newsroom of the *Capital Gazette* newspaper in Annapolis, Maryland in the US and shot dead Gerald Fischman, Rob Hiaasen, John McNamara, Rebecca Smith and Wendi Winters as well as wounding two others. The paper's crime in the shooter's eyes? Accurately reporting his harassment of a former classmate on social media, to which he pleaded guilty, and then successfully defending the defamation lawsuit he brought against them because of that reporting.

In April 2018, Ahmad Abu Hussein, a Palestinian journalist covering a protest along the Gaza-Israeli border and wearing a vest marked "Press" and a helmet marked "TV", was shot in the stomach by an Israeli soldier. He died after two weeks in hospital. Earlier the same month, Yasser

Murtaja died after being shot while covering the same ongoing protest. He was one of nine Palestinians who died that day. Another 491 were wounded. He was the only one who died simply doing his job.

In 2019, Reporters Without Borders (AKA Reporters Sans Frontières) listed 39 journalists and 10 citizen journalists as well as three media assistants as having been killed and a further 231 journalists, 115 citizen journalists and 14 media assistants as currently imprisoned. In 2020, 19 journalists and three media assistants were killed up to the middle of August and those numbers are likely low only because of the coronavirus pandemic. Those figures don't even begin to come close to the numbers of writers who are forced to relocate from their home countries to avoid being jailed or killed and who live in exile for the remainder of their lives while attempting to shed light on censorship, oppression, corruption and general abuses of power.

It isn't just non-fiction writers. Salman Rushdie spent years in hiding and under police protection after a fatwa was issued calling for his death in response to the publication of his novel *The Satanic Verses*. Inspired in part by the life of the Prophet Muhammad, some Muslims felt that the novel was blasphemous and mocked their faith. Ayatollah Khomeini of Iran called for his death and there were several failed assassination attempts. As recently as 2016, money was being raised to pay any successful assassin.

The top 10 countries in the world for press freedom are currently Norway, Finland, Denmark, Sweden, Netherlands, Jamaica, Costa Rica, Switzerland, New Zealand and Portugal. The bottom 10 countries are Cuba, Laos, Iran, Syria, Vietnam, Djibouti, China, Eritrea, Turkmenistan and North Korea. Australia is 26th, mostly due to the heavy concentration of print media ownership in two corporate organisations. Canada is 16th because of attempts to force reporters to reveal sources and the recent closures of over 40 independent newspapers, which threatens media pluralism. The UK is 35th because of insufficient protections for whistleblowers, journalists and sources and repeated heavy-handed media approaches in the name of national security. The US is 45th (ironically due in large part to the 45th president). Despite press freedom being enshrined in the Constitution, Donald Trump often refuses to deal with media he considers unfavourable, suggests the revocation of press credentials (again of media he considers unfavourable), routinely uses the term "fake news" to describe unfavourable media coverage and calls the press "the enemy of the American people". Additionally, reporters run the risk of being arrested for covering protests and attempting to ask public officials questions as well as being subjected to physical assault while on the job. Yeah, okay, Australia, Canada, the UK and US aren't exactly at the level of North Korea but they're clearly not at the level of Norway either. They can do better.

And still we write. And still we should. If we stop writing, then censorship is successful, even when it's self-censorship. Of course, our lives are important but our voices are important as well. "But I'm nobody!" I hear you say. Hi, nice to meet you. I'm nobody, too. Our voices are more important than ever in a world where corporates increasingly determine whose voices are heard, usually based on whether it impacts on their ability to make money.

I'm unlikely to meet an untimely demise because of my writing (the most controversial thing I've ever written was calling out another writer who wrote a particularly ill-informed and badly researched article). In fact, as a white woman in Australia, the most likely causes of my death will be old age, illness or intimate partner violence. Wendi Winters probably thought the same things would be the cause of her demise. Would she have stopped writing had she known ahead of time it would contribute to her death? I doubt it. Will I? No. Will you? I sure hope not.

WHAT HAPPENS TO YOUR UNPUBLISHED
WRITING AFTER YOU DIE?

In March 2015, Terry Pratchett, the British author of over 70 books and creator of the Discworld series, lost his battle with early onset Alzheimer's. He was just 66 years old. In June and September 2015 respectively, *The Long Utopia* and *The Shepherd's Crown*, his two final completed books, were published. In 2017, the manager of Pratchett's estate used a steamroller to flatten a hard drive containing all his unpublished, incomplete works and tweeted a picture of the destroyed device. It was Pratchett's wish fulfilled.

Pratchett's estate and heirs were in an enviable position. With 70-odd books already published, the royalties will be flowing in for many years to come so their decision to respect his dying wish was, it would seem, a relatively easy one.

However, it doesn't always appear to be the case. Despite her immense success, after Virginia Andrews's death in 1986, her estate hired a ghostwriter to keep penning works in her name. Some of them were begun by Andrews but not completed before she succumbed to breast cancer at the age of 63.

And seven years after the publication of his last single-author novel, Tom Clancy began collaborating with a variety of other authors, publishing five co-authored books. Since his death in 2013, six novels have been written using the characters he established and with his name the most prominent wording on the covers. Three more are already planned (at the time of writing this). Also at the time of writing, Clancy's widow has filed a lawsuit to have ownership of the character of Jack Ryan clarified. She believes it belongs to the estate of Tom Clancy. The personal representative of the estate disagrees.

It's unclear whether Virginia Andrews had any preferences regarding her unfinished writing at the time of her death but Tom Clancy seems to have embraced the commercialisation of his characters and his name (even if the legalities could have been a little bit clearer).

Anne Frank is perhaps the most famous of all posthumously published writers. The writing was her own – intimately and perfectly so – but when her diary was first published in 1947, certain details and entries were omitted to avoid offending the conservative moralities of the time. These deleted components were reintroduced in subsequent editions. But Anne always intended for her diary to be read by others (although it is unlikely she suspected it would be posthumously). An entry dated 20 May 1944 noted that she had begun redrafting her diary with future readers in mind after hearing a radio broadcast in which the exiled Dutch Minister for Education, Art and Science called for the preservation of ordinary documents such as diaries and letters as a testament to the suffering of civilians during the Nazi occupation.

These are some fairly famous examples but the options for what happens to your writing after you die appear to be as follows:

- It is destroyed – this probably isn't anyone's first choice if you're not Terry Pratchett. Writers work hard to put words into an order that elevates them from language to art and the idea of all that effort going to waste is generally unpalatable. (Whenever I plan what to save in the event of a house fire, it's always cats first, hard drive containing all my back-ups second. Of course, life is what happens while you make other plans. When I did have a house fire in 2009, I saved the cats and forgot all about the hard drive. Luckily, the fire was contained to one room and didn't get anywhere near my computer.)

- It languishes in obscurity – this probably isn't anyone's first choice either. The majority of people who write, just like Anne Frank, do it to be read. Languishing tends to suggest it's ready to be read but isn't anywhere accessible that would allow it to be.

- It is published by your family/estate – an interesting proposition. This means that someone found, read and thought your writing worthy of going to the effort of putting it out there. Sure, you won't get final book cover approval but they've hopefully given your writing the respect it deserves by doing justice to the editing, designing and publishing processes. It's what most writers dream of, dead or alive.

- It is completed and then published by your family/estate – a more problematic proposition. I'm currently 85,000 words into writing a novel with about 25,000 to go and I have no idea how I'm going to finish the book. I made some notes several years ago when I first started writing it but since then I've decided that I don't like the ending I initially came up with and I'm not going to use it. But if I die before completing it, someone might find those notes and think I still intended to use those plot points. It's also still in first draft format. Of the four books I've published so far, three of them were onto the third drafts when I published them and the other was on the fourth or fifth. I suspect my family/estate wouldn't be prepared to put in another two, three or four drafts of my incomplete works because they're not invested in my writing the way I am.

And then there's one last option that has nothing to do with your writing and everything to do with money:

- Your family/estate slaps your name on something you had little or nothing to do with – I don't know about you but I find this a little distressing. You're either forever associated with something that is simply a poor imitation or another writer who has expended time and energy writing something great is denied proper recognition for their work.

I suppose the answer is, as much as it is within your control, to write and publish as much as you can while you're still breathing and to leave clear instructions about what you want done with your incomplete or unpublished writing when you do depart this earth. There are no guarantees, of course. But if it bothers you, remember this: you'll be dead, unable to do anything about it and likely completely oblivious. Besides, if one of your legacies is to provide a source of income (no matter how small) to the loved ones you leave behind, it might just be worth it.

PART 6

READING

THE RULES OF READING

I sometimes have a love-hate relationship with reading. I love to read. I hate finishing a book and wishing it had been better. One third of the way through reading a non-fiction book that has been well-reviewed, that has set the author up to write a series of similar books and has established her as a figurehead of the "fuck up the patriarchy" movement (I'm paraphrasing but that's definitely the kind of language she would use), I was finding it a bit... tedious. So much so that the idea of picking it up again made me not want to read at all.

I looked longingly instead at my TBR pile. And then had guilt. The most ridiculous kind of guilt. As if I was considering cheating. On a book. Because of some arbitrary rules that I must have set for myself somewhere along the way without realising it.

So I'm creating a new set of reading rules (as much for myself as for anyone else).

YOU DON'T HAVE TO BUY A BOOK

If you want to own a book, then you have to buy it. But if you just want to read it, then you can borrow it from a library or someone you know who has a copy of it. But whatever you do, you must never steal a book. Never download a pirated copy of a book. It is stealing from the author. If you can't afford to buy a copy, become a member of a library and borrow it. Some authors will even give you a free copy of their book if you ask nicely. It doesn't cost anything except a little bit of your time.

YOU DON'T HAVE TO READ ALL GENRES

Reading widely is a great way of expanding your knowledge of the world. But most of us read simply for pleasure and the expansion of our knowledge is just a by-product. If we are reading for pleasure, then it's unlikely we are going to enjoy all genres of writing. If you don't enjoy a particular genre, then you don't have to read it. It's completely counterintuitive. If you only enjoy one genre and you only want to read that one genre, then you are perfectly within your rights.

YOU DON'T HAVE TO STICK TO ONE GENRE

There is also nothing that says you can't read more than one genre. Read them all if you like. Read any combination of genres that satisfies your reading appetite. Read the popular and the obscure, read the bestsellers and the flops, read the critically acclaimed and the universally panned, read fiction and non-fiction, read romance and horror, read thrillers and dramas, read sci-fi and historical, read steampunk and erotica, read fantasy and urban realism, read crime and westerns, and when you're done reading all the genres that exist now, look for new ones because they are being invented every day.

YOU DON'T HAVE TO READ AGE-APPROPRIATE OR DEMOGRAPHIC-APPROPRIATE BOOKS

Most fiction seems to get divided up into categories based on which age group it is meant for: pre-school, new readers, middle grade, young adult and adult. And then there are the categories we're told we should like based on who we are: women's fiction for women, adventure for men, sci-fi for nerds and so on. But you can read books from any or all of these classifications. Most publishers stumble into books that go on to be bestsellers and that's if they aren't too busy falling all over themselves to reject them completely. The idea that they know who should be reading what, better than the readers themselves, is laughable.

YOU DON'T HAVE TO READ A BOOK JUST BECAUSE EVERYBODY ELSE IS

FOMO (fear of missing out) is real, even when it comes to reading. But just because everybody else is reading a book because it was Oprah's pick or it had a billion-dollar marketing budget or it's currently being made into a movie that may or may not suck doesn't mean you should feel obligated. Getting sucked into reading a book that everybody else seems to be talking about often means it will fail to meet expectations because it's almost never as good as the hype suggests. It's perfectly reasonable to instead spend that time reading something you actually want to read rather than something you have just been tricked into reading.

YOU CAN READ THE LAST PAGE OF THE BOOK BEFORE READING THE FIRST

Oh, how it pains me to write that! You will never catch me reading the last page of a book before reading all the other pages before it linearly. Mostly because the words have no real meaning to me if I haven't read all the words before them. But if reading the last page of a book before diving in at the start is what floats your boat, then go for it. If it's a crime, then it's certainly a victimless one.

YOU DON'T HAVE TO FINISH READING A BOOK JUST BECAUSE YOU STARTED IT

On several occasions, I've read books – struggled through them actually – only to find that getting to the end made all of that struggle worth it. And with just as many (probably more), I've struggled through only to find that it wasn't worth it at all. And then there are the books that I never finished. The one I always cite is *Jane Eyre* by Charlotte Bronte. It just didn't speak to me. But there have been a few others. *The Haldeman Diaries*, a memoir kept by HR Haldeman for the four years he was Richard Nixon's Chief of Staff. It's still in my library with a bookmark marking the place where I gave up over a decade ago. I might go back to it one day. But I might not. And that's perfectly okay.

YOU DON'T HAVE TO FINISH READING A BOOK BEFORE STARTING TO READ ANOTHER

Ah, the dilemma that propelled me into writing these rules. I'm not very good at remembering what happened in a book if I don't read it all in one go, so I try to stick to one book at a time. But whether it's circumstances or the book itself, sometimes you feel like reading but don't feel like reading that particular book. So it's completely acceptable to read something else instead. You might go back to the other book. You might not. It's entirely up to you.

YOU DON'T HAVE TO LIKE A BOOK JUST BECAUSE EVERYBODY ELSE DOES

I won't name the two books that I dislike the most but one of them is considered a classic (my review: "this is the story of – to be frank – nothing very interesting and nothing much happening... the kind of bad novel a teenage boy might write before compiling a manifesto and then going on a killing spree") and the other was made into a TV show (my review: "the only redeeming thing about this book is that it serves as an important lesson for everyone out there writing: if something as bad as this book can be published, then there's still hope for the rest of us"). Different books speak to different people for different reasons and just as often they don't speak to us at all. There's no right and there's no wrong when it comes to opinions, there's just lots and lots of them.

YOU DON'T HAVE TO LIKE EVERYTHING ONE AUTHOR WRITES

Some writers write to the same formula in book after book. If you like the formula, then you'll probably consider that a good thing. But it's possible that you might get tired of the formula after a while. Similarly, some writers bore themselves sticking to the same writing formula, so decide to try something different. They might like the results. You might not. It is not compulsory to like everything that comes from one writer. And if the day comes that it is compulsory, then they're no longer an author, they're a cult leader.

YOU DON'T HAVE TO REVIEW A BOOK ONCE YOU'VE FINISHED READING IT (BUT THE AUTHOR WOULD PROBABLY APPRECIATE IT IF YOU DO)

If it isn't clear by now, let me spell it out for you one last time: when it comes to reading, you don't have to do anything you don't want to. And that includes posting reviews. Yes, writers like reviews (particularly positive reviews) and if you can manage it, they'll be eternally grateful. But if you can't, then don't worry. You don't owe them anything. In fact, if you've read their book, then you've already done more for them than most people have.

∞

So that's it. And the rules of reading all really come down to one thing: do whatever the hell you want. As long as you keep reading. After all, as Mark Twain so eloquently put it, those who don't read have no advantage over those who can't read.

FOR THE LOVE OF LANGUAGE

I like knowing stuff. It doesn't matter what that stuff is, I just like knowing it. Knowledge is cool. I haven't figured out what to do with it all yet but in the meantime, I'm continuing to accumulate it.

In that spirit, I was watching a couple of documentaries about Tourette's syndrome – one focused on children struggling with the condition and the other explored the difficulties in obtaining employment when unable to control muscular and vocal tics. And as I commonly do (because I always want to know more), I Googled Tourette's syndrome and began reading on Wikipedia about the details the documentaries weren't going into.

One of the children in the documentary and one of the men looking for work had what I discovered was called coprolalia – "the utterance of obscene words or socially inappropriate and derogatory remarks" – and that only a small minority of people with Tourette's exhibit this symptom. When I clicked through the link to find out more about coprolalia, I discovered that "copro" came from the Greek for "faeces" and "lalia" came from the Greek for "to talk". Coprolalia literally means "to talk shit".

Knowledge is one thing but language is another entirely. And for someone who loves language as much as I do, this was a glorious find. This was wonderful. This was bliss! My heart skipped a nerdy beat. And it went on and on as I read about copropraxia and coprographia. Copropraxia is "involuntarily performing obscene or forbidden gestures" – "copro" from the Greek for "faeces" and "praxia" from the Greek for "actions", literally "shit actions". And coprographia is "involuntarily making vulgar writings or drawings" – "copro" from the Greek for "faeces" and "graphia" from the Greek for "to draw", literally "to draw shit". It doesn't get much better than this!

I know I'm not the only one. During the episode "Mr Willis of Ohio" from *The West Wing*, Aaron Sorkin writes the following exchange as the main characters play poker.

President Bartlet: There are three words, and three words only, in the English language that begin with the letters "DW".

Josh Lyman: This is a pretty good illustration of why we get nothing done.

President Bartlet: Can anyone name them for me please?

Sam Seaborn: Three words that begin with "DW"?

President Bartlet: Yes.

Sam Seaborn: Dwindle.

President Bartlet: Yes.

Toby Ziegler: Dwarf.

President Bartlet: Yes.

Toby Ziegler (to Sam Seaborn): C'mon, Princeton, we've got dwindle, we've got dwarf.

President Bartlet: I see your five and raise you five by the way.

Toby Ziegler: Dwarf, dwindle…

Leo McGarry: Fold.

Josh Lyman: Fold.

CJ Cregg: Last card down.

President Bartlet: "Witches brew a magic spell, in an enchanted forest where fairies…"

Toby Ziegler: Dwell, dwell, dwell! Dwindle, dwarf and dwell!

I've written previously about how much I love my dictionary, randomly thumbing through pages to discover new and fantastic words. I've also written previously about how my beloved dictionary was more than a decade old and even though I gave in and finally purchased an updated version, I still love my old dictionary more than my new one. This was confirmed when I arrived at the end of the "D" section to find that there were no longer only three words beginning with "DW". My new dictionary (which I loathe more and more each time I pick it up) also lists:

- Dwale – the deadly nightshade
- Dwang – a short piece of timber fixed horizontally between vertical framing members, to which lining materials may be attached
- Dweeb – a person who is despised as lacking vigour or personal style
- Dwine – to waste away or fade

As far as I'm concerned, none of these other "DW" words are all that worthy, certainly not enough to render the scene from *The West Wing* irrelevant. And none of this is apropos of anything except that I'm a great big word nerd. (In "The Midterms" episode, Aaron Sorkin manages to work in the term "acalculia" and there are so many more examples of his love of language. I love *The West Wing* almost as much as I love my old dictionary. And for anyone who wants to write, watching all seven seasons is like taking a crash course in how to do it well.)

When I looked up "coprolalia" in my new dictionary, it wasn't there, although there were several other "copro–" words. But when I looked up "coprolalia" in my old dictionary, there it was – "the uncontrolled use of violent and obscene language, especially as a result of an illness such as Tourette's syndrome". Just another black mark against the new dictionary. And further evidence of both my love of language and the fact that I'm more than a little bit unusual – who else looks up the same word three times in three different places, two of them different versions of the same dictionary? I'm sure it isn't just me even though I've never met anyone else who would admit to it. When I do, maybe my love of language will be matched by my love for that person. Until then, it's just me, my old dictionary and *The West Wing* as I continue to accumulate knowledge and appreciate language.

ON READING THE BOOK THAT BEAT ME FOR THE 2016 TEXT PRIZE

In 2016, I entered the manuscript of my unpublished young adult novel *Black Spot* in the Text Prize competition for young adult and children's writing. I wasn't holding my breath about winning because I'm not a holding-my-breath kind of person. And when I received a blanket email from the Text Prize people thanking everybody for their entries and saying that the shortlisted authors would be contacted individually, I assumed I wasn't one of them because I hadn't heard anything.

A couple of days later, my phone rang. I didn't recognise the number. I thought it might be about a job I'd applied for. Instead, it was a woman named Ally, who told me she worked at Text Publishing. She was calling to let me know that *Black Spot* had been shortlisted for the Text Prize. And to invite me to the announcement of the winner in just under two weeks' time.

If it sounds like I was very calm during that phone call, I wasn't. I was stunned. I was overwhelmed. But I was happy. This was an achievement. This was amazing. This was bliss.

From 297 entries, the five shortlisted novels were mine, *Eternal* by Sarah Bainbridge, *Waste* by Claire Christian, *Never Let Go* by James Cooper and *Rosebud* by Fiona Hardy. And two days before the official announcement, we each received a phone call to let us know if we'd won or not, presumably to avoid those "What the fuck?" or break-down-crying reactions that sometimes happen when you only find out on the night. As I said at the time to my honorary manager, I was bummed that I hadn't won but I'd get over it. And I have.

At the official announcement party, Claire Christian was declared the winner and as she gave an impressive speech, I was 1) thankful I hadn't won because I don't do public speaking and 2) certain she was going to be a much better marketing proposition for Text Publishing. (Look at her official author portrait; she has colourful hair! Blue, red and yellow at various times since I met her! If that doesn't say marketer's dream, then I don't know what does! Okay, I don't know much about being a marketer's dream, if I did I'd be better at it, but Claire seemed to me to be it.)

Towards the end of August 2017, her book was published under the revised title of *Beautiful Mess*. In September, I bought a copy and in October, I read it (you can read my four-and-a-half-star review on my blog). I sent a message to Claire saying I thought the book was wonderful and I hoped it wasn't too awkies having someone you'd lost to writing a review of your book and she responded by thanking me, saying it wasn't awkward and she was glad I had enjoyed it.

I was always going to read Claire's book because 1) it won a writing prize and that's a pretty great endorsement, 2) I wanted to know what she had done better than me and use it as a learning process, and 3) I'm a little masochistic (but mostly the first two). I was very pleased to be able to report that it's an amazing book because 1) it justifies that it won the Text Prize and 2) I got to write a glowing book review and avoid looking like a sore loser.

It struck me, though, that there were quite a few similarities in our books. Explorations of death, the tricky time of being a teenager, identity, power, relationships with parents, relationships with significant others (friends and lovers) and mental health (specifically depression). There were also two big differences. Claire had approached her story from a place of realism, pure gritty realism, while I had written a piece of escapist fiction. And it was clear that she spent a lot of time with real teenagers. If I didn't have a sister 20 years younger than me and a teenage niece and nephew, I wouldn't have spoken to a teenager in decades, pretty much since I was one.

One thing that was really reinforced for me was that books aren't really the kind of thing that can be definitively ranked as better or worse. They're not like science tests and they can't be objectively marked correct or incorrect out of 100. The reason that both of our books were shortlisted was because they were both good. Her book isn't better than mine. It just spoke more clearly and more powerfully to the people at Text Publishing. It was closer to what they were looking for, something that neither of us could have known about, so it was a bit of a crapshoot in the end in that respect.

And the other thing is that I haven't really been beaten. My book still exists. It will be published. It will be read. My success will come differently and later than Claire's but it will still come. Her book is fantastic. And my book was good enough to be shortlisted with it. It doesn't get much better than that.

THE NINE TYPES OF BOOK REVIEWS

Once a book is published, there are two things an author hopes for: sales and reviews. Sales are good because they allow a writer to be financially supported as they write their next book. Reviews are good because they lead to more sales. And the more stars each review has, the more validated the author feels and the more confidence potential readers have.

But regardless of whether a book is good, bad or somewhere in between, and assuming it has had enough exposure, it will have each of the following types of review.

THE NEVER-READ-IT REVIEW

Obviously, someone who reviews a book they've never read has a nefarious purpose, either to promote or prevent the reading of it. Platforms like Amazon usually don't allow a review of a product that hasn't been bought directly from them so that helps a little. Platforms like Goodreads rely on the honesty of the reading community they have assembled. It doesn't always work.

Authors might suggest they don't mind so much as long as it's a good review but reviews aren't really for authors, they're for potential readers. And there's nothing worse for a reader than relying on a review and being time-wastingly deceived.

THE NEVER-FINISHED-READING-IT REVIEW

Everyone has started reading at least one book that they just haven't been able to get through. *Jane Eyre* is my most famous example. And if you run through the Goodreads list of all my reviews, you won't find it there. How could I justify reviewing a book I haven't actually read? But plenty of people do it, usually using their inability to finish it as evidence of the book not being good enough to hold their interest. I prefer to interpret it as evidence of the reader's inability to persist.

Some books that have impressed me are those that I really hated reading. *The Godfather, The Fourth Estate, Life of Pi* – I really struggled reading these books. I just didn't understand what the point of any of them was and I found them difficult… until I read the last pages of each, at which point they suddenly became profound.

Any review that starts with "I didn't finish this book…" is one I automatically disregard.

THE RATING-WITHOUT-EXPLANATION REVIEW

I understand that most people don't have the time to write lengthy reviews but I also automatically disregard one-star and five-star ratings if they don't have an accompanying review that explains why. After all, a book has to be awful to be rated one star and amazing to be rated five stars. At least, they should be.

The rating without explanation bothers me less for two-star, three-star and four-star books (although I always appreciate even just a sentence as to why). But a one-star or five-star rating without going into the reason why is open to interpretation. Is it one star because the reader doesn't like that genre but thought they'd give it a go anyway or is it one star because it was a truly terrible book? Without the explanation, the rating is close to meaningless.

THE NITPICKING REVIEW

The nitpicking review gets caught up on one tiny little thing and is then based entirely on it. I saw it in a review where the reader couldn't get past the fact that the story was set during a southern hemisphere Christmas, making it hot and entirely lacking in snow. Even though this is how half the world celebrates Christmas, the reader was particularly annoyed that it didn't reflect their experience. So I have no idea whether the book was any good, just that they didn't like that aspect of it. It's especially unhelpful.

THE RELATIVE REVIEW

Families can be great. They want to support the creative (although slightly fanciful) efforts of their sons, daughters, fathers, mothers, brothers, sisters, uncles, aunts, nephews, nieces and so on. So when a book is released, they're among the first reviewers.

I have one of these reviews myself. My mother kindly wrote to accompany her five-star rating of my debut novel, *Enemies Closer*, "This is a great read. Not finished it yet. But enjoying it very much. Looking forward to each chapter. Have holidays coming up and will be engrossed." To the best of my knowledge, she has never finished reading it. Even though she used to be, she's not much of a reader anymore. It's perfect evidence of why reviews from relatives should be approached with at least a little caution.

THE SPOILER-REVEALING REVIEW

A great many books rely on plot points being revealed to the reader only as the book is being read and yet some reviewers feel the need to let us know them in their reviews. "Rosebud's the sled," Herman Mankiewicz whisper-shouts at people filing into the first screening of *Citizen Kane* in the movie about its making, *RKO281*. At least he had some comic timing. Most reviews with spoilers simply give away all the good bits, making reading the book itself entirely unnecessary or entirely unsatisfying.

THE SHORT THOUGHTFUL REVIEW

A sentence or a paragraph is all that most writers want because a sentence or a paragraph is all that most potential readers will read before moving onto the next review. "A traditional romance with feisty main characters and a lovely fairy tale ending. Three stars." It doesn't get much shorter or sweeter than that. And while a writer might prefer four or five stars, it's the kind of review that will speak directly to the target audience for a book of that genre.

THE MID-LENGTH MUSING REVIEW

The mid-length musing review is more likely to be seen and read in full on a book blog and is more likely to be written by an amateur book reviewer and appreciated by bibliophiles. You will know exactly why the reviewer did or didn't like the book and, in most cases, it will have just enough detail for the author to think, "Hmmm, I must remember this part of the critique when I'm writing my next book." Unless it devolves into a rant (always a possibility when someone feels strongly enough to write a mid-length musing review), then it's always worth giving it some consideration.

THE LONG ESSAY REVIEW

This is the kind of review most writers can only dream of, thousands of words dedicated to a genuinely thoughtful consideration of the author and their book. These will usually appear in newspapers and magazines and will be written by professional critics who weave the story of the author and their writing of the book into their review of the book itself. They're flattering for authors (assuming they're positive) but they're mostly for hard-core readers and they're few and far between for writers who aren't already famous.

∞

Reviews are a bit like publicity; there's no such thing as a bad example of it because the only thing worse than being talked about is not being talked about, as Oscar Wilde so wittily put it. Still, authors hope for a little bit of thought and effort when their books are being reviewed. After all the thought and effort they've put into writing their books, it's what they deserve.

WHY I DON'T GO TO LIBRARIES ANYMORE (AND WHY I LOVE THEM ANYWAY)

My local council has recently built an architectural award-winning building (even though I've heard people describing the outside as looking like Donald Trump's hair) and moved both its offices and the library into it. I'm assured it's beautiful inside. I wouldn't know. I haven't gone in and don't have any plans to. Because I don't go to libraries anymore.

The last time I went to a library was with my sister and her then pre-school-aged daughter on one of their weekly trips to return the children's books they'd borrowed and select some more. Before that? A meeting of unit owners where I lived that just happened to be in a hired meeting room at a library. And before that? During my undergraduate studies, which I finished when I was 22 (nearly half my lifetime ago).

A FEW REASONS WHY I DON'T GO TO LIBRARIES ANYMORE

Time constraints on reading

If I really get into a book, I can read straight through and finish it in one sitting (assuming I have the time, which I rarely do these days). If I don't really get into a book or if it's really long or if there are other things I have to prioritise, it can take me months to read a book. When this is the case, I don't want to have to return to a library to renew my borrowings or even have to return them unfinished, I just want to put it on my bedside table and be able to pick it up whenever I have a few spare reading moments.

I don't like being pressured to read, particularly not within a set period of time. I read for enjoyment and pressure is not enjoyable.

I prefer to read in private

I know plenty of people like to take a book to the beach or a coffee shop or a park or even simply pick one up in the library and start reading right there and then, but I feel weird reading in public. I will do it on the train (sometimes it's safer than making eye contact) or at the airport bookshop when I'm waiting to catch a flight but, for the most part, I do all my reading at home (and most of it in bed – the term for a person who does this is a "librocubicularist").

Although I know it's not the intention, reading in public or even just in company feels like someone is being ignored. I've got guilt about enough things, I don't need to add any more to the list.

If I want to read a book, I buy it

For some girls, it's shoes. For me, it's books. There is nothing that feels as good to a bookworm as buying a book. Certainly, it's nothing like merely borrowing one (because you know you'll eventually have to give it back).

There are so many second-hand books that need forever homes (and I often buy them from charities so it's a win-win scenario) that I might never have come across if I was browsing in a bookshop. And purchasing brand new books means I'm supporting writers to be able to support themselves and write more books.

I don't have any children

I think libraries are so important to children learning to love reading. My sister and her three children virtually live at the library. But I don't have any children. And I already love reading. So, in conjunction with the other reasons I've espoused above, this is why I don't go to libraries anymore.

A FEW REASONS WHY I LOVE LIBRARIES ANYWAY

Libraries are where I learned to love reading

Like I said, libraries are so important to children learning to love reading. It's certainly where I learned it. My family wasn't flush with cash when I was growing up so if we wanted to read books, this is where we found them. And since my parents were divorced and lived two hours apart, we had not one but two local libraries to spend hours in, as well as our school libraries and for those years we lived in a rural town, the mobile library in a truck that would come and park outside the school periodically.

It's such an important formative experience to read as a youngster, to discover books that you love reading as a child. Let's face it, if you don't learn to love reading as a child, you're unlikely to learn to love it at any other time in your life. And everyone can learn to love reading if they find books that speak to them. Where better than at a library?

Libraries are where I learned

Okay, yes, this is what schools are for but when I think about it, school is where I was taught but libraries are where I learned. There's only so much information that can be conveyed in a classroom during very short classes (although at the time, they never felt short) but to reinforce it, to read opposing points of view, to learn more deeply about what are essentially a teacher's talking points, there is nothing better than a library. Libraries might be where children learn to love reading but they are also where children learn to find things out for themselves instead of just accepting what they're told.

I went through my primary, secondary and tertiary studies before the internet was the all-consuming and all-informing (some say ill-informed) thing it is now. There was no such thing as Google Scholar to find academic resources so we had to actually go to the library and physically look things up. It might sound tedious but actually it was a glorious process of discovery because you so often stumbled across things that you never would have if you hadn't been walking past a shelf full of books that were technically outside of the area you were interested in.

Libraries are the reason for my first ever published pieces

During the second year of my second undergraduate qualification, I did a subject called Small Press Publishing. Essentially, the whole subject was about publishing a book. Everyone in the class proposed topics for the book, we chose one and then everyone was assigned a job that would get the book written, edited, designed and printed. The book was called *InRoads* and profiled the great streets of Melbourne in Australia (where we were living and studying).

I was assigned responsibility for coordinating the Toorak Road section. We put out requests to the student body to submit pieces and were looking for about six per street. We only received three for Toorak Road and so it became my additional responsibility to write the three extra pieces we required.

I'd never been to Toorak Road before but suddenly I needed to become an expert. I visited. I walked up and down the street. I noticed shop after shop with recognisable names and that became the first piece I wrote called, "What's in a Name?" I took the free tour at Como House, a historical residence previously home to a high society family and now a National

Trust property flush with tourists, and that became the second piece I wrote (you can read it on my blog). And then I went to the local library and researched everything I could about the establishment and history of Toorak Road. It became the third piece I wrote. All three were published in the book, the first time I was ever published. (My father accompanied me on one of my visits and took dozens of photographs – particularly of Como House, St John's Church and Fawkner Park – and that's how he was published for the first time in the same book – on the front cover no less – but that's another story.)

If it hadn't been for that local library, I never would have been able to write that sixth and final piece to complete the Toorak Road section.

Libraries hold events for writers and readers

There is nothing better for a writer than connecting with readers who appreciate what they've written and readers clearly enjoy it as well or they wouldn't turn up. "Meet the Author" events are offered in many libraries and while social media connections are common these days, there's nothing quite like meeting your favourite writer in person. My nephew met Andy Griffiths when he was nine (another formative experience).

When I was younger, I would be in awe at the thought of seeing a writer whose work I liked in person but the thing that struck me when I finally heard them speaking was that they were just regular people with a particular skill. Now that I'm older and a writer myself, I cherish those connections even more because finding people who are prepared to read your work and want to talk to you about it is difficult. Thank God for libraries facilitating it.

Libraries buy books and some governments offer lending rights payments to writers

Obviously, in order to have books on the shelves, libraries usually have to buy books, which is good news for authors. And in some countries (28, according to Wikipedia at the time of writing this, including Australia, New Zealand, Canada, the UK, Israel and quite a few European countries), there are public lending rights (for public libraries) and educational lending rights (for educational libraries) programs. These programs differ by country but generally seem to be cultural programs administered by the governments to compensate authors for the loss of royalties from potential sales due to the books being available for free to those consuming them. We don't get to say this often these days but yay to governments who recognise the importance of libraries and the authors of books that make libraries possible.

LOUISE TRUSCOTT

∞

If you need more convincing that libraries are wonderful places, I could give you plenty of reasons (computer access for people who don't have it at home, historical record preservation, lending of films and music and now digital products as well, being a public gathering place along with general health and wellbeing benefits – seriously, there have been studies, look it up!) but if you're reading this, then I suspect you're already a library enthusiast. And I hope you still call into your local library from time to time even though I don't. Because they rely on visitors through the doors to convince people obsessed with commercial priorities that they're still worth funding. They are and always will be.

HOW FAR SHOULD WE GO TO SUPPORT
WRITERS WE KNOW?

I'm a writer so it probably won't come as any great shock that I know other writers. People I've studied with, people I've worked with, people I've been published with, people I've been shortlisted for awards with. Some of these people I know better than others. Some I know only a little. But at some point in the past, our paths crossed.

Whenever these writers I know release a new book, I'm the first in line at a bricks-and-mortar bookshop to buy a paperback if they're being physically published or online if they're only being released as an ebook. I'll sometimes buy more than one copy and give them to other people I know. I always read them and I always review them honestly. (I'm probably very lucky that none of the writers I know have ever written a terrible book so I haven't been faced with a difficult decision in that respect.)

Books by writers that I know include *Beautiful Mess* by Claire Christian (winner of the Text Prize 2016), *How to Make a Movie in 12 Days* by Fiona Hardy (shortlisted for the Text Prize 2016), *Pickle to Pie* and *Something Missing* by Glenice Whitting (Glenice and I studied writing together at Holmesglen TAFE), the Lachlan Fox series, the Jed Walker series, the *Alone* series and *The Last Thirteen* series by James Phelan (James and I studied writing together at Swinburne University), *The Girl from France* by Laurent Boulanger (Laurent was one of my tutors at Swinburne University), *Messenger*, *Visioner* and *Destroyer* by KK Ness (KK is a friend of a friend who did a beta read of one of my books) and *The Ultimate SMSF Trustee's Guide* by Reece Agland (Reece is a friend and former colleague from when I worked in the accounting industry and okay, I'm going to confess that I've never read his book but I did buy a copy of it and give it to my dad to read because he has a self-managed superannuation fund).

Another friend of mine has released his first book this year, a non-fiction investigative piece about an industry he has significant experience in. He spruiked its impending release for months and when it was finally available for purchase, he provided a link to his publisher's website on his social media accounts. I clicked through to the main page, fully expecting that my next step would be to find his book and order a copy.

But the main page of his publisher's website stopped me cold. It listed all the latest books in its stable and as I scrolled through them, I realised it was a who's who of Australian far-right conservatives. People I have little respect for. People with whom I fundamentally disagree. People who have made their names discriminating against and belittling minorities and the many, many other classes of people they don't like.

I know this friend of mine is a conservative. He watches and promotes Sky News After Dark (Murdoch far-right propaganda for anyone not in Australia) relentlessly. But despite that, I've always found him to be a reasonable person. He likes rules, he likes fairness, he likes checks and balances. I suspect, even without having read his book, that it will be a perfectly fine book, supported by meticulous research and logical conclusions. But I am conflicted about how supporting him by buying a copy of his book might also be supporting these other authors.

My purchase – or lack thereof – won't be the difference between this new author making it or not. It will only reflect how far I'm prepared to go. I don't know how far that is yet.

THE 30 BOOKS THAT SPARK MY JOY

Anyone who doesn't live under a rock will have heard of Marie Kondo, the tidying expert. She helps people to declutter their homes and their lives and when it comes to books, she lives by the following motto: "I now keep my collection of books to about 30 volumes at any one time."

As happens frequently on the internet, this statement went through a huge round of Chinese (or perhaps that should be Japanese, in light of her nationality) whispers and suddenly everyone was saying that Marie Kondo was telling people to throw away most, if not all, of their books.

She wasn't saying that. Her general advice is that the items you do keep should spark your joy. And if books spark your joy, then feel free to have as many of them as you want.

Books spark my joy. I have thousands. I have a library. That's not a description of my books. It's an entire room just for my books. I could have bought a cheaper house if books didn't spark my joy so much. Still, I thought it would be an interesting exercise to find the 30 books that really spark my joy.

It was a lot harder than I thought. Mostly because I read a lot of books that are thematically dark, fiction and non-fiction about many different but difficult topics. But I got there in the end. So here, in alphabetical order because it was hard enough choosing them without trying to rank them, are the 30 books from the thousands in my collection that spark my joy.

BLUEY TRUSCOTT BY IVAN SOUTHALL

A biography of the famous Keith "Bluey" Truscott. My grandfather and Bluey had the same great-grandfather so there's a family connection. It's more like propaganda than a proper biography and given the fact that he was a champion Aussie Rules footballer as well as a fighter pilot and war hero who died during World War II, it's not surprising.

CLEO BY HELEN BROWN

The tragic story of how Helen Brown and her family coped with the death of one of her children and the key role in that process played by Cleo the kitten.

EATS, SHOOTS AND LEAVES BY LYNNE TRUSS

You have to love a book that takes its title from a joke about punctuation. What? You don't have to? Okay, you don't. But I do. One for the language purists.

ENGLISH DICTIONARY

My favourite book. The one book I can't live without.

FREEDOM TO LOVE BY CAROLE MORTIMER

The first Mills & Boon I ever read so it holds a special nostalgic place in my heart. Written in the 1970s, it hasn't aged well but then again not many Mills & Boon books from that time have. There was a copy of this book in my high school library and I found a copy of it in a second-hand bookshop many years later.

HORNET'S NEST BY PATRICIA CORNWELL

My favourite Patricia Cornwell book, perhaps surprisingly not about her most famous creation, Kay Scarpetta. But perhaps not, considering one of the main characters is a cat.

JENNIFER GOVERNMENT BY MAX BARRY

A book that ingeniously skewers the path of global consumerism we're on and it's written by an Australian. Just one of Max Barry's brilliant books.

NINETY EAST RIDGE BY STEPHEN REILLY

The one and only published novel from the brother of famous Australian author Matthew Reilly, it contains my most favourite description ever, "star spangled smile".

NO WAY BACK BY MATTHEW KLEIN

A deceptively simple book that is brilliantly written, about regretting the life choices we make and how we go about rectifying them. That makes it sound pretentious but it's actually mainstream fiction. An amazing ending.

NOT A PENNY MORE, NOT A PENNY LESS BY JEFFREY ARCHER

I love Jeffrey Archer's early career novels and this was his first. The backstory behind it is as good as the book itself.

PAULA AND ME BY JOHN "JJ" JEFFERY

The first published book edited by me that I didn't write. It wouldn't generally be the kind of book I am drawn to but I was trusted by JJ to help him honour his wife and I think we achieved something wonderful together.

POSTCARDS FROM PLANET EARTH

The book of poetry I studied in Year 12. I hated it at the time but it has grown on me. Some of the poems suffer from their age and societal changes but it is an amazing collection from various poets.

REVERSE DICTIONARY

A book from Reader's Digest that lists simple words and gives various complex synonyms. And much, much more. Great for word nerds like me.

SENSE AND SENSIBILITY BY JANE AUSTEN

Pride and Prejudice gets all the glory but I actually prefer *Sense and Sensibility*. The Misses Dashwood kick the asses of the Bennet sisters in my opinion.

SOMETIMES GLADNESS BY BRUCE DAWE

The collected poems of my favourite poet. There is a real sense of Australian-ness to Bruce Dawe's poetry but then he mixes it up with sentiments, ideas and language that are universal.

TEXTS FROM DOG BY OCTOBER JONES

Comprised entirely of text messages between October and his dog, it's hilarious and a lovely escape from the neverending serious books out there.

THE BIBLE

I'm not especially religious but I recognise a good story when I read one. The Bible is full of brilliant tales, regardless of whether you think it's word-for-word truth, completely made up or somewhere in between.

THE BLAIR WITCH PROJECT: A DOSSIER BY DA STERN

A side project, I imagine much of it made up from the research that went into creating the movie, that made my jaw drop in an "Oh my God" moment in a way that the movie by itself never did.

THE DIARY OF JACK THE RIPPER: THE DISCOVERY, THE INVESTIGATION, THE DEBATE BY SHIRLEY HARRISON

Written and published before the diary was proved to be a hoax, it's still a fascinating book.

THE ERN MALLEY AFFAIR BY MICHAEL HEYWARD

It's ironic and appropriate that *The Ern Malley Affair* comes after *The Diary of Jack the Ripper*. After all, they're both books about literary hoaxes. Ern Malley was the creation of James McAuley and Harold Stewart. In the middle of the 20th century, they wrote what they considered to be bad poetry and submitted it to a literary magazine. Modernists loved it and then the hoax was revealed, embarrassing them. Michael Heyward's tale of the affair is delicious.

THE GREAT FLOOD MYSTERY BY JANE CURRY

The Great Flood Mystery is the first proper chapter book I can remember reading as a child. This must have been the beginning of my lifelong appreciation of a good mystery being revealed layer by layer.

THE LADY AND THE CHOCOLATE BY EDWARD MONKTON

An absolute gem about a bar of chocolate convincing a lady that she must give meaning to its life by eating it.

THE LAST VICTIM BY ANNE E GRAHAM AND CAROL EMMAS

The story of Florence Maybrick. Fascinating on its own, the authors used the claims that her husband, James Maybrick, may have been Jack the Ripper to spice it up even further. She was convicted of murdering him and went to jail. Was she Jack the Ripper's last victim? Probably not, but still a terrific read.

THE PIG OF HAPPINESS BY EDWARD MONKTON

He is so happy. Another gem, this time about a happy pig. It's as simple as that.

THE POET BY MICHAEL CONNOLLY

The first Michael Connelly book I read and the reason I've read every other book of his since.

THE POET'S MANUAL AND RHYMING DICTIONARY

As I'm sure you can already tell, I love a good dictionary and for anyone who likes to write rhyming poetry or songs, this takes the hassle out of coming up with rhymes. It gives you rhymes you would never, ever have thought of.

THE WATCHER'S GUIDES (VOLUME 1 BY CHRISTOPHER GOLDEN AND NANCY HOLDER, VOLUME 2 BY NANCY HOLDER, JEFF MARIOTTE AND MARYELIZABETH HART AND VOLUME 3 BY PAUL RUDITIS AND ALLIE COSTA)

Only for the true *Buffy* fans, these books go into all the details that nobody else cares about.

30-SOMETHING AND OVER IT BY KASEY EDWARDS

In the 1960s, Betty Friedan's *The Feminine Mystique* coined the term "the problem that has no name". This was the equivalent book for me. I was desperately unhappy working in the corporate rat race and couldn't quite put my finger on why until Kasey Edwards helped me realise I was just 30-something and over it, doing a job and living a life that didn't "spark my joy", as Marie Kondo would put it.

20ᵀᴴ CENTURY RUSSIAN POETRY SELECTED WITH AN INTRODUCTION BY YEVGENY YEVTUSHENKO

Okay, I can't read Russian but these poems have all been translated into English and they cover a period of huge tumult in Russia. It's like a history book from the unique perspective of Russia's poets.

WILLIAM SHAKESPEARE: THE COMPLETE PLAYS

The tragedies, the comedies, the histories, the romances, Shakespeare's plays have everything. *Much Ado About Nothing* is probably my favourite but there's something for every mood and for every day.

LOUISE TRUSCOTT

∞

So that's it. One of the most surprising things to me was how many Australian books I chose. It shouldn't have been surprising since I'm Australian but I'm more glad about it than I thought I would be. I like that local content is sprinkled amongst the books from the rest of the world. But it probably also shows that I need to expand my horizons a little to read more books from authors of non-English speaking backgrounds. As I write this, I'm doing a year of reading Australian women writers so it's a longer-term goal. But I've got plenty of reading years left in me. I hope you do, too.

ABOUT THE AUTHOR

Louise Truscott was born, brought up and still lives in Melbourne, Australia. She tried not being a writer and editor, then tried being a corporate writer and editor, but she's only truly happy writing and editing when she chooses what to write and what to edit. With a blog called Single White Female Writer, there are lots of hints in the name about who she is.

She published *Enemies Closer*, her debut novel, under the name LE Truscott in 2012. *Project December: A Book About Writing*, her second book, was published in 2015 and *Project January: A Sequel About Writing* was published in 2017. *Black Spot*, her upcoming novel, was shortlisted for the 2016 Text Prize.

www.ingramcontent.com/pod-product-compliance
Lightning Source LLC
Chambersburg PA
CBHW060314030426
42336CB00011B/1036